Heap of Bones

A Baja Surfer's Chronicle

by

Steve Sorensen

Heap of Bones: A Baja Surfer's Chronicle

Published by Picacho

5578 Coyote Ct.
Carlsbad, CA 92010

Email correspondence may be addressed to:
picacho67@gmail.com

Second Print Edition ISBN 978-0-9629418-9-4

Ebook Edition ISBN ISBN 978-0-9629418-6-3

Edited by Heather Goodwillie

Cover illustration and design by Jessica Millis

Table of Contents

I, on my side, require of every writer, first or last, a simple and sincere account of his own life, and not merely what he has heard of other men's lives; some such account as he would send to his kindred from a distant land.

— Henry David Thoreau

August:

Pilgrimage to Mount Rushmore

August 12, Cook Lake, Wyoming

For three days now we have been camped at this remote lake in the Black Hills of Wyoming, waiting patiently to make our first pilgrimage to the most revered site in the cosmology of a Baja surfer: Mount Rushmore, South Dakota. We are required by faith as much as by law to visit this pagan shrine once every five years, but because the sun, moon, and tide are not yet in their most favorable alignments, the three of us—my wife Claudia, our neurotic Australian shepherd Kirra, and I—must wait, and wait, and then wait a few days more. Surfing is always a sport of waiting. We wait for the right season, we wait for the right swell, we wait for the right tide, we wait for first light, we wait for the night wind to cease, and then we wait for the right wave. All this waiting for just a few seconds of the most dazzling beauty a human can ever know. So for us, waiting a few more days means nothing all.

I know it's unfortunate that a story about surfing in Baja must begin at an unheard-of lake in the Black Hills of Wyoming, 2,500 miles from Cabo San Lucas, and 5,000 feet above the ocean. But every story has to begin somewhere, and because this work is a chronicle—that is, a factual account told in the order of time—it must begin at the beginning.

When I was a younger man, just starting out in my career as a journalist, I believed it was the writer's duty to bend, hammer, and twist both time and the facts until they conformed to his will. If I wavered from that task, there were always humorless editors waiting to enforce their more powerful will. But now that I'm in my sixties, lazy, indifferent, and too stubborn to follow direction from anybody, I'm beginning to appreciate the beauty of chaos. I accept that stories told in a natural order can start and stop, lurch and flounder, wander aimlessly in circles, or dribble to a finish without ever finding a conclusion. Or, they can head off again in a direction never expected, which is what happened to Claudia and me.

For the last five years or so, my wife and I have lived in an odd little town called Zacatitos, on the tip of the Baja peninsula. The population varies with the seasons, but I doubt that it ever exceeds one hundred, and almost all of us are gringos. There are so many capes along that coast—Cabo San Lucas, San José del Cabo, Cabo Frailes, Cabo Pulmo, even a Cabo Falso—that it can become confusing, and for that reason Mexicans call that entire region Los Cabos. The area where we like to surf, on the east side of the peninsula, is called the East Cape.

That word *gringo*, by the way, is considered impolite by most Mexicans, who are among the most polite people on earth, so they rarely utter it except in anger. Calling us *americano* is not strictly correct, either, since everybody on this continent, as well as the one to the south, has a right to that title, including Mexicans, Guatemalans, Peruvians—even Canadians. The most commonly heard alternative to *gringo* is *norteamericano*, though you sometimes hear the word *estadounidense* (United Statesean), which to my ears sounds

unbearably awkward. So we sunburned immigrants call ourselves gringos and accept with good humor whatever slander
comes with that word, knowing we well deserve it.

The reason hardly any Mexicans live out on the East Cape,
except for an occasional rancher, is that for centuries that land
was considered worthless desert, good for nothing but raising
a few scrawny longhorns. One of the Jesuit priests who lived
in the Los Cabos region during the eighteenth century, Johann
Jakob Baegert, wrote of the place: "Everything concerning
[Baja] California is of such little importance that it is hardly
worth the trouble to take a pen and write about it." And, "…
from top to bottom and from coast to coast [it] is nothing else
than a thorny heap of stones, or a pathless, waterless rock
arising between two oceans."

It took people who had witnessed the modern rape of
upper California to appreciate the rare beauty of the East
Cape, and many of them, at least at first, were surfers. Most
came from San Diego, but others came from San Clemente,
Santa Barbara, Santa Cruz—all the disgraced saints along El
Camino Real. Those places had once been heavens on earth
but now have become manmade hells, with their carbon
monoxide freeways, toxic beaches, and neurotic residents
chasing each other in a manic orgy of lust and greed. Surfing,
more than anything else, is a celebration of nature, and surfers
know they don't belong in such ghastly places. But god, or
perhaps the devil, had played a cruel trick on them by creat-
ing most of North America's finest surf breaks in southern
California. It was only a matter of time before the frustrated
surfers had to break out. Eventually it became clear to them
that Baja was the only place left to go, not just because the
surf was spectacular down that way, but also because the international border served as a kind of filter through which
most Americans could not, or would not, pass. I like to think
of those first California pioneers to the East Cape as surf

refugees—that is, immigrants who fled their ravaged home-
land looking for a new start.

The waves that break on the East Cape begin as horren-
dously powerful winds generated by winter storms in the
southern hemisphere, near Antarctica, six thousand miles
away. We can't get a north swell at all; we never see waves
from due west or due east, and only rarely from the southeast.
Our swells come from the south or southwest, which is why
we call them "southern hemis," and for a Baja surfer they're
one of the great wonders of the world. Because the waves
travel such tremendous distances before they reach the East
Cape, they have time to become well organized. Faster waves
overtake smaller waves, combining into even larger waves.
Waves that begin as random, violent wind energy gradually
settle into clean sets, with something like eighteen seconds
between waves, and three to six waves per set. These sets can
be five, even ten, minutes apart, with almost total calm in between. Waves organized in patterns like this can travel very
long distances—one-fourth the diameter of the earth—with
little loss of energy. By the time they reach Baja's East Cape,
these southern swells are smooth, clean, surprisingly powerful, and shockingly beautiful.

Because we're dependent upon nature's winter tantrums
off the coast of Antarctica, the natural surfing season on the
East Cape begins around the first of March—autumn in the
Antarctic—and continues into late October, when relative
calm returns to the southern hemisphere. But there's another
natural force of nature that generates large waves in Baja—
hurricanes, or *chubascos,* as they're sometimes called in
Mexico. Hurricane season becomes active here in July, grows
agitated in August, violent by September, and doesn't begin
to calm down again until mid-October. The engine driving
those hurricanes is heat—hurricanes require water temperatures of 80 degrees Fahrenheit or higher. Baja land temperatures by July are in the high 90s, but that doesn't even begin

to describe the insane intensity of the tropical sun, or the insufferable humidity.

One surfer friend who spends the entire summer in Zacatitos told me that when it gets unbearably hot, he and his wife take a little fishing *panga* off the coast and dive over the bow as deep as they can go to enjoy the cool water for a few brief moments. "Then we have to make a decision," he said. "We can either stay cool, or we can breathe."

There is no escape from that kind of heat at any hour of the day, but it gets worse after the sun goes down, when you might expect things to cool off. Then all breezes cease, and the heat begins to radiate up off the ground. The only respite comes with rain, when the temperature sometimes drops a few degrees. But summer rain in Baja is nothing like a gentle spring rain in California. The water often comes in violent, torrential bursts that flood the arroyos, rip out the roads and bridges, and leave a shocked gringo wondering why he ever moved to a desert.

So Los Cabos, you see, might be paradise nine months of the year, but it can be hell for three. The Mexicans who have lived there all their lives are used to hurricane season, of course, but for anybody else living without air-conditioning, those months are unbearable. And because our house is run off solar panels—there are no power lines, water lines, or phone lines anywhere in Zacatitos—we have no air-conditioning. So, like most gringos, for two or three months of the year, we choose to go elsewhere, and this year it is South Dakota.

The Texas and Florida surfers who occasionally find their way to Baja think we're nuts for leaving during hurricane season. Where they come from, on the Gulf of Mexico, hurricanes provide the best surf. But I don't care what they think. First of all, hurricane surf is ugly. The storms aren't far away, often less than 1,000 miles, and the waves don't look anything like our miraculous southern hemis. Second, a fair percentage of those Pacific hurricanes eventually travel directly over southern Baja, and while they aren't the terrifying class 5 hurricanes seen on the Atlantic and Gulf coasts, a class 3 hurricane, with winds over one hundred miles per hour, is not my idea of fun. And finally, I'm 62 years old. Between the months of March and July, I see more spectacular surf than many surfers see in a lifetime; by July my body is tired, sometimes beat up, and I'm ready for two or three months of rest.

And there's yet another reason why we leave Zacatitos in the summer. No matter how much an immigrant professes to love the desert, eventually he begins to crave the colors of the latitude where he was born and raised. A Canadian friend who lives in Los Cabos told me that one year, while watching the winter Olympics on TV, he broke down and cried at the sight of falling snow. One moment he was a manly hockey fan, and the next he was a blubbering sentimentalist. "I wouldn't go back to those brutal winters for anything," he said. "But, oh my god, to be able to look up and see snow falling out of the sky."

By June or early July, most *norteamericanos* who live in southern Baja begin to suffer from a craving for the color green. For me, the craving comes in the form of recurring dreams in which I am lying on my back in a lush meadow high in the Sierra Nevada, listening to the sound of a rapidly flowing creek, while staring up at the tops of pine trees swaying in the breeze. For my wife Claudia, who was born and raised in Southern California, the craving is more often for juicy cheeseburgers and supermarkets stocked with things you can't find in Mexico, like pickles, horseradish, and baking yeast.

Every gringo has to solve this problem of latitude longing. Some expats refuse to sell their house in the U.S.—if they can afford to keep two residences—just so they'll have a place to stay for those few weeks of summer. But Claudia and I wanted a simpler solution. So we store a 22–foot Winnebago in California, and during the months of summer we wander in circles through the Rocky Mountains, Canada, Oregon, or the eastern Sierra Nevada. We don't like leaving our home in Zacatitos, but we know we'll be back in October, and if we're lucky, there might be four or five more weeks of surfing at the season's end.

August 14, Cook Lake, Wyoming

So this is how and why we ended up in the Black Hills, waiting our turn to visit Mount Rushmore.

One of the many puzzling dilemmas for U.S. citizens who choose to live in Mexico is how to keep their motor vehicles legally registered in the U.S. For Californians this is especially difficult because in California, car owners are required to get a smog inspection every other year. We've lived a thousand miles from the California border for years now, never owned a vehicle that failed a smog test, yet we still have to pay for the inspection and certification. Without the smog certification, you can't register the vehicle. If you try to postpone the smog check until those months when you're actually in the U.S., you'll likely end up paying a hefty late fee. Worse yet, if the Mexican police catch you driving a vehicle without current registration, they may impound your vehicle, and you may never see it again.

So before we set off on this summer's tour of the Rocky Mountains, I made a trip to the DMV in Oceanside, California to see if there wasn't some logical solution for this problem. After living in a foreign country for so long, I'd fallen into the lazy habit of thinking my government might want to help me. I took a number at the counter, then sat down and waited my turn. The holding pen there at the DMV was filled with the strangest menagerie of people I'd seen in some time. Just about everybody in the room was pierced, tattooed, surgically enhanced, hyped-up, semi-delusional, or sedated. In Mexico, Americans are respected for their individualism, but I couldn't help thinking that in California things had gone a bit too far.

After an hour or so of waiting, my number finally came up. I went to the front counter to plead my case to the stern-looking woman on the other side. "Is there some kind of smog exemption," I asked, "for residents who don't actually live in California?"

"Yes," she replied, "but we don't give those out." This woman was a grizzled veteran of public service who thirty years ago had already heard and rejected every possible motor vehicle excuse, and with retirement in sight, she wasn't about to begin doling out leniency to the likes of me.

"I see…. Well, if you don't give them out, what are they for?" I wondered.

"Don't even ask. You won't get one."

"But see, my problem is that I'm retired and live in Mexico nine months out of the year. I can't just drive to the local inspection station like everybody else. And I've already paid fines for late registration and late smog certification on two different vehicles now for four years in a row."

She nodded, obviously not surprised, and already scanning the holding pen behind me for her next lying, wheedling motorist.

"Well, isn't there something I can do about this?" I asked.

She leaned forward and mockingly whispered, "Do what everybody else does—register your vehicles in another state."

"But … I don't have an address in another state," I said.

She gasped at my stupidity. Then she lowered her chin, leaned a little closer, glared at me over her pearled reading glasses, and said, "Get one."

August 16, Cook Lake, Wyoming

Claudia and I had driven our Winnebago all the way to Cody, Wyoming, and were headed for Sheridan before I finally processed the information the woman at the Oceanside DMV had given me. And then suddenly I understood. "How far do you think it is to South Dakota?" I asked Claudia.

Claudia, who is five years younger than I am, and that much more nimble of mind, said immediately, "I know what you're thinking." She studied the road map for a moment. "It's something like four hundred miles from here."

"Did you ever want to see Mount Rushmore?" I asked.

"Not really, but I'll go if you will." Claudia's been saying things like that to me now for twenty-five years, and it's one of the reasons I love her.

We had planned on turning north into Montana. In my mind North America ended at the continental divide, and there was no sense in driving through endless wastelands of corn and wheat if mountain creeks and green pine trees were what you were longing for. But now I was beginning to understand what so many of my Baja surf buddies had been telling me about the importance of making a pilgrimage to South Dakota.

"How much did we pay in California income tax last year?" I asked.

Claudia got out her laptop and in a couple minutes gave me the figure. For two retired people, it was an unreasonable amount.

"And what services did we receive from the State of California that were worth that much money?" I asked.

We both mulled that for a mile or two but couldn't come up with any.

The rest of the facts and figures were easy enough to sort out. South Dakota has no income tax. South Dakota has no smog inspection. The cost of registering a vehicle there is about a third of what it costs in California. The cost of insuring a vehicle in South Dakota is considerably less than it is in California. And South Dakota has Mount Rushmore.

Almost all the surfers living on the East Cape register their vehicles in South Dakota. In fact, South Dakota license plates have become a kind of vanity plate for Baja surfers. And while it's true that the whole vehicle registration process can be handled by an agent in Rapid City, for a small fee, the only way to become true South Dakota residents, and therefore benefit from zero state income tax and cheap insurance, is to make the pilgrimage all the way to Mount Rushmore.

But the notion of surrendering our California citizenship turned out to be a surprisingly difficult and emotional one for Claudia and me. One morning in Springdale, Utah, the manager of a supermarket had told us that the only place in town where we could buy wine was the state-owned liquor store, which wouldn't be open until noon. "Ma'am," I said, "We're from California. We need liquor now."

"Welcome to Utah," she replied.

In Sheridan, Wyoming, we had stopped at a Walmart to buy groceries but found no beer on the shelves. When we asked a clerk what was going on, she explained, "In Wyoming a store can sell either beer or bullets but not both. We chose bullets."

I had been born in San Francisco, and Claudia in San Bernardino—two of the oldest communities in the state. We had met and married in Encinitas—the capital of surfing (as far as I'm concerned) in North America. We had survived two governors who were movie actors, and three with the name Brown—one of those had kept Linda Ronstadt in the governor's mansion as his first mistress. California had produced the Grateful Dead, boutique marijuana, chocolate raisins, boxed wine, and the Boogie Board—all in our lifetimes! Between the oppositely charged poles of San Francisco and L.A., California had produced a jolt of brilliance the world hadn't seen since the Renaissance. But like so many of its vain and foolish celebrities, California had burnt itself out early. Now our state was best known for outrageous property taxes, stop-and-go freeways, and smog. Over sixty years, the population of California had grown from about ten million to nearly forty million, yet the state hadn't added a single surf break. Claudia and I weren't eager to surrender our California birthright, but we had run out of choices.

At a coffee shop in Gillette, we got online and looked at a dozen or so websites whose proprietors specialized in helping out-of-state scofflaws register their vehicles in South Dakota, or become legal residents, if they so chose. I arbitrarily picked one called "America's Mailbox," in Rapid City, and called ahead to let the office manager know we were coming.

"Do not, under any circumstances, show up in South Dakota this week," the woman warned me. It seemed a rude reception for two California pilgrims who had just crossed the plains in a covered wagon seeking a better life. "This is bike week in Sturgis," she continued, "and you won't find so much as a parking place in this town."

We had unwittingly timed our arrival in South Dakota for the week of the largest gathering of Harley-Davidson owners in the world. More than 400,000 bikers would be descending on a town with a normal population of 6,000.

We should have guessed that something was up, because as we meandered through Wyoming, every little town had at least one bar with forty or fifty choppers parked out front and a scabrous pack of paunchy old bikers trying their best to look menacing. There were also a surprising number of women old enough to be somebody's grandmother determined to flash their breasts at every passing motorist. It takes courage to be an outlaw when your hair's gray and you're living on Social Security, but then I could say the same about a lot of surfers I know too.

Our Australian shepherd Kirra, a spirited blue merle with two white eyes, decided somewhere around Greybull that she couldn't tolerate the sound of Harley-Davidsons, which, it's true, do have a throaty growl all their own. As we drove across eastern Wyoming, Kirra warned us each time a Harley was approaching from behind long before we could spot it in the rearview mirror. As the Harleys roared past our Winnebago, Kirra would leap at the window and show the bikers her teeth.

So after speaking with the woman at America's Mailbox, we knew we were heading into a hornet's nest and we'd better come up with an alternate plan. We stopped at a little Forest Service office in Sundance, studied a map of the Black Hills, and picked this spot, Cook Lake, Wyoming, at the end of thirty miles of dirt road that no Harley would ever travel.

And we sit here now, waiting for the geriatric bikers of Sturgis to finish raising hell.

August 17, Rapid City, South Dakota

To become residents of South Dakota, we first needed to establish legal residency. We assumed that not just any Californian would be allowed to wander in and demand citizenship, along with cheap vehicle registration and zero income tax. Otherwise, the place might be overrun by the sort of people I had seen at the Oceanside DMV. But to our astonishment, we learned that to establish residency in South Dakota, the hopeful applicant must produce a campground receipt for one night. There are no other requirements of any significance.

Rapid City is the second-largest city in South Dakota, which might sound impressive, but if it were in California I don't suppose it would require more than two freeway exits. Yet even with the bikers gone, it still had a surprising amount of traffic and congestion, which we assumed was a result of the seasonal surfer pilgrimage. We checked into the Rapid City KOA, making sure that the receipt the manager wrote specified both Claudia and me as residents—we didn't want to spend two nights in our new home state if we could avoid it.

August 18, Lame Deer, Montana

After breakfast, Claudia and I drove to the Rapid City DMV, where we were the only pilgrims seeking refuge on this particular day. In fact, we were the only people seeking the DMV's assistance in this entire corner of the state. The courteous, well-groomed attendant was so cheerful that in California he might have been mistaken for simpleminded. He examined our proof of South Dakota residency and found it flawless. Then he administered the standard eye test, which we both passed easily. We surrendered our California driver's licenses, the man took out an extra large pair of scissors, and with two quick snips our combined 119-year relationship with the state of California was severed. The man asked us to be seated, and in less than ten minutes our new South Dakota licenses and plates were ready. He winked as he handed them over to us and said, "See you in five years."

Outside in the DMV parking lot, I knelt on the asphalt and removed our old battered and lusterless California plates. As I attached the shiny new plates, I saw that the logo read "South Dakota—Great Faces," which reminded me that we still had one solemn responsibility to fulfill before we left our new home state.

En route to Mount Rushmore, we passed on the opportunity to visit the Flintstones Theme Park, Reptile Gardens, Cosmos Mystery Area, and a dozen other family tourist traps. We had read somewhere that admission to Mount Rushmore was free, which is technically true, but when we were a mile away, a National Park Service sign posted alongside the highway informed us that the private concessioner that managed our country's largest defacement of stone would be demanding twenty dollars for parking. There was one small roadside turnout where the patriotic landmark could be viewed without cost, but we found that it was already occupied by cheapskates like us. So we decided a slow, California drive-by would do. If the spectacle was really worth twenty bucks, we'd pay the money and take the official tour when we came back to renew our licenses in five years.

As we cruised past the bleak, almost-grotesque, granite depictions of four dead presidents, Claudia and I felt only disappointment. "For some reason I always thought they were bigger than that," I said. "And how the hell did Teddy Roosevelt ever make the final four?"

"Yeah, but imagine what a beautiful mountain it must have been," Claudia added.

August 31, Gallatin River, Montana

We still had six weeks to kill before we could return to our home in Baja, and our only plan was to spend the time wandering around the northern Rockies. Perhaps because I spent so many years living out of a backpack, this sort of life suits me fine. I never grow tired of new scenery, and if it weren't for the price of gas, I would drive all the way to Alaska and back, staying at a new campground every night. Kirra agrees with me. As long as she gets a few miles of trail to explore and a fresh mound of cow manure to roll in every day, she's happy to curl up under the Winnebago every night, no matter where it's parked. But Claudia has trouble adjusting to the aimlessness of our life, and she's growing restless to be settled again in the comfort of her Baja home.

To pacify Claudia, after we'd loaded up with groceries at the Walmart in Helena, I spread out the road map on the table of the Winnebago and said, "See, this is as far north as we're going. From here on out, every mile takes us closer to home."

"Are you sure?"

"Absolutely."

"How far is it?"

"I don't know …. Maybe a thousand miles to San Diego. And, of course, another thousand to Zacatitos. At fifty miles a day, we could be there in forty days."

This afternoon we stopped at a beautiful spot on the Gallatin River, just outside Bozeman, Montana. Claudia put on her bathing suit, opened her collapsible camp chair on the cobbled shore, and pretended she was at the beach. Even in the sun, at high noon, the air temperature couldn't break 70, and the water had surely been ice just minutes before it flowed past her feet.

But then, to our great surprise, a large party of college kids on stand-up paddle surfboards (SUPs) floated into sight around the bend and passed directly in front of us. The flat-water boards had been fitted with shallow fins that wouldn't scrape on the rocks, and because the boards had to move faster than the current for the rider to have directional control, the Montana surfers were laying into their paddles with vigor. The girls in the group wore bikinis in tropical colors, and the boys sported stylish surf trunks. One of them was wearing a rash guard, but none had a wetsuit, or even seemed to need one. They were all laughing and splashing one another and apparently having a wonderful time. The scene reminded me of the song the Beachboys wrote almost fifty years ago, "If everybody had an ocean, across the USA, then everybody'd be surfing, like Californ-i-a."

Kirra

September:

Down the Spanish Trail

September 8, Snake River, Idaho

It was a fairly warm morning in southern Idaho, so we flung open the door and windows of our Winnebago to enjoy the cool canyon breezes. Claudia, wearing earphones, practiced Spanish by repeating the lessons recorded on her iPhone, while I listened to CNN Español on the satellite radio. I couldn't help but notice that other campers strolling by our motorhome appeared puzzled by the babble coming from inside, perhaps wondering if a group of illegal aliens had commandeered this Winnebago.

Claudia and I chose to live in Mexico—we weren't deported, running from the law, or forced to flee our native country by economic or political necessity. Therefore, we believe it is our responsibility to learn the language of our adopted country. In Baja we know gringos who have lived there twenty years and can't buy fish at the market because they never learned to count from *uno a diez*. We know people who insert one Spanish word in an English sentence, think they're speaking Spanish, then become frustrated when their meaning isn't understood. We know gringos who refuse to believe that not every Mexican speaks English and that their failure to comprehend what we're saying is actually an attempt to embarrass us. The typical gringo's solution for any miscommunication is to keep raising his voice until he's shouting in anger.

It's not easy learning a foreign language. What school children pick up almost effortlessly, adults must struggle to learn. (Which should remind us that we're born intelligent and grow more stupid with each passing year.) But Claudia and I are determined to become as close to fluent in Spanish as we can. So every day, no matter where we happen to be, we spend an hour or so practicing Spanish.

For my studies I have a stack of colorful Spanish readers printed by the Mexican government for children learning to read. They cover everything from Cabeza de Vaca to Cervantes and Gabriel García Márquez. Without the aid of a dictionary, I might be able to read at the sixth-grade level now, though I admit I sometimes rely on the drawings for clues. But what I need most is to converse with Spanish speakers every chance I get. Fortunately, with eleven million illegal Mexican immigrants living in the U.S., I get plenty of opportunities. I speak with ski-lift operators in Idaho, ranch workers in Montana, cherry pickers in Washington, car washers in Nevada, and waitresses in California. Always in my conversations, I am impressed by how many Mexicans from the most humble origins speak English far better than I speak Spanish, and I can't help thinking that's a testament to their intelligence and determination.

English is rightly valued worldwide for its versatility and flexibility, but because of its Germanic roots, it will always sound cold and harsh compared to Spanish. In North America, the African influence has helped to round off the square corners of spoken English, and our children should be encouraged to imitate that influence. But compared to Spanish, English will always grate the ears.

Spanish is a language in which the sound of speech is as

important as the meaning. While English comes in square blocks that can build straight and sturdy walls, Spanish comes in spirals, like a seashell, that can grow into any shape you can imagine. Spanish is meant to flow. Because the articles and adjectives in a Spanish sentence must agree in gender with the noun, and because most verb conjugations end in a vowel, there's a built-in harmony and fluidity. That's why the illiterate construction workers who built our house in Zacatitos could curse in long stanzas of the most vulgar language imaginable and still sound more poetic than an American professor of English reciting his own work.

September 30, St. George, Utah

On our way down I-15, most of which follows the route of the old Spanish Trail, we stopped in St. George, Utah, to visit my elderly parents, who live there in an assisted-living facility. My father is 98 years old, and my mother is 93.

Because the facility where they live doesn't allow pets, we had to leave Kirra out in the Winnebago. It wasn't a very warm morning, so we parked under a big, shady mulberry and opened all the windows so she would have the cool breeze while we were gone.

We found my mother to be doing reasonably well. She couldn't walk anymore but got around okay in a wheelchair. Her spirits were high, and her mind was mostly clear. "Every morning when I wake up, I think to myself, What am I still doing here?" she said. "There must be a reason, I just don't know what it is."

But my father's condition had deteriorated badly since we'd seen him last. His hearing had been getting worse for years, which didn't concern him in the least but drove my mother mad because she thought he was intentionally ignoring her. He refused to wear a hearing aid, and now he scarcely speaks to her at all.

About four years ago, my father lost most of his eyesight to macular degeneration—it might actually have been longer than four years ago because he had pretended he could still see perfectly well long after most of his sight was already gone. In fact, he refused to quit driving until recently. He had convinced himself that he could get around well enough in their car if my mother sat next to him and told him where to turn and when to brake. You can imagine the results—or you can actually see them by looking at their Chevy Cavalier, which has only about 8,000 miles on it but is dented and scraped on every panel.

A couple of years ago, when I called the Utah Department of Motor Vehicles to ask why a blind man was allowed to drive in that state, the woman told me bluntly to mind my own business. (I may have mentioned that I was calling from California, which, of course, meant I was a godless heathen bent on undermining a Utahan's individual liberty.) Thankfully he didn't kill anybody before he finally gave up driving on his own—I know he came close to it more than once.

The worst part of losing his eyesight, though, was that my father could no longer read his scientific journals, which had always been an important part of his life. Sometimes, when I stayed with my parents for extended periods, my father would lie on the sofa in the afternoon while I read *Scientific American* to him. He was like a child at story time then, closing his eyes tightly yet absorbing every word, struggling to visualize the multiple dimensions the new physicists were describing and which he hoped might provide some clue to the mystery of death.

My father loved the outdoors and had always been an avid hiker. He and I had crisscrossed much of southern Utah together, and Claudia and I had backpacked with him when he was nearly eighty. Even after he became almost totally blind, he would still go on long neighborhood walks by himself every day, until finally his knees got so bad he had to give that up too.

Now I saw that he was beginning to lose his memory, which was the most shocking loss of all. He asked me the same questions over and over again, because he couldn't retain the answer. And because he was just lucid enough to know he wasn't very lucid, he was embarrassed and frustrated and was beginning to withdraw into his own world, as if he'd decided that trying to communicate wasn't worth the effort anymore.

Finally, after a couple of hours of trying to talk with him and seeing we weren't going to have anything like a normal conversation, I asked my father, "Would you like to meet our dog Kirra?"

My father, who had grown up on a sheep and cattle ranch, loves dogs and had always owned one until late in his life. Actually he had met Kirra on previous visits, though I knew he wouldn't remember her now, so I pretended she was a new dog. His face brightened at my suggestion, he nodded vigorously, and he said, "Yes, I would like that very much."

Kirra is very bossy at times. Being a herding dog, she has an inflated sense of her own importance and a low opinion of human intelligence. For Kirra, humans are dumb sheep incapable of managing anything without her supervision. She isn't mean, but she warns every person she meets that she is in charge, and if they are going to be friends, it will be on her terms. If somebody tries to pet her before she has given permission, she will give that person a warning nip on the fingers. Once people agree to her conditions, she accepts them as conforming members of her herd. She repeats this behavior even if she has met somebody several times before. So I wasn't sure what would happen when she saw my father again.

I went out to the Winnebago and asked Kirra if she would like to come and say hello to my parents. She trembled with anticipation. I gave her a stern lecture on how important it was for her to be on her best behavior, then I smuggled her across the rear parking lot of the facility and through the back door of my parents' apartment.

Somehow—don't ask me to explain it—Kirra knew what her role was in this situation. She wagged her stub of a tail at the first sight of my father, went straight to his side, sat down calmly at his feet, and let him pet her and rub her ears. My father giggled and laughed as if he were a little kid again, which in a sense he was. I believe that might have been the most fun my father had had in a long time.

When we finally left my parents this afternoon, one of the last things my father told me was, "If there's any way you can avoid it, try not to live as long as I did."

I thought he was joking, so I said, "Well, Dad, you always warned me not to smoke or drink. Maybe it's not too late to start."

My father, who has always had a good sense of humor, didn't laugh.

Yamaha Rhino Surf Rig

October:

Exorcising Demons

October 6, Carlsbad, California

After three months of wandering the icy tundra of Idaho and Montana, Claudia, Kirra, and I finally arrived back in north San Diego County to prepare for our three-day, thousand-mile journey home. We have been staying with our oldest son John and his family—all surfers and Baja lovers who will fly south to visit us in the coming year. (Our two younger sons, Kyle and Jens, are in college, and they will visit us at Christmas or Easter break.)

Early this morning, before daylight, we loaded our Tacoma pickup and started south on I-5. The first winter storm of the year had arrived earlier than usual, and it was raining hard outside. We didn't mind the wet weather—living in Baja you come to love the rain, since you so rarely see it. The problem was that we had to find our way to a surfboard shaper's workshop in the industrial part of San Diego so we could pick up a new racing standup paddleboard for Annie, the wife of my old friend Mike Doyle, who lives in San José del Cabo and has been an East Cape surfer for more than thirty years. And now the hard rain had snarled the morning traffic and made it difficult to find our way.

In November, Annie is going to compete in a SUP race from the beach near our house at Zacatitos to Punta Palmilla, a distance of eleven miles. Annie won that race last year, but this year some of the best women paddlers in the world will be competing, and to improve her odds she ordered a new 12-foot racing board. She had been training hard all summer, paddling five or six miles per day, but she needed that new board to complete her training.

I was seriously worried about the hazards of transporting a board that long down a thousand miles of the transpeninsula highway. I'd felt the powerful blast from oncoming trucks on that narrow road, I'd seen nylon straps separate like string cheese, I'd seen much shorter boards snapped in half, I'd seen surfboard racks torn from the roofs of cars, and I'd seen $1,000 surfboards go floating into the desert sky like UFOs.

Mike Doyle, who is now 70 years old, has probably been on more surf expeditions than any human being alive. So when it comes to transporting surfboards, he's the loadmaster. He and I had already exchanged several emails discussing strategies for securing the board. I had bought new straps and foam padding in preparation, and I had lost half a night's sleeping worrying through our various strategies. No matter what method I tried in my sleep, though, I still woke in the morning imagining a thousand new ways things could go wrong. But then I owed Doyle a thousand favors. Most of what I know about wind and tides, surfboard design, surfing strategy, and surf history, I learned from Doyle. So I wanted to do this favor for him if I possibly could.

With Claudia helping me navigate through the wind, traffic, and rain, we finally found the shaper's shop on a busy one-way street behind the Sports Arena. The shaper had left a key outside so I could enter his shop in the predawn hours, and I let myself in. I switched on the lights and found Annie's board waiting there on the shaping racks. I'd never seen anything quite like it before. It was long and narrow, bright yellow and shiny, like some magic rocket. I picked it up and turned it over—even though it was 12 feet long, it weighed only about eighteen pounds. What a beautiful piece of work! Seeing it in real life, though, and knowing it had to have cost a couple of thousand dollars, only made me worry even more about how to deliver it safely.

I carried the board out into the steady rain and placed it on my roof racks with extreme care. Then I began to arrange my complex system of foam pads and thick straps, a fail-safe system of padded bungee cords in case one of the straps broke, and a specially rigged bungee from the nose of the board to a hook under the hood of my truck. But just as my work had begun, an angry blast of wind and rain pounded me in the face until I couldn't see at all and rattled the board so I could barely hold it down. I had no rain jacket—who thinks of a rain jacket when you're headed for Baja!—so I took my beating and finished securing the board while Claudia and Kirra, who could do nothing to help, watched and worried from inside the truck.

With the paddleboard finally secured the best I knew how, we headed for the border. In addition to Annie's board, I was hauling a new surfboard for me and a full truckload of assorted gringo goods, plus I was towing a small trailer that carried a Yamaha Rhino—a rugged, four-wheel-drive, two-passenger vehicle that I hoped would give me access to some of the more remote surf spots on the East Cape.

On the Mexican side of the border, we stepped out of the truck while the female customs officer checked our vehicle registration and searched our load of goods. Meanwhile, a young Mexican soldier in camo fatigues stood close by, eyeing our Rhino. He had a black rifle slung over his shoulder, and his face was without expression. Still, he looked like a boy, hardly old enough to shave. He stepped closer to the Rhino, leaned inside, felt under the seat, and peered behind the steering wheel. What is he looking for? I wondered. Does he think we look like gun smugglers? I was distracted for a moment by the customs officer's questions: Where are you going? How long do you plan on staying? When I turned back again, I saw the young soldier had climbed up the side of our trailer and into the driver's seat of the Rhino, where he had both hands on the steering wheel and was pretending to be racing across the desert, perhaps in the Baja 1000. His smile reminded me of a little kid at a go-kart track. And then in an instant he regained his composure, crawled out of the Rhino, shifted his rifle onto his shoulder, and became the stiff-jawed soldier again.

The customs officer finally decided we were just two gringos on vacation, and she waved us through.

As soon as we crossed the border, the familiar sounds and smells of Mexico washed over us in waves: the rumble of loud mufflers, the blaring of car horns, the acrid stench of burning tires and diesel fumes, and the wonderful aroma of freshly baked bread. And the colors! Lavender houses, pink taxis, flaming-red buses. How is it possible that two cultures that have lived side by side for three hundred years can look, sound, and smell so different? Many Americans visiting Mexico for the first time say they are shocked by these sounds and images, but for those of us who make our home here, it's a comfort and relief to return to them again.

We hadn't been in Mexico more than five minutes, though, when we were pulled over by a motorcycle cop. He was small, had a face like a rodent, and I knew by the look in his eyes he was trouble. The crooked cops in Tijuana like to target tourists, who they know will be carrying cash, and one of the sure marks of a tourist is somebody with a surfboard on top of his car.

The little rat-faced cop said to me, "You were driving too fast, and you must pay a fine. We can go see the judge, who will fine you about five hundred dollars, or we can settle this matter now for one hundred dollars in cash."

In recent years there have been horrendous incidents of narco-terrorist violence in Tijuana—bodies hanging from freeway overpasses and burned corpses found alongside the road. The local police have been implicated in some of these atrocities. Our son John has a surfer friend who was robbed at gunpoint by Tijuana police in the early morning hours. When the young man explained that he didn't have much cash in his wallet, the police escorted him to an ATM machine where he was ordered to withdraw the maximum amount on his debit card.

Like most seasoned travelers to Baja, I'd already had my share of problems with the Tijuana police. But this was daylight, on a busy highway, and I suddenly decided I wasn't going to play their game anymore. "Let's go see the judge," I said in Spanish. "I want to talk to him."

The cop smiled enough to display his gold teeth, and he said, "The judge is eating breakfast right now. You might have to wait a very long time."

"We're in no hurry," I said. "I'll wait as long as necessary, because I want to tell the judge that you stopped the slowest car on the highway this morning—for speeding!"

Cops like that guy are the biggest reason tourism has declined drastically in northern Baja, where a lot of hardworking Mexican people depend on tourist dollars to feed their families. I knew the Tijuana police had been ordered to leave tourists alone, and in fact, tourists had been told they no longer need to pull over for Tijuana policeman at all anymore—they can simply proceed to the federal toll road, a mile or so away, where the Tijuana police have no jurisdiction. So I had a pretty good idea this crooked cop had no intention of dragging me before the judge on a trumped-up speeding charge.

Finally the cop said, "We can settle this for the price of a soda."

I gave him twenty pesos—enough for two sodas. The cop

wished us a nice day, and we went on our way. And now I wish I hadn't given him anything at all.

Tijuana is a stressful place, but from there on, Baja gets better every mile for the next thousand miles.

Claudia slept while I drove through Ensenada and the vineyards of Santo Tomás. We passed slowly through the string of gritty stop-and-go farm towns: San Quentín, Camalú, Colonet, San Vicente. These are not tourist havens but dusty, wind-blown pueblos that bear more resemblance to mainland Mexico than Baja. Born from the miracle of drip irrigation, free trade, and cheap labor, these towns thrive by providing consumers in the U.S. with tomatoes, celery, and strawberries. They may be poor and ugly, but they are vibrant with life and sometimes remind me of a Pieter Brueghel painting depicting European villages in the sixteenth century, with chickens and cows, drunkards and priests, young children and hobbling old folks, teenage lovers holding hands, pregnant dogs, and a fruit merchant pushing his handcart through the street.

Passing through Camalú, I watched in my rearview mirror as a cat waited on the shoulder of the highway until there wasn't a car in sight before crossing to the other side. I doubt there's a cat in the whole USA with enough sense to do that.

At a roadside turnout in the mountains south of Santo Tomás, I saw a group of tense *federales*, and Mexican soldiers with AR-15 rifles guarding a large mound of crumpled cardboard boxes that looked as though they had been shoved out the back of a truck. I slowed down to get a better look, but I couldn't see what the boxes contained, and the rifles that quickly pointed my way reminded me to mind my own business and move along. I couldn't say for sure what had happened there, but a reasonable guess would be that a nervous drug smuggler had felt reality ratcheting down on him as he approached the border. What a dilemma that driver must have had: If he gets caught at the border with a load of drugs, he could spend years in jail, but if he dumps his load and runs, the drug lords will hunt him down and kill him. I suppose that's the price you pay when you make a pact with the devil.

We spent the night in El Rosario, at Mama Espinosa's, a famous landmark for Baja travelers. Before the highway was finished in the mid seventies, this was where the pavement ended—the jumping-off point, where you left behind the comforts of a clean bed and a hot meal and ventured across 800 miles of dusty, rutted road. The entire Baja highway is paved now, but Mama Espinosa's rustic restaurant and hotel still has its nostalgic charm.

I was worried about thieves in the night tampering with the Rhino or with my new surfboard still strapped in back— not to mention Annie's new paddleboard. So we parked as close as we could to the window of our room, then put Kirra inside the truck and opened the sliding rear window so she could keep watch. It can be a headache traveling with a spirited fifty-pound dog, but it has its benefits too, giving a measure of security you wouldn't otherwise have.

I knew I had something like 500 miles to drive the next day, and I would have liked to get some sleep. But I have suffered from insomnia for years, and all I could do was lie awake waiting and listening for Kirra to bark. But she never did.

October 7, San Ignacio, Baja California Sur

We left just after daylight, without coffee, eager to be on the road. Early morning can be a beautiful time to drive the Transpeninsula Highway. After El Rosario the real Baja begins—the land of fierce deserts, extinct volcanoes, oddly eroded boulders, giant cacti, and the bizarre-looking *cirios*, which look like an imaginary plant from a Dr. Seuss book and grow nowhere else in the world. But we knew we had to be careful too. This highway has a well-deserved reputation for being extremely dangerous. The lanes are narrow, and shoulders are nearly nonexistent. If one tire should wander too far to the right, the pavement simply ends, and the drop-off could be six inches or it could be sixty feet. Because the highway was built on a small budget, most of the asphalt was laid without a gravel base, which means the thin pavement is constantly eroding. Fatal accidents are common, minor accidents routine, and mechanical problems almost inevitable. I've seen many big trucks overturned here, their contents spilled across the desert. I've seen many passenger cars demolished. And once I saw a double-decker bus burning to the ground while the passengers stood on the side of the road watching.

They say that before this highway was paved, in some places it wasn't even one road but a threaded labyrinth of unmarked ruts—choose one and it might lead you to where you wanted to go or it might just as well lead you to an alkaline sinkhole in the desert. But the highway gets better every time we drive it. The Mexican government wants to encourage tourists to venture here, and they are working hard to make improvements.

Gringos are more vulnerable to accidents on the Baja highway than Mexicans are. We're too accustomed to well-engineered roads with wide lanes, ample shoulders, and adequate signs. We're not expecting to encounter potholes the size of bathtubs, a curve too tight to accommodate two cars at the same time, a herd of cattle sleeping in the road, or a car passing another car on a blind curve.

The Mexican truck drivers along this highway have one of the most difficult jobs I can imagine. If they put their outside tires on the very edge of the pavement, their inside tires are nearly on the centerline. One moment of inattention in a thousand miles, and their journey can end in another roadside memorial. But they have no choice other than to carry on as best they can, hour after hour, day after day. Some are still teenagers, which means they might be traveling this deadly highway for the next fifty years.

Mexicans have a more fatalistic attitude about highway accidents than gringos do. They routinely ignore speed limits, stop signs, and red lights. They pass on blind curves, turn in front of oncoming traffic, and appear determined to tempt fate in every way possible. Between Tijuana and Los Cabos, hundreds of roadside memorials mark highway fatalities, and in some exceptionally dangerous places, there are a dozen or more per mile. These memorials are called *descansos*, or resting places. In the old days, when the pallbearers carried a coffin from the church to the *camposanto,* they would stop along the way, put down the coffin, and rest while they told stories about the deceased; later, the families would decorate the *descansos* with crosses and flowers, and usually leave *ofrendas,* or offerings, for the dead. Some *descansos* are as simple as a mound of white stones, or a cross painted on a rock, and many are nothing more than a bundle of plastic flowers; but a few are practically mausoleums, probably larger than the mortal home of the deceased.

One of our favorite *descansos* is on a hillside just south of El Rosario. We passed it not long after the sun came up, when the morning light cast a beautiful orange glow across the hillside, and I decided to stop and take a photo. This *descanso* is for a truck driver named Hector, and his name is spelled out on the hillside in six-foot letters made of painted rocks. Hector's loved ones constructed a realistic truck cab about a fourth the actual size, complete with a windshield, steering wheel, and exhaust stack. Inside the cab, a picture of Hector as a handsome young man was placed behind the steering wheel; looking over his right shoulder is a picture of the Virgin Mary. Hector's family also rigged up a small solar panel that charges a battery, and after the sun goes down, the inside of the cab is lit with a golden light, so Hector won't have to spend his nights in darkness.

Travelers who had stopped to pay their respects at Hector's *descanso* had left behind *ofrendas* they thought might be useful to him in the afterlife: cigarettes, a can of Tecate beer, ten-peso coins in a now obsolete currency.

We gringos are easily amused by such raw Catholic sentimentality. It's part of our sense of cultural superiority. But I suspect that we gringos also envy a man like Hector who inspired such love that his family still devotes their time to his memory and that our amusement is just a mask for the anxiety we feel when we wonder if we will ever be so passionately missed.

As we left the villages behind and began crossing the long, straight stretches of desert highway, I began to worry even more about our first encounter with a big truck moving at full speed. Doyle had told me that because Annie's board was so long and lean, with ideal hydro-dynamics, it would also be aerodynamic. In other words, he thought it would cut through the air cleanly. But there was a problem with Doyle's aeronautical analogy. Truck blasts don't just come at you straight on—they come upward too, like wind shear, which can tear a small airplane to pieces. So I wasn't sure what would happen when we hit that first horrific blast.

Just before Cataviña, on a long straightaway where oncoming trucks could open up their speed to eighty miles an hour, we got our first real test. I slowed down when I saw the speeding truck coming, and I tried to veer slightly to the right. But because of the narrow lanes, the most separation I could gain was a few inches. I gripped the steering wheel, glanced up at the tip of Annie's board, and cringed.

To my great relief, Annie's board barely budged.

Our good luck didn't last, though. Fifty miles north of Guerrero Negro, where a long section of the highway was being repaved, we had to drive several miles on a rough dirt road. I drove slowly, but I could see in my rearview mirror how the trailer carrying the Rhino bounced and lurched erratically. Finally, a support on the neck of the trailer broke, and the weakened neck began to sag until the front end of the trailer was dragging on the ground.

I pulled off the road as far as I could, turned on my warning blinkers, then got out to inspect the damage. This is the kind of thing you worry about while driving the Baja highway—broken down out in the middle of nowhere, baking under the midday sun, no cellphone service, and no help of any kind for miles in either direction. If we tried to limp into Guerrero Negro, the trailer neck might break off completely and we could lose the Rhino or cause an accident, or worse. If we left the trailer while we drove to Guerrero Negro for help, the Rhino would likely be gone when we got back. (Mexicans treat an abandoned vehicle as if maritime law applied—salvage rights belong to the first person who gets there.) If we asked a passing car to send a tow truck, we might wait all day and night, and help still might not arrive. And I didn't want to spend a night along a Mexican highway if I could avoid it. In Mexico, risk multiplies after dark.

Finally, after weighing our options for half an hour, I decided to see what would happen if I backed the Rhino off the trailer. To my relief, I saw that without the weight, the trailer no longer dragged on the ground. I wrapped a tow chain around the neck supports and fastened it to the truck hitch in case the neck snapped completely off. Then I fired up the Rhino and began driving down the highway at thirty miles an hour, in the hundred-degree heat, while Claudia followed behind with the truck and trailer.

The big semis roared past at seventy miles an hour, tooting their horns in glee at the sight of a gringo making a fool of himself. But at least now we were making progress.

It was fifty miles to Guerrero Negro, a city where I knew we could find help, though I wasn't at all sure the damaged trailer would hold together that long. But I had forgotten about the little town of Villa Jesús María, and I was pleasantly surprised when I saw it appear out of the flat desert ahead.

Luckily, the first building we came to was a *llantera*. Almost every town in Baja, no matter how humble, has at least one of these dusty little tire shops. Often they have a mechanic there as well—or one can be found in minutes. Like most *llanteras* in Mexico, this shop at Villa Jesús María was strewn with decades of old tires and rims, flattened oil cans, fifty-gallon barrels overflowing with trash, and heaps of rusted junk. Several idle men were waiting there in the shade of a block wall. They reminded me of spiders waiting patiently for their prey, and that brutal highway that ran in front of the shop served as their web. I asked them, "Hay un soldador aquí?"

A middle-aged man stepped forward and replied, "Sí."

I showed the man the problem with my bent and broken trailer, and I explained in Spanish what I believed the solution might be. He patiently indulged me until I was finished speaking, then he motioned me out of the way and leaped into action. He disconnected the trailer from the truck, then quickly wrapped a length of chain around the neck. Then, using an eight-foot length of bent steel as a pry bar and a wooden block for a fulcrum—both of which had looked like worthless junk to me just seconds before—this mechanical genius coaxed the crooked trailer neck back into perfect alignment. The first half of the repair had taken him sixty seconds.

All I could do was watch in befuddled admiration.

Next, the *soldador* arc welded the broken support. After a moment's consideration, he barked an order to his assistant, who disappeared behind the shop and came back carrying a long piece of angle iron. Then the *soldador* cut the angle iron to length with a hacksaw and quickly welded it into place as an additional support for the trailer neck. Not only was the trailer repaired, but it was improved so the problem would never happen again.

I asked the *soldador* what I owed him. He eyed my Rhino, then my truck loaded with toys and treats, my beautiful but pampered wife, my odd-looking and probably expensive dog, and he replied, "Mil pesos!" I could see by his defiant expression he considered this amount (about $75) to be an outrageous fee.

Mexican mechanics have the amazing ability to fix anything with nothing. I don't know if this is a talent bestowed by god or if it's a skill developed through necessity. Wherever it comes from, Mexicans in all the skilled trades have it in abundance. I considered this *soldador*'s marvelous ingenuity a great bargain, and I paid him gladly.

Claudia and I had planned on making it to Ciudad Constitución—three hundred miles farther—but now with this delay, our plan was clearly impossible. So we decided to stop at San Ignacio, a beautiful little town with lovely palm groves and a ficus-shaded *zócalo*. It's one of our favorite towns in all of Baja. An underground river emerges there, providing water that makes the place a true oasis in the middle of a very harsh desert. Before the Spanish arrived, one of the largest populations of Indians in Baja lived there and left their cave paintings in the surrounding mountains.

That evening we had an excellent meal at a restaurant across from the old mission, which is decaying into the rubble of stones it was built from. All of Mexico, even remote Baja, is changing so rapidly that it's becoming difficult to find remnants of the Old Mexico. But sitting in San Ignacio, across from the town square, we wouldn't have been surprised to see one of the old, cantankerous Jesuit padres come riding in on a burro, drinking wine from a goatskin.

October 8, Zacatitos, Baja California Sur

We started driving again before first light, which in Baja is never a good idea. It's not so much the danger of *bandidos*, though that can be a concern too. It's mostly the danger of free-roaming livestock that wander at all times but are far more difficult to see at night. A few years earlier, on this same stretch of highway, driving in the evening twilight, I came close to hitting a group of wild horses that had charged like phantoms out of a thicket of mesquite and onto the highway directly in front of me. I had been watching for them too. The truckers who drive this highway every day have cowcatchers welded onto the front of their rigs that can launch a steer halfway into orbit—the drivers never even slow down. But we have a neighbor in Zacatitos who totaled a Ford pickup by hitting a cow at moderate speed.

Still, Claudia and I had hopes of making it home today, if we possibly could, so we decided to take the chance and start driving early.

By the time we reached Santa Rosalía, a rusty old copper-mining and shrimp-fishing town on the gulf side of the peninsula, the sky was beginning to brighten. We stopped at a roadside coffee stand, where the proprietor waited under a bare incandescent bulb for his first customer of the day. He greeted me politely and asked me to sit in a plastic chair while he heated water in a lidless aluminum pot on top of his single-burner gas stove. Then he poured the boiling water into two Styrofoam cups, measured a teaspoonful of instant coffee into each, and invited me to add my own sugar and cream.

It was a simple and common transaction—buying from a roadside vendor—yet it reminded me why I have so much respect for the Mexican people. Nobody in this country is ever unemployed, even if they earn only a few pesos per day. They never feel sorry for themselves, they never lose hope for the future, they never lose their dignity, and they never stop trying to improve their lives. Mexico, for me, has become the perfect antidote for the anger, self-pity, and greed that have become commonplace in the U.S.

We drove all day long, passing through Loreto, where the

oldest mission in Baja, built in 1687, still stands; through Ciudad Constitución, a hot and dusty farm town; and through La Paz, a modern, sprawling city where Walmart, Costco, Home Depot, and McDonald's are sprouting up along the highway like in any American suburb.

By late afternoon my back was stiff from sitting so long, and my mind was fuzzy from hours of concentration. But we were so close to Los Cabos now that we decided to push on.

After thirteen hours of driving, we finally reached our home in Zacatitos. The sun was setting behind the Lagunas to the west, and the sky was wild with colors of blood orange and magenta. I got out of the truck to unlock our iron entrance gate and saw that our coco palms, which we had planted four years ago, had grown lush with the summer rains, and one had even produced its first tiny coconut. We opened the house, removed the hurricane shutters, turned on the lights, and found that after our three months absence, all was well.

October 9

After coffee and toast, we went to work putting order to the chaos that had accumulated while we were gone. I checked the voltage level on the photovoltaic system and added a little water to the deep-cycle batteries; then Claudia plugged in the refrigerator. We swept and mopped, scrubbed toilets and showers, and knocked layers of dust from the window screens. Soon we discovered that it had been a good summer for cockroaches—like moths and mice, they have fat years and lean. We found them behind the toilets, under the washing machine, between the clean towels, and just about everywhere. They left their droppings wherever they went, but the only real damage they had done was to nibble on a papier-maché clownfish that Claudia had made the year before. "I don't know why they didn't eat the dorado," Claudia said. "It's a much better-tasting fish."

Kirra went right to work marking her old boundaries along the fence line, then took her post on the upstairs terrace, where she spends most of her days and nights watching diligently for wild burros and the occasional stray cow.

We had barely begun our cleaning when the water ran out. The house has two *pilas* that contain a total of 10,000 liters, which ordinarily lasts us about six weeks. I had hired Moisés, a young man from La Playa who collects our trash, to stop by once a week during the summer to water our five coco palms and a row of *bugambilias* (bougainvilleas) that grow under the stairs. The *pilas* had been nearly full when we left in July, and I had left money with Moisés so he could have the *pilas* filled again in September. But it hadn't rained much during the summer, and apparently Moisés had used all that water too. It wasn't a big deal—we just needed to order another truckload of water. This was a Sunday, though, and I was reluctant to disturb José, our water deliveryman, on his day of rest. On the other hand, I knew José would be delighted to earn 700 pesos any day of the week. So I charged up my Mexican cellphone, went up to the rooftop terrace, where we get the best reception, and called José to ask if he could bring us a load of water right away.

"Sí, señor. Mañana."

"But, José, our pilas are empty. We have no water. Can you come today?"

"Sí, señor. But my truck cannot. It needs repairs."

"Okay. But you can definitely come tomorrow?"

"Sí, señor. Mañana temprana."

One of the adjustments gringos have to make when moving to Mexico is learning that in this country it's considered rude to say no to somebody, even when that is what you mean. Mexicans know the difference between yes-yes and yes-no, but sometimes foreigners struggle with that concept.

Another thing gringos struggle to learn is that time doesn't have the same urgency to a Mexican that it has to us. Our friend Pete once had a problem with his water pump, so he called a repairman from San José to drive out and have a look at it. The man came, said he could fix the pump, but he would first have to buy the parts in town.

"So when can you come back?" Pete asked.

"Viernes," the man said, two days away.

But on *viernes* the man never came—or the next day, or the day after that. Finally, Pete found somebody else to repair his pump. Almost one year later, the first repairman showed up at Pete's house, saying he had the parts now and he was ready to fix the pump. And it was a *viernes*.

So when José told me he would bring us a load of water early tomorrow morning, I knew that might not be what he meant at all. Still, there was nothing we could do but wait and see.

Later this afternoon, Mike and Annie Doyle, who had been out surfing on the East Cape, dropped by to pick up Annie's new paddleboard, which was still sitting on top of our truck.

Throughout the sixties, many surfers around the world considered Doyle to be the best all-around surfer of his generation. He was powerful in big surf, agile in small surf, a tireless paddler, yet still creative and playful enough to have been one of the greatest tandem surfers of all time. He still surfs almost every day and SUPs, kites, or swims almost all the others. He's like some mutant amphibian that has to wet its scales in the ocean every few hours. He has all the aches and pains you would expect from any former professional athlete. He has suffered several broken bones over the years, and his joints creak and moan. He's carrying a few more pounds than when he was in his prime, but he carries them well. With his salt-crusted beard, roaring laugh, and charismatic presence, he reminds me of some medieval king who has enjoyed many decades of lustful plundering, and far too many bottles of wine. He has enjoyed his victories, survived his defeats, and apparently he still isn't finished.

The grizzled old loadmaster of 10,000 surf expeditions walked completely around our truck, stroking his beard in contemplation. He tested the straps and bungees I'd used to secure the paddleboard, then patted me vigorously on the back and declared my work "an excellent job."

After we'd carefully unstrapped the paddleboard and placed it on the ground, Annie picked up the tail and eyed down its sleek lines. Annie, who scarcely weighs a hundred pounds, has become one of the most respected female surfers on the East Cape. She's not only athletically talented but fearless. I've seen her charge ferociously into double-overhead waves when tough guys all around her were caught thinking twice. "It's absolutely beautiful," she said, giving me a hug. "I can't wait to try it out."

"Boca de Tule was ten feet today," Doyle told me. "A true southern hemi. Tomorrow won't be as big, but it's gonna be good. Also, we've got two hurricanes working off the Mexican mainland, and one of them is already putting out winds of a hundred and thirty miles per hour."

Nobody I know follows the weather patterns on the East Cape better than Doyle. He learned it all the hard way thirty years ago, when surf forecasts weren't readily available, and surfers had to rely on the wind and clouds to tell them what to expect. Now that we can get instant surf forecasts on the internet, Doyle takes that information, blends it with his hard-earned experience, and makes judgment calls that often amaze me for their accuracy and intuition.

I showed Doyle my new board—a 9'0" shaped by John Kies at Encinitas Surfboards. Doyle had once been a shaper himself and has a better eye than any surfer I know, and I was eager to hear what he thought.

Most younger surfers would consider a board 9'0" much too long. It's a fact that shorter surfboards are more maneuverable than longer boards, but it's not always that simple. Once, about ten years ago, I was surfing with Doyle at La

Pastora, on the Pacific side of the peninsula. A big winter swell was running and it grew all morning with a receding tide. The waves were about 10-foot at dawn, 12-foot by 10:00 a.m., and by noon they were at least 15-foot and extremely powerful. The place was packed with talented young surfers from all over the world, and they had been dominating all morning on their shortboards. But they began having trouble in the afternoon. They couldn't generate enough paddling speed to catch the waves, and if they did catch one, their boards couldn't handle the power, or the chop. They were spinning out of control like hapless victims in some video game. Doyle, who had been riding a 9'0", came in and switched to a gun in the 10'6" range. Then Pat Curren showed up too, riding a board that must have been about 11'0". Pat, the father of former world champion Tom Curren, had helped design the first big guns used to ride giant waves at Sunset and Waimea back in the fifties. Over the next two hours, a pack of the hottest young surfers I had ever seen sat on the beach and watched these two old masters, both in their sixties, put on a demonstration of how to ride big surf.

So it's not really about shortboard versus longboard, and it's not about age. It's about having the right board for the conditions, and the right board for you. Fortunately, surfboard design has been improving over the years, and it's possible now to get longer boards, like my new 9'0", that perform like much shorter boards.

Doyle studied the new board carefully, turned it over three or four times, sighted down the length from the nose, and then from the tail. Finally he gave me his opinion: "This might be the best board you've ever owned. But don't listen to me. Get out there first thing in the morning and see for yourself."

October 10

I was awake by five, had coffee, and loaded my new board onto the Rhino. There wasn't even a glimmer of light in the sky, but I could hear the surf, and it sounded big. Sound can be deceptive, though, making even average surf on a low tide seem bigger than it really is. I puttered around in the garage, where I wouldn't wake Claudia, until I saw the first blush of orange light to the east; then I fired up the Rhino and headed off.

The roads on the East Cape are a god-awful bitch—dirt and mud, no culverts, washboards with skull-rattling ruts, and a new hazard around every curve. I wouldn't have it any other way. If you build four-lane freeways to the best surf breaks on the continent, what you end up with is crowded disasters like Swami's, Trestles, Rincon, and Malibu. No heavy truck or SUV can hold up under these East Cape conditions—their weight just beats them to pieces—but I was pleased to see that this little Rhino floated over the holes and ruts as if they weren't even there.

I quickly covered the three miles to Shipwreck—the first good surf spot heading east—then sat by myself on the bluff, waiting for enough daylight so I could see the waves breaking below.

Shipwreck is a fast wave that breaks on a reef close to shore. It can be a thrilling ride, but it isn't that long, and it's better suited for a board shorter than my 9'0". I stopped there anyway to get an idea of what the swell was doing before I headed farther out.

Finally, the sky grew light enough for me to see white froth below, and in a few more minutes I could see the waves themselves. They were only about head high, which probably meant this was a dying swell. Still, it looked like clean, rideable surf—certainly better than anything I'd seen in South Dakota.

I drove along the beach to Punta Espina and found that I was the only person there. Most surfers who live along the East Cape leave in the summer. This year I happened to be among the first to return.

I dearly love Punta Espina. In the last four years I've ridden more waves there than at any other place in my nearly fifty years of surfing. I've shared wonderful hours there with friends, and I've made a lot of new friends there too. Out of respect for all of them, I have chosen to use a fictitious name for this break, in the hope that it can remain hidden and secluded for a few more years.

Punta Espina has a mixed rock and sand bottom, and the waves refract off a submerged point. I like to think of it as a combination reef break and point break. The normal takeoff spot is about three hundred yards straight out from shore—a long paddle—and far enough away that it's easy to underestimate how big the waves are when you're standing onshore. The first half of the wave is the best—with long, fast walls—but if you choose to ride from the outside all the way in, the ride can be up to four hundred yards long. For me, this break starts to get fun when it's about head high, and it gets more fun as it gets bigger. If you start deep on the wave (farther back), it can be a real challenge to make it across the first section, and the penalty for failure is getting caught inside and pounded on the head by the next several waves in the set.

Though the morning sky was brightening now, the sun hadn't risen above the horizon. I took my new board out of the bag and gave it its first coat of wax. The board is white, except for two bolts of yellow down the rails, and it has no gloss coat—an absolutely gorgeous piece of work.

I took a few minutes to stretch my legs, back, and shoulders. When I was younger, I never stretched before surfing, convinced that stretching was like playing golf—something you avoided until you got so old you had no choice. But after the pains in my shoulders, knees, and lower back started at around forty, I learned that stretching can not only prevent injury but improve the performance of an aging surfer like me. I still haven't taken up golf.

I carried my board to the water's edge, slid onto the deck, and pushed through the small shorebreak. The water was at least 85 degrees—warmer than the air. Cold water causes old bones to ache, even with a good wetsuit, but water can be too warm too, and this water felt too warm.

I paddled slowly across the cove, trying, after three months out of the water, to go easy on my shoulder muscles. The new board glided well. Once I was outside, I took my time before edging toward the takeoff spot.

Some people say that surfing alone is foolish and irresponsible, and maybe they're right. When I was in my twenties, it always felt a little spooky to be out alone at dawn without another person in sight. But it feels like a real pleasure now. I know if something went wrong and they found my fish-nibbled body washed up on the beach, nobody would be standing around saying, "What a shame he died so young." If I want to surf alone at dawn on a remote beach in Mexico, that's nobody's business but my own.

I let a full set of five waves pass under me, trying to get a feel for this swell. The truth is, I was nervous, because at my age, every time I paddle out, I'm not sure if I can still get it done.

Most guys my age, if they're in decent shape, can paddle fairly well. Our wave judgment improves as we get older, and once we get to our feet we can rely on years of muscle memory. The crucial test for an older surfer is that quick transition from belly to feet. Younger surfers take for granted the complexity of timing and coordination involved, but older surfers learn the hard way how much athletic ability is required. Failure to make that simple maneuver is what puts an end to surfing careers. You can't fake it, no amount of bravado can substitute for it, and fancy new surf trunks don't help in the least.

I slid easily into a head-high wave and wallowed to my feet just in time to take full control. I'm sure it wasn't pretty, but at least there was nobody watching. My new board accelerated quickly and felt smooth as I headed down the line. When I laid into a sharp cutback, it gained speed, which is what a good board should do; completing the turn, it made a clean, seamless transition from one edge to the other. Most important, the board felt comfortable, with no surprises, as if I'd been riding it a long time. It was a good match for my age and size, and I couldn't wait to see what it would do in bigger surf.

Usually, I stay out in the water about three hours, but today I managed only about an hour and a half before my shoulders were exhausted. And I only rode about ten waves, all in the head-high range.

I was home before nine o'clock and found to my shame that Claudia was hard at work again cleaning house. She didn't say anything about my sneaking off for a morning of surf—she never does—but I felt guilty just the same.

I'd had my fun—now it was time for the drudgery.

October 11

Around nine o'clock this morning, after I'd returned from surfing, we heard the familiar low-gear whine of José's water truck coming around Punta Gorda, about a mile west of town. José hadn't showed up yesterday, so we had to clean house the best we could with little one-liter bottles of drinking water. It was sort of like your mother cleaning your dirty face with spit and a Kleenex.

It's about ten miles from where José fills his truck at the big arroyo east of San José del Cabo to Zacatitos, and about half those miles are dirt road. José's truck is easily the oldest in the fleet, and he drives slowly to avoid expensive repairs. I don't think I've ever seen him drive faster than twenty miles per hour, and his average is more like ten. Maybe his truck won't go any faster, I don't know. His bald tires wobble like hula hoops, and on some days he backs up steeper sections of the road to take advantage of the lower gear ratio. But José is a patient man, and he prefers to drive the old, rugged, unmaintained beach road because, as he says, it's *más tranquilo*, and it's the route his grandmother used decades before the newer road was built.

Many Mexican truck drivers make their living hauling water to the East Cape, but my favorite has always been José. I used another deliveryman when we first moved here, but I didn't like the man's surly attitude, and I wasn't impressed by the speed of his truck or his fancy paint job. So I switched to José, and he has been our water deliveryman ever since.

José is perhaps 38, weighs around 300 pounds, and holds his pants up with a piece of rope. I had never heard him speak a word of English, but this year he had a surprise for me. He climbed down out of his truck, shook my hand, cleared his throat, stuttered twice like a schoolchild delivering a carefully practiced recital, and said in halting English, "Welcome home."

"Muchas gracias," I replied.

José fired up his little Honda pump and began filling our *pilas*. Then we moved a few feet away where it was quiet enough to talk. "Is everything at your house okay?" José asked, reverting to Spanish.

"Yes, everything is good," I said. "Yesterday I found a small water leak in the pipes in the garage, but I was able to fix it."

"Gracias a Dios!" he replied.

"How is your family?" I asked.

"Everybody is well, gracias a Dios."

"And your truck?"

"Better now, gracias a Dios."

Years ago, when he was in better physical condition, José surfed on the East Cape, and he always likes to ask me now how the surf has been.

"The surf was head high today," I said, "and very clean."

"Gracias a Dios!"

Many Mexicans aren't aware that Baja has world-class surf—they think gringos come to fish, play golf, or make fools of themselves in the bars at Cabo San Lucas. But José knows all about the surf here, and he's proud that surfers come from all over the world to ride his favorite wave, Shipwreck, which he calls "Mexican Pipeline." The surfers appreciate José's enthusiasm too, which is why the hood and side panels of his truck are speckled with decals from Rainbow, Volcom, Reef, Sanuk, Bubblegum Wax, and many other surf manufacturers. José has become the unofficial water deliveryman for East Cape surfers.

The water José brings is not potable. I treat it with chlorine, which kills many microorganisms, and it is treated again by an ultraviolet system, which, hopefully, kills everything else. Theoretically, the water is then drinkable, but we don't. Instead we buy water in San José that has been filtered by reverse osmosis and is literally purer than rain. We buy the water in refillable plastic jugs, and it costs only about eighty cents for five gallons. Using this system, nobody at our house has ever gotten sick, *gracias a Dios!*

Now that we had water in our *pilas*, Claudia and I were able to continue cleaning house, which excited Claudia more than it did me. Claudia's standards of cleanliness greatly exceed my own, and I soon lost interest in the work. Part of my rationale for shirking my duties, which I didn't share with Claudia, was that we were Mexicans now, and it might be considered culturally inappropriate for me to be involved with indoor household chores. A man's place, after all, is outdoors. The flaw with my thinking, which I have been struggling to improve, was that I have few outdoor chores. We have no lawn, no shrubbery—only five coco palms and six *bugambilias*. Everything else on our lot is native desert landscape. Also, because the house is nearly new, there is nothing to repair. Even washing the truck, in my opinion, would be a senseless act, since we drive almost daily on dirt roads and the truck would be dirty again in less than a mile.

My real focus of concern was for my surf gear. The old wax on my eight surfboards had hardened after three months of disuse. What the boards needed was to be carried into the sun so the wax could melt and then be scraped off. Also, leash cuffs needed to be inspected for salt rot and for corrosion around the metal swivels. Obsolete tide charts taped to the garage wall needed to be thrown away. My gear bag needed to be cleaned out, old scraps of wax discarded, empty sunscreen bottles tossed, tool kit inspected and replenished. Unfortunately, all these chores combined didn't require more than thirty minutes, though I managed to extend that time to nearly an hour. Then, rather than submitting to household chores, I decided it would be a good idea to prune the low-hanging palm fronds, which had been tattered by the summer storms and, in fact, had scraped the roof of the truck when we drove under them.

Claudia, however, soon noticed my absence and went looking for me downstairs. "I'm completely overwhelmed with cleaning everything in this house," she said, "and you decide you need to prune your palm trees?"

I started to explain my chain of logic but decided it sounded less convincing out loud than it had in my head. Besides, I knew that no surfer's wife has been more tolerant of this famously irresponsible lifestyle than my own. So I swallowed my macho pride and spent the rest of the day mopping floors.

October 13

Although Claudia doesn't surf more than a couple of times a year, she grew up in west L.A. and understands how a lifestyle can be built around the beach. She accepts my urgency for getting in the water early in the morning to avoid the winds that will inevitably develop later in the day, she loves to watch the sunrise over the ocean, she likes to walk along the beach with Kirra, and if the surf is good and I stay out in the water for three or four hours, she doesn't mind reading or sketching until I've exhausted myself. So today, with our house chores finally finished, Claudia drove with me to Punta Espina at first light.

Today, though, was full moon, and at dawn the tide was unusually high. Some surf spots aren't hampered much by a high tide, but Punta Espina isn't one of them. Unless the surf is big enough, the waves tend to roll in without breaking. In addition to the high tide, the night wind, which comes from the north here, was still putting an ugly bump on the surface of the water. I watched a couple of sets from the beach before deciding it was hopeless.

On our way home, we stopped on the bluff above Shipwreck and watched a couple of sets. It looked to me like there was only one wave in every other set worth riding, but because Shipwreck breaks on a shallow reef, the high tide doesn't hamper it as much. The night wind had backed off a bit now, and the faces of the waves looked fairly clean. Only three guys were in the water, but they were patient and selective and they were getting some decent rides. So we drove down the arroyo to the beach, parked under one of the *palapas* there, and I paddled out.

As I said, Shipwreck isn't really my kind of wave. It breaks fast and can get hollow, but it breaks in shallow water, has a rocky bottom covered with urchins, and has just one takeoff spot, which means with four or five guys in the water it can feel crowded. But I figured with my longer board, I could take off a little bit deeper than the others, and maybe I would get my share of rides.

Before long two Mexican guys paddled out, which I was surprised to see. When I first started surfing in Mexico in the sixties, there were almost no Mexican surfers at all. But Mexicans are blessed with great athletic talent, enormous energy, and fierce determination, and now that Mexico has a rapidly growing middle class, Mexicans are beginning to find the time and disposable income to pursue a sport like surfing. Much of mainland Mexico's Pacific coastline can receive swells from the north and south, water temperatures are ideal, and today Mexico is starting to produce outstanding surfers.

Many Mexican surfers are even more aggressive in the water than Californians. Their competitive instincts have been honed by *fútbol* and boxing, and even though most Mexican surfers will go out of their way to be courteous and friendly, they think of surfing as a contest, and they consider waves breaking in their territorial waters to be their Mexican birthright. In other words, Mexican surfers can be the same sort of obnoxious jerks you find in California, Hawaii, Australia, and every other place in the surfing world.

When I finally paddled for an exceptionally clean, outside wave, one of the Mexican surfers, who was not even in a position to catch the wave, paddled in front of me, effectively blocking me out so his friend, farther inside, could have the wave for himself. I had never seen that strategy employed in Mexico before, and I certainly didn't like it. But I kept my mouth shut. Mexicans expect arrogance from *norteamericanos*—they've been seeing it all their lives—and I was determined not to fit their stereotype.

So I paddled even farther out, using my strategy of taking off deeper than everybody else. I caught a couple of decent waves, but they both closed out before I'd ridden them more than fifty feet, and I was beginning to feel a bit frustrated.

Then I caught one very clean, hollow, overhead wave and rode it nearly to the beach.

When I paddled back out, even the Mexicans were howling in Spanish and giving me the thumbs up.

As José says, "Mexican Pipeline!"

October 14

With our house in good order, Claudia and I needed to drive into San José to buy groceries, drinking water, beer, minutes for my Mexican cellphone, and a lot of other things. But even before the sun came up, I knew by the sound from our bedroom window that the surf today was going to be good. And I knew that this late in the fall surfing season, there wouldn't be too many more days like this. So I got up, made coffee, ate a banana and a peanut butter sandwich, and told Claudia I was only going as far as Shipwreck and I wouldn't stay long.

I decided not to take my new 9'0" Kies. Call it a hunch. Even when Shipwreck isn't big, it can break very hard, and I wasn't comfortable risking my new board there.

The board I took instead was an older, slightly smaller Kies that I had bought used. It was light, very maneuverable, and rode as though it was much shorter than it actually was. I loved that board, but it was getting old—dinged and showing the yellowing of age—and I was thinking it might not have much life left in it. That was why I had taken its dimensions to John Kies and asked him to make me another one just like it. In other words, my new board was almost a replica of the old board I loved so much.

The Shipwreck regulars were already out when I got there, sitting on their shortboards (around 6-foot in length) in a little pack, with the sun just breaking the horizon. I knew this group of guys only slightly, and though they had always been friendly, surfers are surfers, and I knew they wouldn't welcome my presence. Shipwreck is a tight wave, with that one little takeoff spot and not enough room for a lot of surfers.

As I paddled by the other guys on my way outside, I nodded good morning but got nothing in return. I respect these guys who surf Shipwreck regularly. They know the bottom conditions down to every rock and urchin, their boards are the perfect size for that wave, and their wave selection is seldom wrong. They have the place wired. But I had no intention of competing with them. Instead, I hoped to use my strategy from the day before of sitting farther outside and catching waves they couldn't get.

By sitting deeper, I would have a chance to catch larger waves, but with a hard-breaking wave like this, in shallow water, there was always the possibility of injury. The year before, I'd scraped bottom here, and even with booties on, I'd taken five urchin spines deep into my heel. It had taken me nearly a month to get them out.

So I was selective—at least at first. I caught a couple of medium-sized waves and rode them cautiously. But, eventually, I became eager to catch something bigger, like the amazing wave I'd caught the day before. I waited for a good-looking set to appear on the horizon, and I let the first two smaller waves pass me by. Then I saw a wave in the overhead range welling up, and I decided to try for it.

I caught the wave easily—too easily, really. The wave jacked up quickly, and I could see the drop was going to be steep. I stomped on the tail of my board and carved hard to the right. I survived the drop, but as soon as I was angled down the line, the shoulder lurched up in front of me, and I knew I was way too deep. If I had tucked under the lip, I might have made it, but I didn't want to take a chance in that shallow water. So I turned hard into the face of the wave and lifted the nose of my board. Just as my shoulders cleared the lip, I shoved my board hard with my feet so it would fly out the back of the wave.

No problem. The wave crashed inside of me with a terrific, hollow-sounding thump. But I was out the back now, free and clear. I tugged on my leash to retrieve my board, but only half of it came back to me. And then I realized that my board had gotten sucked back into the breaking wave; it had been pounded hard off the bottom and broken in two.

I removed the leash from my ankle so I wouldn't get it entangled in the rocks, and I swam in, pushing half the board in front of me. When I overtook the other half, about halfway in, I collected it too. Broken fiberglass is very sharp, and I didn't want anybody to get cut.

I've broken only five or six surfboards in my life. A couple of those I didn't care about and was maybe even happy to get rid of. But to lose a highly prized board like this one hurt. It was like losing an old friend—somebody you've laughed with, suffered with, and even shared a few triumphs with. And, yes—no getting around it—the wide hips of a good surfboard are feminine, and though I know better than to say anything of the kind to my wife, I can still recall the sadness of losing a favorite girlfriend, and I can't help but feel that losing a good surfboard is a similar kind of pain.

But at least when a surfboard breaks, nobody bleeds. No bones are broken. Nobody dies. Not usually. Surfboards are not permanent, and they can be replaced.

As I was stood on the beach with two pieces of surfboard in my hands, trying to make sense of what had just happened to me, one of the Shipwreck regulars came up to offer his condolences. "Too bad about the board," he said. "But you know, any surfer who doesn't break a board once in a while probably isn't charging hard enough. For whatever it's worth, though, I thought you were sitting a little too deep."

October 16

The surf reports do not look encouraging. Two hurricanes

had been spinning off the coast of mainland Mexico when we first got back, but they ricocheted around in the ocean until they finally wore themselves out without producing much in the way of surf. That's what happens this time of year. The Pacific begins to cool, and hurricanes moving north from warmer waters just melt away. There are still some big storms 6,000 miles away, off New Zealand, and with a bit of luck we might get another decent southern hemi or two. But I'm afraid this year's fall surf season is already beginning to shut down.

October 19

Claudia has always had more restless energy than I have. She's the sort of person who has to be doing something all the time. If she's sitting on the beach while I'm surfing, she has to be knitting or sketching. She doesn't nap easily in the afternoon, like I do, and has never mastered the art of sitting quietly in the evening with a cold beer, just watching the sunset. Even in her sleep she's busy, constantly twitching and jerking, though she claims she has no awareness of this habit. She's a compulsive cleaner, and when there's nothing left in the house to clean, she will go to work in the kitchen baking bread, mango pies, or coconut-oatmeal cookies. After that, she begins experimenting with new recipes from her library of cookbooks. This has certainly made my domestic life enjoyable, but I have always wondered—even worried—what would happen if she ever ran out of things to do.

Last winter Claudia decided she wanted to learn some form of sculpture, and one of the first things she wanted to make was a whale's tail. I suggested clay, but as it turned out, an artist here in Zacatitos was offering a three-day course in cement sculpture, using wire mesh as the skeletal framework and cement as the malleable skin. In Mexico, almost everything is made of cement and steel, so we figured that was an appropriate medium for a sculptress here. Claudia took the course and in three days produced a gray, fifty-pound whale tail that reminded me of the tailings a cement-truck driver leaves behind after he cleans out his chute—pretty much just a gray, shapeless blob. Claudia wasn't happy with the result either. Trying to be supportive, I told her it was a good first effort, and the next one would be better. I applied an acid wash to the tail that gave it an aquamarine color, and I mounted it on one of our fence posts for all the world to see. After a few days she asked me to take it down.

Then Claudia heard about a weeklong sculpture course offered in San José, this one in papier-maché. I recall that week clearly because there was a big south swell at the time, and Claudia needed our truck every day so she could drive into San José to attend her course. After missing two days of 10-foot surf, I emailed Doyle to ask if I could ride along with him and Annie. I felt like a teenage kid in San Diego trying to hitchhike on the Coast Highway.

At any rate, after the course was over, Claudia brought home a beautiful, blue, three-foot whale tail. We placed it on a corner shelf in our house, where it has stayed ever since. The very next day, Claudia set to work producing papier-maché fish, and she hasn't stopped since. We now have a dozen red snappers, five or six yellow-fin tuna, marlin, dorado, several parrotfish, a roosterfish, a clown fish, and more. Every one of her attempts showed an improvement, and they continue to improve, until now each fish has individual scales, glass eyes, and complex color schemes. After giving away most of her early efforts, we still have whole schools of fish hanging on every wall. Sitting in any room of our house is like being submerged in a large aquarium with several species of fish circling overhead.

To be a happily married surfer, it's important to seduce your spouse into accepting a life of indolence. So today I helped Claudia set up a new workbench in the garage, where

I hope she can spend many happy hours producing papier-maché fish.

October 23

The surf forecasts have been calling for a south swell—maybe the last of the season—to arrive on the 23rd. But that forecast was for mainland Mexico, and south swells usually arrive at Los Cabos a day or so later. All night long I listened for the sound of big waves, but all I heard was the soft sound of bubbling mush. We walked down to the beach this morning just after dawn, but we saw no sign of a new swell, and now I'm thinking the surf forecast is wrong.

October 25

I woke about three this morning to the sound of powerful waves cracking on the beach. I went out on the terrace and listened in the dark to the pattern of four or five waves to a set, followed by long lulls in between—the signature of a classic south swell. I went back to bed and told Claudia I was leaving for Punta Espina in two hours.

"I'm going too," she said.

When we got up again at five, Kirra trailed us back and forth from the bedroom to the kitchen, worried she was going to be left behind. She always knows when we're going to the beach—I think her clue might be when Claudia puts on her bathing suit While we threw together a quick breakfast, Kirra began nipping at our ankles to hurry us along and yapping at us when she didn't see progress toward the door. Finally, I ordered her out of the house. Even then she stared defiantly at me through the window screen until I clapped my hands and shooed her away. She slinked down the stairs to wait by the Rhino, where she knew we couldn't sneak off without her.

The sky was still dark when we started out the East Cape road, but as usual, there were a few trucks on their way to some job site. In Mexico the workers often ride standing in the back of the trucks, holding on to the stake-side panels. As we dropped into a narrow arroyo just west of Shipwreck, we saw to our surprise that a party of Mexican marines, all wearing black masks and carrying automatic weapons, had set up a roadblock at the bottom of the drainage, where they were vigorously inspecting every vehicle. We were used to military checkpoints—there are seven between Tijuana and Los Cabos—but we had never seen one out here on the East Cape before.

My Mexican friends have told me they have more confidence in the military than either the federal or local police. They say the military is the least corrupt of all government institutions, and they respect the young soldiers for being the only authorities in Mexico with the courage to stand up to the narco-terrorists. I'm inclined to agree. I've never felt in danger around the soldiers, never been asked for a bribe, and never known them to steal anything from my car while conducting inspections.

I chatted with the polite young soldier while he inspected our Rhino, both to put him at ease and to let him know we had nothing to hide. When Kirra growled at him, he stepped back and said, "Muy bravo!"

Knowing that Mexicans respect an aggressive dog, I said, "Sí, muy bravo, pero un poquito loco también."

The soldier laughed, wished us a good day, and waved us through the checkpoint. But I couldn't help wondering what was going on.

At Punta Espina I could see right away, even in the dim light, that the tide was still too high. But at least this was a real swell. I paddled out as the sun came over the horizon and surfed alone for an hour or so, struggling to catch the slow-breaking waves. When the tide began to drop, though, the waves became bigger and crisper. The swell was still building too, and by nine o'clock some of the waves were a foot or two overhead and breaking in wrapping lines nearly 300 yards long. Punta Espina doesn't get much better than this, and to have such a good swell this late in the season was a joy.

For the second day in a row, I surfed for four hours, which is a long time in the water for anybody. But I knew this was the tail end of the fall surf season, and I figured I'd better get it while I could. I went home tired but happy.

Later this afternoon, I read in the local newspaper, *La Tribuna*, that in San Lucas a homicide investigator had been killed by a narco hit man (actually, hit woman, the paper said), and all vehicles leaving Los Cabos were being inspected.

Friends and family back in the U.S. have accused Claudia and me of being reckless as hell for moving to Mexico. We've given up arguing the point. We don't want to encourage Americans to move here, so it's not an argument we want to win. It's a fact, though, that Mexico can be a dangerous place—almost as dangerous as the United States. Mexico is in a kind of civil war with the drug traffickers right now, much like the war the United States government had with organized crime during the Prohibition era. I believe the Mexican people are at a crossroads, trying to decide whether they want to be a true modern democracy or if they will allow the country to slide back into the old corruption and economic inequality. The war has been violent on mainland Mexico and along the U.S. border, but Los Cabos, for the most part, has been free from bloodshed. Some Mexicans say the narco-traffickers bring their families to Los Cabos to be safe, and they don't want the violence to spread here. I don't know if that's true or not. Maybe Los Cabos has just been lucky. But one thing is certain: the economy of Los Cabos is built on tourism, and if Los Cabos is no longer seen as a safe place for families to visit, the results will be disastrous for the Mexican people who live and work here.

We have learned since moving here that the image Americans have of Mexico as a violent and dangerous country is greatly distorted. Here are a few facts about violence in Mexico that most Americans don't know:

— The murder rate in Tijuana, one of the most violent cities in Mexico, is lower than the murder rate in New Orleans.

— The murder rate in Mexico City is lower than the murder rate in Washington D.C.

— The murder rate in Houston is about the same as the murder rate in Mexico.

— The murder rate in Baja California Sur (the state we live in) is lower than the murder rate in California.

When I read American newspapers, I see that gun violence in the U.S. is so common it's hardly considered news anymore, and even mass murders have become almost routine. But for reasons I can't understand, a lot of Americans consider the idea of getting murdered in Mexico to be far more horrifying than getting murdered at home.

October 26

As I drove past the beach huts of the *panga* fishermen at Punta Espina this morning, I could see the light of their kitchen fires inside, which meant the women were up fixing breakfast already. Outside, the thick Mexican blankets the men roll themselves up in at night lay abandoned in the sand like cocoons. The men had taken their morning coffee down to the beached *pangas*, where they could discuss the day's prospects without waking the children, who were still sleeping inside the huts. I nodded and waved to the fishermen as I passed.

The *panga* fishermen and surfers share this beach every

day, and our interest in the weather and tides is similar. Yet, I'm sorry to say, we don't interact much. In the past, there has been some trouble between the gringo homeowners who live along the bluffs and the fishermen who camp with their families on the beach. The friction has to do with trash, the disposal of fish guts, the sound of loud mufflers at four in the morning, and the Saturday-night festivities when music and laughter often last until dawn. What the homeowners have trouble understanding is that these fishermen and their families have been using this beach for decades—long before any gringos arrived. Plus, in Mexico, the beaches are federally owned and considered public property. The fishermen have every right to be here.

Owning a beachfront home is not always the dream some people suppose it might be. Corrosion from the salt air makes home maintenance difficult. Landscape plants suffer from salt burn. The price of a beachfront lot is at least ten times higher than an ocean-view lot set back a ways. But the biggest problem is that everybody in the country has access to the route in front of your house, and ATVs and pickups pass by at all hours of the day and night.

We own a lot in this subdivision, allowing us access to surf here. We've never been involved in the *panga*-fishermen dispute, yet we can see it from both sides. I always make it a point to smile and say *hola* when I pass the fishermen, and they have always been courteous to me in return.

Some of the homeowners here, I heard later today, are talking about paying the *panga* fishermen to move their huts elsewhere—perhaps even buying them a lot outside this subdivision. Anything that eases the tension is okay with me, but it worries me that our two cultures so often find it difficult to get along.

October 27

I paddled out alone at Punta Espina just as the sun rose over the water. The high tide—a 7.0—was even higher than yesterday, so I spent an hour chasing lazy rollers that refused to break. In frustration, I moved in closer to the rocky point, where the waves were breaking a little better, and I was able to catch a couple of decent waves. But the water there was frighteningly shallow. The rock here is volcanic—sharp and jagged—and flesh wounds in these tropical waters easily become infected and are slow to heal.

I was wearing my Sea Specs (polarized sunglasses made for water sports) because the day before I had burned my eyes staring into the low morning sun. And now, with the polarized lenses, I could see rocks beneath me more clearly than I really cared to see them. I rode a couple of waves high on the lip to avoid the rocks looming below me, but that was more risk than I was comfortable with on my new board. So I moved back to the normal takeoff spot and tried to wait patiently for the tide to drop.

Finally, around nine o'clock, the tide began to recede. Not only were the waves breaking more cleanly now, but the lower tide was causing them to jack up higher than the actual swell size. And still there was no wind.

With conditions this good, and nobody out but me, I should have been having my best surf session in months. But something was wrong, and I couldn't figure out what it was. My timing was off, my energy level was lagging, and my focus was wandering. On one of the best waves I'd seen in weeks, I bobbled and nearly blew what should have been an easy takeoff. I recovered and ran out in front of the peak, but then sank a rail on the cutback and got pitched out into the flat.

I paddled back outside and let a perfectly good set pass me by while I tried to understand what was wrong. At my age, anytime you blow an easy takeoff, you wonder if you're losing the physical ability to surf anymore. It happens to everybody sooner or later. But I'd had several excellent rides in the past few days, and I refused to believe my time had come. I had a suspicion my problem was mental, but I couldn't figure out the cause.

After several dark minutes of soul searching, I recalled that the night before I'd fallen asleep reading a book about the stock market collapse of 2008, in which the words "New York" had been repeated over and over. And now I came to the horrifying realization that, without even being aware of it, I'd been singing "New York, New York" to myself all morning. I had been infected by the highly toxic and debilitating Sinatra virus.

Experienced surfers know that the song you have in your head while you're surfing is crucial to how well you perform. Obviously, there's the rhythm of the music, which functions as a timing mechanism, or mental metronome, lending fluidity to a surfer's movements. Plus, there's the attitude of the music, which inspires the surfer to fully express himself. But it's more complex than that. Music switches off the thinking part of the brain that is useless in any activity that develops as rapidly as surfing. Thinking is helpful as you prepare for an approaching wave, but once you begin paddling, intuition must take over.

We modern humans spend most of our time wrapped in a fog of technological illusion in which it is difficult to know what is real and what is imagined. In powerful surf, though, things are about as real as they can ever get. Everything happens quickly, not always in the way you expect, and the penalty for not correctly interpreting reality can be severe. The right music can help a surfer create a mood of relaxed alertness, which is really the essence of good surfing.

But nobody can surf with a Frank Sinatra song in his head. It's the arrogant, pretentious music of boozy urbanites who wear toupees, shiny suits, and neck jewelry. Worse yet, it's arrhythmic. And "New York, New York" might be the most virulent of Sinatra's songs, with that horribly flat voice straining to sound hip. Somehow that cursed tune had oozed into my brain and become stuck there, like an amoebic cyst, and was taking over my bodily functions. Worse yet, I was out in the Sea of Cortez, all alone, with nobody who could come to my aid.

I knew I had to exorcize this demon, I had to do it by myself, and I had to do it fast.

I began flipping through the songs in my jukebox memory. Luckily I have a large repertoire, which is another advantage of getting older. Over five decades I've surfed to the Beach Boys, the Rolling Stones, the Grateful Dead, the Pretenders, Willie Nelson, and now, more and more, to Lucinda Williams. But when I know I'm in trouble, as I was today, the song I always try to conjure up in my head is Billy Joe Shaver's "Black Rose."

> *The devil made me do it the first time*
> *The second time I done it on my own*
> *Lord lend a hand to a simple-minded man*
> *Learn to leave that black rose alone*

I began repeating the lyrics in my head, like a mantra, until the tune itself emerged. It was plain-old Southern hillbilly and had nothing at all to do with surfing. But it was the perfect antidote for Sinatra. The wretched demon that had tortured me all morning howled like a banshee as it fled for the darkness of some smoke-filled bar, and my relief was immediate, like sliding a needle under a crushed fingernail to bleed off the pressure.

As I sat astride my board, repeating Billy Joe Shaver's lyrics and waiting for my courage to return, I began pondering the meaning of Shaver's song. The irresistible thrill of temptation? Interracial sex? Maybe the pure joy of recklessness?

Not long after becoming a born-again Christian, Shaver shot some guy in a Texas bar for having the audacity to tell him to shut up. So Shaver knew something about reckless-ness. Fortunately for Shaver, shooting somebody in a bar is considered a constitutional right in Texas, not a crime, and he was acquitted.

I probably could have sat out there all morning, happily pondering the meaning of Shaver's song. But I'd come to surf, the sun was getting high and hot, and I knew it was time for me to get moving. Soon a new set of waves began to form on the horizon, and with my nerves calmed, my timing re-covered, and my courage restored, I caught the second wave of the set and rode it cleanly to the beach.

Thank you, Billy Joe Shaver.

October 28

Long before dawn I could hear waves breaking out our bedroom window, but they didn't sound as loud as they had the day before. I knew the tide was going to be even higher today and, of course, forty minutes or so later than yesterday. Plus, I was still tired and sore from wrestling demons. So I rolled over and went back to sleep.

Just after sunrise a powerful wind began blowing out of the east, and I knew I'd made the right call by sleeping in, even if I'd done it more out of laziness than anything else.

One surf forecast says we could see a small swell some-time early next week, but I'm doubtful.

October 30

Every plant in southern Baja has a strategy for surviving in this harsh desert. Cacti store water in their fibrous flesh during the rainy season and slowly draw from that storage during the rest of the year. Their beautifully designed trunks expand and contract like an accordion to accommodate the change in volume. Deciduous plants drop their leaves and shut down during long droughts, like plants up north do in winter. Other plants take their moisture from the nightly dew. Animals have their strategies for surviving in this desert too. Snakes, lizards, and chipmunks take refuge underground. The cattle and wild horses grow tremendously fat during the rainy months, then gradually consume that fat through the rest of the year until they look like walking skeletons. Many birds migrate north in the hottest months and return in the cool of winter. In Zacatitos, large flocks of doves have developed the creative adaptation of sticking close to swimming pools, where they can drink their fill every night after the gringos go to sleep.

Los Cabos has more natural sources of water than most places in Baja, and when those fail, we have a desalination plant at San Lucas. But we still have to conserve water if we want to survive here. At our house, the gray water, which is all the household wastewater except that coming from the toilets, collects in a buried 400-gallon concrete tank. Every time we shower or wash a dish, that water is saved. Our greatest water use by far is laundry. Our washing machine uses about fifty gallons of water per load. Because almost every day here is warm and breezy, we hang the wet clothes on lines strung across a sunken terrace on the roof, where they dry faster than they would in a gas dryer. Laundry day is Saturday, so by Sunday the gray-water tank is full, and for me that's the time to water plants.

At the bottom of our gray-water tank sits a one-horse-power pump, with a switch in the garage and an automatic shutoff that works on a float, so we won't burn out the pump by running it after the tank is dry. Because the pump draws about 500 watts of electricity, I wait until mid-day to do my watering, when our big Surrette storage batteries are full but the solar panels on the roof are still producing about 2,000 watts of electricity. I have three gray-water hoses that will reach our five coco palms and five *bugambilias*. The gray water comes out a bit smelly at first—sort of like perfumed sulfur—but the smell is gone the moment the water soaks into the ground.

Kirra loves the smell of the gray water and tries to roll around in the wet mulch. The plants here, both native and non-native, thrive on the gray water, which is rich in organic nutrients and phosphates. The coco palms, especially, love it.

Mexican fan palms are native to the deep canyons of northern Baja, stubborn remnants of a wetter era. The coco palms are not native to Baja, but they grow naturally all over the Pacific, and they do well here when given a little care. They grow quickly when given water, but they also tolerate long droughts. I've seen coco palms that haven't been watered in a year yet still look reasonably healthy.

I bought our coco palms from a nursery in San José, where they grew almost wild in the bottom of an arroyo. I selected five palms with trunks about one meter high, the nursery woman flagged the palms with orange tape, and later a crew of laborers dug them out of the ground by hand and wrapped their roots in burlap. The next day another crew delivered them by truck. Since then they have doubled in size, providing badly needed shade to our house.

When mature, coco palms produce an abundance of coconuts, which the locals have warned me to remove before hurricane season. Doyle told me once, "The first time I saw a full-scale hurricane here in Los Cabos, I watched coconuts flying through the air like projectiles fired from a cannon. I was so terrified, I put on my snowboard helmet and sat in the middle of my biggest room for two days."

Coco palms don't do well in upper California—not even in San Diego—because of the cold, so for Claudia and me, looking off our terrace and seeing their graceful fronds swaying in the breeze is a pleasant reminder that we live below the Tropic of Cancer now. But everything else growing in our yard, except for the five crimson *bugambilias*, is part of the natural Baja landscape, which we consider so beautiful that it doesn't require any human meddling.

The most unusual plant we have in Los Cabos is the *torote*, which some people call "elephant plant" because its trunk is short and thick, like an elephant's legs. It has beautiful golden bark, bright green foliage, and a wonderful spicy scent. Mexicans value it highly for ornamental use, and it is protected under Mexican law. When we built our house, we temporarily moved several *torotes* with the help of Tomás, the town's backhoe operator, and we later replanted them around the house. I'm proud to say that not a single *torote* died, and with just a little extra water now and then they have grown to be thick and beautiful. We also moved a few *cardon* cacti, which also survived. We didn't have such good luck with the *palo blancos* or the paloverdes, though, which have deep roots and can't tolerate much stress. It's too bad, because they're both gorgeous plants.

One of the blocklayers who worked on our house for several weeks, on his last day on the job, brought us a small *lomboy* he'd dug up and placed in a rusted tin can. He promised us the tiny plant would grow large and give our house shade. This man liked to listen to music on his car radio while he worked, and he was surprised every day to find that his battery was dead when it was time to go home. So I would get out my jumper cables and help him start his car. The *lomboy* in a rusted can was his way of thanking me.

Lomboys look like stunted cottonwoods, or perhaps poplars, with large green leaves—not at all like desert plants—which causes me to wonder if they are remnants of an age when Baja was much wetter than it is now. Normally, they only bear leaves during the summer rainy season, but if watered they can bear bright green leaves that riffle in the wind year-around. We planted the *lomboy* in front of our house, and I give it a little water every now and then too. I have a hard time imagining it ever growing big enough to offer much shade.

October 31

I read in the paper this morning that there was a violent shootout in San Lucas last night, about 40 miles away. The military had been searching for the gunmen involved in the shooting of the homicide investigator. Soldiers followed a suspicious SUV with tinted windows and no license plates to a working-class neighborhood of San Lucas; there the suspected gunmen in the SUV took refuge in a small house, and a raging gun battle took place. One of the gunmen was killed, but somehow the rest escaped. Or, at least, that's what the newspapers reported.

The Mexican people who live and work in Los Cabos are appalled by this incident, which they fear will frighten off tourists right at the beginning of the high season. There are two ways a gringo can look at this: One, the violence has spread from the mainland of Mexico to Los Cabos, and there could be more to follow. Or two, the Mexican government is determined to stop the narcos from becoming entrenched here, and the military is prepared to hunt the narcos down and kill them.

November:

Dancing at Dawn

November 1

Today my father turned 99 years old. I called him on
Skype, but he could barely hear, and I don't think he even
knew it was me.

November 2

Before dawn there was a gusty wind blowing from the
north, but I knew it would stop as soon as the sun came up. I
could hear that a small swell had arrived during the night, so
Claudia, Kirra, and I drove out the East Cape road, just as the
sky was brightening, to have a look.

The temperatures have been dropping a little every night,
and as I stripped down to slip into my thin wetsuit, the morning air felt cold. But as soon as I hit the water, I knew I'd
made a mistake. In California, even on a summer morning,
the ocean water is brisk. But here it was around 80 degrees,
and I was sweating before I had paddled a hundred feet.

I surfed alone for about an hour in mediocre, shoulder-
high surf. When the waves are this small, I usually start thinking of ways to make the session more challenging. One thing
I like to do is take off behind the peak, a hundred feet or so

deeper than I would in bigger surf, and see if I can make it across the wall. It's a good exercise for teaching yourself how to get the maximum speed out of even smaller waves, and it can be fun too.

Finally, my friend Tom paddled out on his standup board. (We have too many Toms here, so we sometimes call this one Fireman Tom.) Tom is a retired deputy fire chief from Carlsbad and a graduate of UC Berkeley. He and his wife Paula keep a motorhome in California too, and they proudly drive vehicles with South Dakota plates. They had arrived back in Baja the day before. Tom's an easygoing guy, but he's also very strong, one of the most experienced surfers at Punta Espina and a serious student of the ocean. Much of what I know about surfing this point—wind patterns, swell angles, lineup—I learned from him.

"How's the neck?" I asked. Tom had a kiting accident last year, and the last time I'd seen him, in July, he was still having trouble with a disc in his neck. He'd even switched from belly paddling to standup paddling so he wouldn't have to arch his neck all the time.

"Better, thanks," he said cheerfully. "I made a little traction device with a rope and a pulley and a jug of water as a weight. I hang that contraption from a doorway, and it separates the vertebrae just enough to give me some pain relief. I think it's helping the disc heal better too."

About a year ago, Tom decided he was going to teach himself how to kite surf. A friend gave him a set of old kiting equipment to learn on, but the friend warned Tom that the old setup didn't have all the newfangled safety equipment, like quick releases, that the new kites have. So Tom drove way out on the East Cape, to an isolated spot called Boca de Salada, where there is a long, empty beach he could practice on without getting tangled in rocks, *palapas*, ATVs, or other people.

In kiting, there's a critical moment: after you have the kite in the air but are still standing on the beach, you need to wrestle with the lines while you get down to the water's edge and mount your board. It can be a difficult thing to do, even with somebody helping you. And Tom was trying to learn how to do it by himself.

A powerful gust of wind came up, and suddenly the kite began to drag Tom sideways down the beach. He ran to keep up with the kite, struggling to regain control, but he could see immediately he was going to lose. The kite lifted him about twenty feet in the air and quickly slammed him into the sand. He struggled to get back to his feet, but again the kite lifted him twenty feet and slammed him into the sand. Then the kite started to drag him along the beach, literally sanding off his skin. Tom knew if the kite lifted and slammed him again, he might not survive the blow.

The vest that came with this borrowed kite did have one primitive quick-release feature—a knife stored inside a pouch on the back of the vest. Somehow, while still being dragged along the sand, Tom managed to reach around, recover that knife, and cut the cord between him and the kite.

Well, now he was lying there by himself on a remote East Cape beach with bloody sand burns all over his body and what felt like several broken bones. So Tom, who had been an EMT in his early days as a firefighter, performed a full-body exam on himself. He was pretty sure he had a fractured pelvis, so he advised himself not to move. But then he realized he had to ignore his own advice, because if he didn't get back to his car, he might sit there all day, or longer, before somebody came along to help, and he would surely die of dehydration, maybe internal bleeding, or even shock.

Tom managed to drag himself back to his car, and when he caught sight of himself in the rearview mirror, he thought, "Jeez, you look just like a sugar cookie." He drove home and washed out his abrasions in the shower; later, when his wife

Paula returned from a day in town, she took him to the hospital.

Fortunately, Tom's X-rays turned out to be negative. No broken pelvis, no broken anything. But now he has that slow-healing herniated disc in his neck, and it might be a while before he can belly paddle again.

November 3

This morning at three, the ocean sounded like an elementary school orchestra tuning its instruments. No order at all, just random noise. Because we live a quarter mile back from the beach and a hundred feet above it, I rely on sound more than sight to let me know what's going on down there, and I knew that what I was hearing didn't bode well for the day's surf. Normally, a swell that has traveled 6000 miles has plenty of time to get organized into some sort of recognizable pattern. But the chaos I was hearing probably meant that the nightly offshore winds were blowing whatever swell was there into shreds. Still, Claudia and I decided to drive out to the East Cape and have a look.

To my surprise, the surf at Punta Espina looked outstanding. Apparently the angle of this swell was too slight for points west but was just right for the East Cape. With the lower tide, some waves were well overhead. Fireman Tom was already out on his SUP, but he was the only other surfer in the water. As I paddled out, I watched Tom take off on a long, beautifully shaped wave that walled up before him; he calmly took a high line and flew across the top of the wave right in front of me. With the low-angled morning sun shining through the back of the wave, it was a wonderful thing to see, and I called out to him, "If I had a camera, you'd be on the cover of *SUP Magazine!*"

My morning session didn't start out so well. I took off too far back on my first wave, the wall collapsed in front of me, and I had nowhere to go. I got pounded hard, and after I floated to the surface, I glanced outside and saw at least three more big waves coming. On the first two, I turned turtle, flipping upside down and grasping the board tightly in my arms as the waves washed over me. Then I flipped over and paddled hard, scrambling to get outside. But I could see that the third wave was even bigger than the first two, and it was going to catch me right in the impact zone.

That's a dangerous situation to be in, with the full arc of the wave landing directly on top of you—and turning turtle doesn't help. Years ago Doyle broke his neck at Sunset doing that, and he's warned me about it more than once. Since nobody was behind me, I abandoned my board and dove as deep as my leash would allow—about eight feet. Even then, I was thrashed violently in the turbulence. The wave tore so hard at my board that my Velcro leash cuff separated, and my board was snatched away from me. I caught just a glimpse of it as the last wave in the set swept it away.

It was about four hundred yards to shore, in rough surf, but I had made that swim many times before, and I knew I could do it again. What worried me most was that the waves might sweep my new board east into the rocks and batter it to pieces. So I swam and swam and swam.

I caught up with my board about a hundred feet from the rocks, where it had stalled inside a calm eddy. I reattached the leash and paddled back out, still hoping to get in at least one good ride.

But it was too late. By the time I got back outside, the wind was blowing the faces of the waves to pieces, and whitecaps were starting to show. Tom and I each took one more sloppy wave apiece and headed in.

Back on shore, Jeff King was sitting on the beach watching us. Jeff is a well-known big-wave surfer who has lived in Los Cabos more than twenty-five years. He's one of the most respected watermen here—for his knowledge of the ocean, his fearlessness in big surf, his understated surfing style, and his unique sense of humor. Jeff has so much physical talent that he might have been a professional surfer in his youth, if it weren't for the fact that he is 6'4" and weighs about 230 pounds—much too big to be a pro in this era of shortboards. Jeff is over 50 now, and lately he's had a hard time with arthritis. It hasn't kept him out of the water, but he has switched to SUP so he doesn't have to make that tough transition from belly to feet. His favorite water sport these days, though, is kite surfing, which doesn't require that transition either. But I've seen him come back from an hour of kiting so stiff his friends have to help him out of his gear.

Wind is the natural enemy of most surfers, but kiters relish days like this—big surf with powerful wind. So when Tom and I came walking up the beach carrying our boards, Jeff said brightly, "Well, the day's already over for you guys, but it hasn't even started yet for me."

Kiters remind me of evangelical missionaries. Everybody looks like a potential convert to them. They think if they can persuade one other person to believe in their sad delusions, they will look less fanatical. "How much do you know about kiting?" they ask earnestly. "Would you like to know more?" But they aren't going to convert me. I don't want anything to do with that sport.

Every kiter I've ever known has a dozen horror stories about the many things that can go wrong. They call them "kitemares." Doyle, a devoted kiter himself, has a bumper sticker on the back of his car that says, "Kiting Ruined My Life." Yet he has been trying to get me to kite with him for years. Once I asked him, "Are you sure you really like kiting all that much?"

"Well," Doyle said, "I've broken two eardrums and three ribs from kiting. One eardrum hasn't healed, and I'm probably going to need surgery to fix it. My ankles always ache, and sometimes I'm so sore afterwards I can hardly walk. But yeah, I like it a lot. You should take it up. I'll help you learn."

Not long ago, Doyle managed to persuade a fellow in San José to take up kiting. The man, who doesn't surf or participate in other water sports, said he was willing to give it a try. So Doyle gave him some old equipment and taught him the basics. Every day he has time off from work now, the man takes the equipment down to the beach, practices setting it all up, and gets the kite aloft. Then, without even getting his feet wet, he hauls it all in, puts it away, and goes home. It's been three months now, and that's as far as he's pursued kiting. Which I think is a very wise decision.

Once Doyle was trying to teach another man how to kite. They had the kite aloft, and the man was standing on the beach holding on to the lines, when suddenly the man let go. In seconds, the kite was a speck on the horizon. "It was like throwing a thousand-dollar bill to the wind," Doyle said.

I don't think I will ever have any interest in kiting. For one thing, I hate the wind. (Annie agrees with me. She refuses to even drive out to the East Cape with Mike on kiting days.) Besides, I still have fun with plain old-fashioned surfing, and though I'm almost certainly deluding myself, I think I'm still getting better at it.

November 4

There was still a bit of leftover swell today, and I surfed for about three hours in semi-windy conditions. There were several surfers out, but Punta Espina was far from crowded. The wave there is so long, surfers can spread out. One surfer looking for a challenge can start deep and try to drive through the first section; another in a more relaxed state of mind can sit farther down on the shoulder and pick up the end of waves that would otherwise go unridden.

The wind started to get bad around ten, and just about everybody had gone in. I was about to head in too, when I had a bit of an accident.

I had just dropped into a head-high wave, when I looked up and saw another surfer, a fellow named Chuck, paddling back out. He was directly in front of me, and we were headed for a collision. I had three alternatives, and I had less than a second to decide which one I preferred: I could drive high for the wall and try to slip above Chuck, but if I failed we would collide very hard; I could cut back left, but then the whitewater would almost certainly sweep me right into him; or I could stall my board and back out of the wave, which still might result in my hitting him but would eliminate the possibility of a hard collision. I stalled as quickly as I could and partially exited the wave, but my momentum swept me forward, and our boards collided.

Who was at fault? Well, there are no laws in surfing, and there are no traffic police. But there are accepted rules of etiquette that have been agreed upon by surfers worldwide. One rule says that the surfer riding the wave has the greatest responsibility because he has the ability to turn. But another rule says that surfers paddling back out should paddle around, never through, the takeoff zone. So, in effect, we were both at fault. Or, at least, that's how I saw it.

Chuck's a good surfer, and a good guy—always calm and respectful of others. No angry words were exchanged between us. We inspected our damage, and the result was that the nose of my board had cut a shallow, five-inch slice through the bottom center of his board, and a one-inch piece of my new board's nose was missing.

If somebody shows me an old board of theirs in perfect condition, I know they probably hated that board and never used it much. Surfboards that get used are going to get dinged. I used to patch all my dings myself, but I lack the skill and patience to do the job right. Fortunately, we have a person right here at Punta Espina who is a master with fiberglass and resin.

I apologized to Chuck, more out of courtesy than acceptance of blame, and said, "Well, I think I'll head up to Rod's house. He can make this accident look like it never happened."

"I think I'll do the same," Chuck replied.

Rod lives with his wife Donna on the hill above Punta Espina, in a beautiful house that has a view of the surf break below. The place is a surfer's dream. The house is painted lime green, a color option available to Americans only if they're willing to move to Mexico. (Fireman Tom's house next door is painted popsicle orange, another color not tolerated by American homeowner associations.) Rod, a burly guy with a deep tan and a growl of a laugh, owned a surf shop in California for many years. He's retired now but still the kind person who has to be doing something with his hands every day. And his craftsmanship is amazing.

When I showed Rod the damage I'd done to my new board, he laughed at my foolishness, then said, "Ah, don't worry. I can fix that."

Rod and I chatted for a while about this and that—Mexican car insurance, heavy-duty leaf springs, ATVs, jellyfish. Just as I was getting ready to go, he pointed across his yard and said, "Will you look at that!"

Lying in the shade behind Rod's house was a very sad, gray-muzzled dog that had once been a stray. His name was Meany. Rod and Donna had adopted him several years ago after he'd been abandoned by Mexican ranchers living nearby.

Like a lot of dogs in Baja, Meany looks a bit strange. All over mainland Mexico you see what I would call the prototype dog: medium size, short hair, angular features, tan to yellow in color. They are probably close to what dogs looked like before human-supervised breeding interfered, and what dogs would revert to if supervised breeding ceased. But in Baja, where Americans have been bringing their hyperbred dogs for years and allowing them to mate with Mexican dogs, that reversion has only partly taken place. As a result, you see many variations of what I call the Mr. Potato Head dog, with a lab's body, a terrier's fur, a collie's coloring, and a boxer's head. This dog, Meany, was that kind of dog.

Rod and Donna had named him Meany because he had been unkind to their other dog, Peso, who had also been a stray. Over time, Meany and Peso had worked out their differences and become friends. But Peso had been an incurable car chaser, and eventually that dangerous habit got him killed. So now, without his buddy, Meany was a pathetically mournful and lonely-looking old dog.

But while Rod and I had been chatting, a feral cat—a skinny calico—had wandered into the yard and cautiously approached Meany. When Meany didn't appear aggressive, the cat circled him a few times, then began rubbing against him. Meany raised his head, as if he refused to recognize that the cat was even there. Finally, feeling safe enough to take a chance, the cat lay down in the cradle between Meany's front legs and took a nap.

"They don't know each other?" I asked Rod.

"As far as I know, they've never even seen each other before," Rod growled. "And I'm not looking for any more pets!"

When I got home later this morning, I told Claudia about Meany and the feral cat. She said, "I bet they've been secret friends for years. They're just now feeling comfortable enough with their sexuality to come out of the closet."

November 5

The big SUP race was scheduled to begin today at 9:00 a.m., in Zacatitos, at the arroyo by Mickey Muñoz's house.

Claudia and I drove down a little early and saw that Mike and Annie Doyle, and a few other competitors, had already arrived. Annie was busy wrapping one forearm in tape because a couple of days earlier a surfboard fin had sliced into her arm, cutting part of the muscle. She'd had two layers of stitches in the arm, and it obviously hurt, but she refused to drop out of the race.

Before long, the other paddlers began to show up in vans, with their extra-long racing boards piled on top. The woman who was ranked the number-one professional SUP paddler in the world, Candice Appleby, arrived with another top-rated professional, Gillian Gebree. They were both young, tall, and blonde, with magnificent physiques, and were wearing nothing but little white bikinis. They both looked as if they could bounce cannonballs off their stomachs.

It's a curious fact that female beginners often do better at SUP than male beginners. Some people say that with their wider hips and lower center of gravity, women have better balance on an unsteady surface. And that theory makes sense. But one old surfer who had coached women's sports told me, "You wanna know the real reason women pick up SUP faster than men? It's because they listen, follow instructions, and learn. Men are such knuckleheads, they have to learn everything the hard way!"

Among those in the men's division were Fernando Stalla, an outstanding young waterman from Sayulita, on the Mexican mainland, and Anthony Vela from California. There was about a 4-foot swell running that morning, and while we were waiting for the race to begin, Vela put on an impressive display of catching waves on his SUP and riding them into the sand. Racing boards are long, straight, and narrow—not at all designed for catching waves—yet he pulled it off with cat-like athleticism.

In the senior division were Mickey Muñoz, age 73, and Mike Doyle, age 70. To any nonsurfing tourists who happened to be wandering up the beach, Muñoz and Doyle would look like two old guys in silly hats trying to prove they weren't dead yet. But an informed observer would recognize them as two of the greatest watermen the world has ever known. Both Muñoz and Doyle had been Malibu regulars back in the fifties and been pioneers of big-wave surfing on the North Shore of Oahu. Doyle had grown heavier with age. Muñoz seemed to have grown thinner. Although friends, they had been competing fiercely against each other in one water sport or another for over fifty years. And now we were about to see them compete in an ocean sport that didn't even exist ten years ago.

Doyle told me right before he entered the water, "I don't care if I finish in last place. I just want to finish." But Doyle had trained for this race for weeks, and I knew him too well to think he would allow his old rival to better him, if he could possibly help it.

Outside the world of surfing, Muñoz hadn't become the nationally recognized figure Doyle had become. (Articles in the mainstream media often mentioned that Muñoz had been the stunt double for Sandra Dee in the movie *Gidget*, but that trivialized his great talents.) No matter. Real surfers know that Muñoz had been one of the first to ride the massive surf at Waimea. They know he had logged a lifetime of surf explorations all over the world. They know he had made important contributions to surfboard design and, especially in the sixties, to surf style. To anyone who knows the history of surfing, Mickey Muñoz is a giant.

Muñoz had arrived late and had to scramble to get his gear ready in time for the start. He decided to wear a leash in the rough seas but he lacked the bit of cord needed to attach his leash to the board. I happened to have a piece of cord in my gear bag, so I offered it to him. Trying to be diplomatic, I said, "Doyle told me all he wants to do is to finish this race.

He doesn't care about winning. Personally, I'd like to see you both crossing the finish line together, or close to it."

Muñoz got a sour look on his face, glanced toward Doyle, and replied, "Right."

The morning had started out calm—absolutely perfect weather for a race—but the race wasn't scheduled to start until nine o'clock. The idea was to have the racers arrive at Punta Palmilla, twelve miles away, around noon so the Saturday-morning spectators wouldn't have to trouble themselves by getting up early to see the finish. But now, at starting time, the wind was blowing about ten knots and white caps were starting to show outside. It was going to be a rough crossing to Palmilla, but at least the racers would have the wind at their backs.

To make it fair, the organizers decided on a water start. The paddlers entered the water at their leisure, assembled offshore, and then the starting horn was sounded. Within five minutes, the racers were dark specks on a frothy sea.

With two hours to kill before the racers would reach Punta Palmilla, Claudia and I drove into San José to complete a few weekend chores. Although the East Cape is mostly primitive desert, San José del Cabo is anything but that. This lovely, Spanish colonial city, nearly 300 years old, has a thriving historical district with art galleries, fine restaurants, and boutique hotels, all centered around the old mission. In addition, San José has an international airport, good hospitals, excellent supermarkets, and a new convention center. With the recent addition of a new Walmart, gringos lack nothing here.

When we arrived at Punta Palmilla, there must have been 500 people waiting on the beach. The first paddler to finish was Candice Appleby, beating Fernando Stalla by one minute. (Stalla later redeemed the men's honor by winning the four-mile race in convincing fashion.) Annie, with her little 99-pound frame, was the third woman to finish overall and first in the fifty-and-over division.

I don't know how old I was when I started handicapping athletic events by age. Perhaps that's one of the first signs of being over the hill. But I couldn't help noticing that the combined ages of Appleby and Gebree didn't equal Annie's age. You always have to admire the power and talent of youth in its prime, but victories come at all ages, and I couldn't get over how impressive Annie's performance had been. For me, she was the real champion of the day.

Twenty minutes after Annie finished, the two old men came into view—first Muñoz, still moving with quickness and agility, followed later by Doyle, who was laboring mightily to gain even one second on his old rival.

Doyle and Muñoz grew up in an era when the young sport of surfing was searching for a competitive format that made more sense than a contest controlled by judges who were often biased, lacking in knowledge or, in some cases, just plain dishonest. During the late sixties and seventies, many surfers around the world rebelled against contests and the commercialization of surfing. That was the era of "soul surfing," and both Doyle and Muñoz became part of that movement. But that doesn't mean they weren't competitive. Even today, in their seventies, if you put them in a race with a finish line, they will cough up blood trying to catch anybody ahead of them.

Later, searching for an explanation for his loss to Muñoz, Doyle jokingly offered this excuse: "He's shorter than me, so he has better balance—it's an unfair advantage! And besides, I'm telling you, after all these years that old guy is still tough as hell! Doesn't he know when to quit?"

November 7

This morning, coming back from our daily walk, a skinny, half-starved dog with yellow tiger stripes emerged from a mesquite thicket and followed us at a distance. Apparently, it was curious about Kirra—perhaps attracted by her blue merle coloring, bobbed tail, and white eyes. When we stopped and encouraged the dog to approach us, it sat down and refused to come any closer. Claudia offered one of the liver treats she always carries with her, but either the dog didn't understand or its fear of humans was greater than its hunger.

Mexicans have many wonderful qualities, but their treatment of animals is not one of them. Dogs in Mexico are rarely spayed or neutered, and it's common in poor Mexican households for several family dogs to live on nothing but table scraps. Many dogs here suffer from lifelong health problems caused by malnutrition when they were puppies, and some dogs end up starving. A lot of Americans here in Los Cabos adopt starving dogs and try to nurse them back to health. The irony is that these rescue dogs, which have had such wretched lives, often have the sweetest personalities. And they can be amazingly loyal.

A couple of years ago, our friends Pete and Pauline took in a rescue dog that had severe health problems due to poor nutrition as a puppy. They named him Yoda, and they spent a small fortune on vet bills as they nursed him back to health. With time, Yoda grew into a wise and loving pet.

Every afternoon Pete goes for a long swim in the ocean, and because Yoda can't tolerate the thought of letting Pete out of his sight, he always goes with him. Not long ago, when Pete went for his daily swim, Yoda was taking a nap on the porch, and rather than wake Yoda up, Pete left without him. When Yoda woke up and realized Pete was gone, he followed Pete's tracks down to the beach, plunged into the ocean, and began swimming out to find him. By now, though, Pete had already completed his swim and was sitting on the beach talking with me and a few other people. I happened to see Yoda paddling for the horizon, and I said, "Hey, Pete, where's Yoda going?"

Pete jumped up and said, "Oh, my god! He's looking for me!"

Pete ran down to the beach, dove through the breakers like a lifeguard, and began swimming after Yoda. But the wind had come up, and Pete couldn't see Yoda for the whitecaps. So I climbed higher on the bluff and gave Pete arm signals indicating which way he should swim.

Fortunately, Pete can swim much faster than Yoda, and he caught up with him about a hundred yards out. But I have no doubt that Yoda would have swum to Hawaii in pursuit of the gringo who had given him a second chance at life.

November 9

I haven't been sleeping well lately, mostly because I'm up half the night scratching my jellyfish stings. Every surfer I know here gets stung, but for most surfers the stings are a temporary irritant, and then they go away. For me, the stings itch and itch—sometimes for days. Often I will fall asleep at night nearly itch-free, but then I will wake in the early morning hours with inflamed hives all over my neck, back, and arms. The itching comes in waves, with thirty seconds of calm followed by thirty seconds of maddening torture. Sometimes I scratch the hives in my sleep and wake in the morning with sores where I have torn my flesh raw.

Once, surfing in Australia, I was stung on the leg by a potent blue bottle jellyfish. Within twenty-four hours, most of my leg had turned black and blue. The wound didn't keep me out of the water, but it itched like a biblical curse, and the itching didn't stop for six weeks.

We have blue bottles here in Baja, but luckily, there aren't very many. The most common jellyfishes we have here on the East Cape are what the Mexicans call *aguamalas*. Sometimes you see their long, hairlike filaments in the water, but most often they're invisible. Even the larval form of the jellyfish has nematocysts, which are the stinging element, and the larvae are so small they are nearly microscopic. The jellyfish go right under surf trunks and a rash guard, so there is no way to avoid them short of a full wetsuit, hood, and booties—a ridiculous solution in water that's 80 degrees or warmer. I've heard that surfers in Australia sometimes wear panty hose to keep jellyfish off their legs, but then those Aussies do a lot of things I would never consider doing. There are creams sold online that are supposed to act as a repellant, but the product reviews I've read say they don't work, and I don't know anybody here who uses them.

I know of only three or four things that can relieve the itching of a jellyfish sting. The best by far is a shower so hot you can barely stand it. The immediate relief from that is so overwhelming it's almost orgasmic, and I'm even a bit embarrassed to talk about it. The hot-shower remedy lasts for a couple of hours, which is long enough to get a little sleep. Eventually, though, the hot-shower effect wears off and the itching returns.

Sometimes in the early morning, when I'm having coffee on the terrace, I'll press the warm ceramic cup against a particularly itchy sting. This method relieves the itching too, for the same reason a hot shower does. But I've burnt myself with a hot cup this way, and I've spilt coffee all over myself trying to reach stings on my back.

Hydrocortisone cream will sometimes provide enough relief that I can sleep, but the cream is gooey, and the effect lasts only an hour or so.

The only other relief I know of, which I do not recommend but which I confess I sometimes resort to, is to strip down to bare skin and rub against a rough stucco wall. This method leaves the skin raw, but it provides medium-term relief when all other means have failed. Claudia calls this my "wild bear remedy," and she forbids me to practice it when other people are present.

November 10

Yesterday's surf report called for a small swell to arrive today, so I drove out to Punta Espina, even though I knew the surf report was probably wrong. All last night I listened for surf, but it never came. Was the swell just a bit late? Was the angle off just enough that it wouldn't hit the East Cape? I didn't know. I made the drive anyway, though, because I was anxious to see how my damaged surfboard had survived its surgery. (True, it was only cosmetic surgery—a little rhinoplasty—but it was enough to cause me worry.)

I parked in front of Rod's house and waited to see if he was awake yet. Fortunately, Rod has insomnia, like me, and he came outside as soon as he heard me pull up. He saw the concerned look on my face, but he didn't say anything until he opened the garage door. "Well, there it is," he said. "What do you think?"

Rather than trying to patch the broken tip to make it look new again, Rod had made a black tip, like an arrowhead, that fit over the damaged nose. It tapered off in elegant lines that perfectly matched the original black pinstriping. Not only did it hide the ding, but it actually made the board look better. "That's beautiful work, doctor. Thank you so much!"

"I'm glad you like it."

"And what about Chuck's board?" I asked. "Did he ever bring it to you?"

"Yes, but that job was a little more difficult. The nose of your board took out the Rusty logo on Chuck's board, so I had to completely reconstruct it. It came out looking good though. I think Chuck will be happy."

I paid Rod 500 pesos for his work; then, as I was leaving I asked him how Meany and the feral cat were getting along. Rod rolled his eyes. "They're like old buddies now. I guess we have another cat."

November 11

Claudia and I arrived at Punta Espina as the sun was coming up and we parked at our usual spot in the middle of the cove, where the beach is almost always empty. On the east end of the beach, perhaps a quarter mile away, there's a large *palapa* somebody built a few years ago. Usually, it's vacant this early in the morning, but today we saw a car parked next to the *palapa*, and we could faintly hear the sound of music drifting toward us. In the dim light, though, we couldn't see who it was. There aren't many tourists around the East Cape this time of year, and they rarely find their way to this beach, anyway. Was it the *panga* fishermen, we wondered? Not likely. They have their own shacks at the other end of the cove. Could it be some local gringos having an all-night party?

"Maybe after it gets light, I'll walk down there and see for myself who it is," Claudia said.

The swell was big enough, but the tide was too high—a 7.4—and the night wind was still chewing up the surface of the waves. But I was afraid if I waited for perfect conditions, the east wind would kick in and blow the waves to shreds. So I paddled out and surfed alone for an hour or so, catching a good wave now and then if I moved clear over into the rocks and rode in the shallow water.

After a while, Fireman Tom paddled out to join me. He has the luxury of watching the break from his terrace while he enjoys his morning coffee, and he paddles out only when he thinks the conditions are good and likely to get better. In other words, I often serve as Tom's guinea pig. If I'm struggling with the waves, he has another cup of coffee. If it looks as though I'm getting some good rides, he comes down and joins me.

Soon Rod showed up too, wearing just an old pair of canvas trunks. Rod's old school—he rarely wears a wetsuit or a rash guard, and he always has a deep tan.

Before long, the night wind stopped, the water surface glassed off, the tide dropped quickly, and suddenly the waves were a couple of feet bigger than they'd been when I'd first paddled out. Conditions rarely get any better than this, in any season, and to have just the three of us in the water was something special. After three hours, when I finally gave in and rode my last wave to the beach, I was thoroughly exhausted and even a bit dehydrated. I sat down in the sand, drank about a liter of water, then started pulling off my wet gear.

Claudia, who had spent the morning reading in the shade of her umbrella, said, "You know that music we heard coming from the *palapa* this morning?"

I'd nearly forgotten. "Yeah?"

"Well, after you paddled out, I got the binoculars to see who it was."

"And?"

"It was an old Mexican couple dancing in the sand."

That was terrible news, as far as I was concerned. Claudia, who is an excellent dancer, has always needled me for not dancing with her at parties and wedding receptions. It's not really my fault—I've always been a terrible dancer and have never found the desire to learn. But apparently that silly, outdated mating ritual has some emotional associations I'm not aware of. And now I had to be taunted again for my romantic failings, even though I was too tired to properly defend myself.

"I thought you told me Mexican men weren't romantic," Claudia said.

"Well," I finally replied, "I suppose Mexican men can be romantic at times. They just need to find someplace where nobody can see them."

November 12

It's finally beginning to feel like fall here in Zacatitos. The noonday sun has lost its bite, the nights are cool, and both sunrise and sunset are violent dramas of color—very Mexican in their excessive animation and emotion. When we first moved here, I was worried that we would miss the changing of the seasons, but I see now that things change in Baja too, just as they do everywhere else.

With no surf in sight, I spent the cool of the morning working in our yard, thinning out the mesquite and *liga*, which are far too abundant and whose roots steal water from the *torote* and *ciruela de monte*, which are more beautiful. With a little selective pruning, I can sculpt the plants into pleasing shapes, but I try not to be too aggressive.

I find the natural desert landscape here close to perfect just the way it is, and I'm always surprised to find that not everybody agrees. One Southern California visitor, who heard me ranting about my love of the desert, said, "Show me what it is you find so beautiful here. Because I can't see it!" Many gringos who move here claim they love the desert, but the first thing they do with their lot is scrape it clean with a backhoe, then set about planting a proper English garden, with flowers and ferns and even a little patch of lawn.

I can understand how some people might consider the southern Baja landscape harsh or even menacing. Almost everything that grows here throws out a snarl of spines or thorns, as a warning to browsing animals that it won't be eaten without a fight. In a land where plants might not get a drop of rain in nine months, growth comes slowly, and must be protected. But even thorns can be beautiful.

There's a tiny bird here, the blue-gray gnatcatcher, that takes refuge in the shade of the boxthorn, a plant that reminds me of the concertina wire coiled over prison walls. The boxthorn has a very bad attitude—one of the least inviting plants in a land where everything that grows can cut, poke, and scrape. But the animated little gnatcatcher flits among the boxthorn branches with impunity, knowing it's perfectly protected in its shelter of thorns.

November 17

Today at noon I saw a bobcat moving through the arroyo below our house. It was about twice the size of a house cat, with a very stocky build, and it swaggered with the muscled confidence of a high school football player. The birds in the *palo blancos* whistled warning signals to each other, which caused the bobcat to stop and wait a few seconds before moving on.

Almost every evening a beautiful fox makes his rounds through our neighborhood. He lives on the rocky hill below our house, and he likes to check out the sandy arroyo to the west of us around dusk. I'm not sure what he's looking for, but he's always in a hurry, as if he has someplace to be and is already late. His tail is as large as the rest of his body, and I think that blanket must be a great comfort to him when the winter nights are cold. Sometimes, when it's dark out, he makes a harsh crying sound, which irritates Kirra. She'll tolerate his cry for twenty minutes or so, then, suddenly losing her patience, she'll charge down the stairs and bark into the darkness until the fox moves on.

We have a lot of chipmunks here in Zacatitos. They're a little smaller than their *norteamericano* cousins; I've watched red-tailed hawks swoop down and easily carry them away as if they weighed nothing. That's probably why the chipmunks choose to live mostly in the cool, protected spaces under and between the granite boulders.

Today I saw a large raven in our yard with the hindquarters of a chipmunk in its beak. The raven was trying to find a place to hide his meal so he could come back later and finish it. He flew onto the palm thatch covering our water tanks and tucked the hindquarters neatly under a palm frond. Then he moved a few feet away, pretending to have no knowledge of his hidden prize, watching as the other ravens circled overhead. He hopped around nervously, becoming increasingly agitated, until finally he decided his hiding place wasn't secure enough; then he plucked out the hindquarters and flew off to look for a better stash.

November 19

This morning we loaded my 10'6" SUP onto the Rhino, drove to the west end of Zacatitos, and parked in the little cove west of the rocky point. There is almost never any rideable surf there, and today was no exception. With no wind, and surface conditions glassy, I figured it would be a perfect day for cruising around in the cove.

I'm what you might call a flat-water paddler. A lot of older surfers I know are switching to SUPs for riding waves, and I may come to that one day myself, but I intend to put it off as long as possible. SUPs remind me of the monstrous longboards we used to ride back in the sixties—thick, heavy, and slow to turn. Why you would want to go back to that after riding a light, fast, modern thruster, I don't know. But I do enjoy taking the SUP out on a calm day and slowly paddling around in circles. It feels like cruising in a big old 1956 Cadillac.

The water temperature has dropped a lot—down to around 75 degrees—so I decided to wear my shorty wetsuit, not because I was cold but because a wetsuit offers at least some protection from the *aguamalas*.

I paddled west to Punta Gorda—a rocky, flat-topped landmark that can be seen for miles in every direction. The water was clear, and with polarized sunglasses I could see an amazing variety of fish below me: shy rock bass that hang close to the shelter of the volcanic pinnacles; poisonous porcupine fish that inflate themselves to appear menacing to predators; bizarre needlefish that look like prehistoric monsters; and big, white bat rays that hover eerily across the sandy bottom like flying saucers. The fishing grounds that start a few hundred yards off Punta Gorda, known as the Gorda Banks, are famous for having some of the best sport fishing in North America, and I could see the white fishing boats glistening in the distance. After an hour or so, I circled around and paddled back—maybe a total distance of two miles.

After I'd finished, Claudia took the SUP out for a while. She's been wanting to learn for some time now. She has the balance and the determination but she needs to overcome her fear of the ocean. I know from teaching our boys to surf that it's best not to push beginners. Let them learn at their own pace. And teaching a spouse how to do anything is far more difficult than teaching a stranger. So I kept my mouth shut and watched admiringly from the shore.

After Claudia was finished, we tried to coax Kirra onto the SUP. Some dogs enjoy riding on the nose of a surfboard. Once at Punta Espina, I saw a small dog riding on the nose of a SUP in 8-foot surf. The dog had learned to crouch down and brace itself when dropping into a wave, just like its master, and it didn't appear the least bit afraid. Kirra, on the other hand, doesn't much care for water and is terrified of waves. We couldn't get her anywhere near the SUP. To appease us, though, she waited for a small wave to wash up on the sand, ran in an arc through the foam, then headed for dry ground— her idea of surfing. She shook herself off vigorously, dug a hole down to cool sand, and hunkered there on her belly till we were ready to leave. The truth is, in spite of her sometimes ferocious behavior, Kirra is a coward.

November 20

This afternoon we were at a neighbor's house, sitting on the terrace drinking cold Pacificos and enjoying the ocean view, when I noticed a pair of feral burros wandering down the arroyo below us. One of the burros was limping badly on its right front leg. Curious, I wandered off from the group so I could watch the burro and maybe learn what was wrong with it.

The burros slowly followed the afternoon shade until the arroyo opened onto the beach; then they started to climb a sandy bluff where there were a few patches of yellowed grass. The injured burro trailed far behind the other one, though it struggled to keep up, and it appeared to be in a great deal of pain.

Burros in Zacatitos are like black bears in Yosemite. They are intelligent, hardy survivors that have managed to turn the human invasion of their territory to their own advantage. Unlike bears in Yosemite, though, burros aren't native to Baja. The Spanish introduced them more than 300 years ago. But burros have adapted well to these desert conditions, which are similar to their native northern Africa. They fear no predators—one solid burro kick to the head could easily send a mountain lion to eternity. Burros can go days without water and can even drink the brackish water that oozes up at the mouth of our arroyo. They eat almost anything that grows, or once grew, and like the bears of Yosemite they love to get into trash. I've seen burros eat empty milk cartons, moldy bread, pineapple skins, and rancid cheese. For some reason they favor cardboard (some say it's the glue they're after), and they will even chew the paper from a sack of cement. Also, like black bears, burros can be real pests. While we were building our house here in Zacatitos, I was constantly shooing them away from the job site because I knew the mischief they could cause. But the Mexican workers didn't approve of my attitude, and sometimes after I shooed the burros off, I would see the workers carrying buckets of water out to the burros as an apology for my poor manners. It was an ass, you might recall, that carried Mary into Bethlehem, and for that kindness, devout Mexican Catholics hold a special place in their hearts for them.

Like most gringos here, I have mixed feelings about the burros. I admire their ability to survive in such a harsh environment, but at the same time, I know they're taking precious resources from the few deer that live in this desert. And farther back in the hills, they're competing with the *borregos*, or bighorn sheep. I would prefer to see the native animals have first shot at survival.

Still, I don't like to see any animal suffer, and I could see that this burro with the bad leg was in big trouble. It would lift its leg as if it intended to take a step, then put almost no weight on it at all, moving forward in lurches. Every three or four steps, it would have to stop to rest. Although burros can survive on almost any desert forage, because the nutritional quality of the forage is so poor, they have to eat a lot of it, which means they have to keep moving or they will die. Resting until its leg healed was not an option for this burro.

I moved down the arroyo a ways farther where I could get a closer look, and I saw that this injured burro was a jenny—a female. The other burro, I noticed, was shockingly male.

Then, to my surprise, the young male burro—or jack—retraced its steps to the jenny and began nursing from it. The jack hadn't yet weaned itself from its mother, even though it was fully grown! He was wandering around the desert, going any direction he wished, knowing he had an easy meal any time he wanted it, while his severely injured mother struggled to keep up. By stealing nutrition from the mother, the jack was making her already desperate condition worse.

At the same time, it was hard to blame the jack. Burros are social animals, and they travel in family groups. The offspring stay close to their mother long after they can survive on their own. And no burro likes being alone very long. The bray of a burro at night, after it has been separated from its companions, is one of the loneliest sounds you will ever hear. The young jack was just doing what it knew how to do.

If I had to guess, I would say the jenny had been struck by a car or truck and her leg was broken. But there are a lot of ways an animal can get injured in this desert. Maybe it had been kicked by another burro. Maybe it had caught its hoof in a rock cleft and wrenched it trying to get free. Maybe it had gotten caught in a wire fence.

Watching the jenny try to put weight on her bad leg time and time again made me feel sick to my stomach. But a burro is a wild animal—it isn't going to let me or anybody else examine its leg. And trying to repair a broken leg is a difficult task even for a domestic horse or burro. For an animal in the desert of Mexico, it would be impossible. Naturally, I wanted to help. But I couldn't think of a single thing I could do.

November 21

I woke in the middle of the night worrying about the injured burro, and then I couldn't get back to sleep. I still couldn't think of anything I might do to help her, but I wanted to know if she was all right, or maybe even getting better. So I got up early and went out on the Rhino to look for her. After a couple of hours of driving up the arroyos searching for her tracks, I hadn't found any sign of her anywhere.

Later this morning, I told Claudia I wanted to do something to help this burro. I wasn't going to let her suffer. I was going to make it my responsibility to do whatever needed to be done, even if I didn't know yet what it might be. In the U.S. an animal like this would be put down, put to sleep, euthanized—whatever you want to call it. On some ranches even today this is done with a bullet to the brain. I've had to do it myself more than once. It's better to do the job with an injection, but this burro was a wild animal, not a pet. Either method of euthanasia was better than letting the animal suffer. The problem is, guns are not allowed in Mexico, at least not without a special permit. Hunters are sometimes given a gun permit, for a price. (The fee for hunting a bighorn sheep is said to be $100,000.) The police in Mexico have guns, but would they drive out to Zacatitos to euthanize a burro? I didn't know.

Then I began to wonder whether I had the right to decide if this burro should live or die. Except for its injured leg, it still appeared to be in decent health. Wouldn't it make more sense, I thought, to wait a while and see if the burro was able to recover on its own?

I decided I would do my best to keep an eye on the jenny for the next few days and see how things developed. With that bad leg, I didn't expect her to travel far. If the leg improved, that would be excellent. If the leg became worse, I would take the next step, whatever that might be.

November 22

To everyone's surprise, including weather forecasters at NOAA (National Oceanic and Atmospheric Administration), we have a late-season hurricane about 750 miles off the tip of Baja and moving northwest. It's already been named Kenneth, and it's a category 4, with maximum winds of about 145 miles per hour. (Hurricane Katrina, you might recall, was a devastating category 5.) Only one hurricane larger than a category 3 has ever struck the Baja peninsula in modern times, and this hurricane likely poses no real threat. It's entering colder water now and will probably fizzle out soon. What's unusual, though, is that it has arrived so late in the season. In fact, in the eastern north Pacific, this is the strongest late-season hurricane ever recorded.

Claudia, Kirra, and I walked down to the beach early this morning to look for the injured burro, but once again we couldn't find any sign of her. Had she already collapsed and died somewhere? Was she maybe resting in a shady spot where she had water?

At the beach we saw there was maybe a 3-foot swell running—nothing more—but the surface of the water looked oddly disturbed; even without much wind, the horizon was lurching and sloshing like water in a bathtub. There were a few clouds in the sky, but the weather was hardly what you'd call stormy.

Later today, our trash collector, Moisés, came around. I usually don't put our bag of trash out until I can hear him coming up the hill because the burros will tear into the bag and have trash spread all across the desert. Fortunately, Moisés's truck can be heard from at least a mile away. The mellow sound of his Mexican-made muffler, as he winds through the gears climbing the hill to our house, is so musical it could well serve as the Mexican national anthem.

When he got to our gate, Moisés shut off his ignition, as he usually does, so we could chat awhile. Because he makes his rounds all through Zacatitos, Moisés knows what everybody in town is up to. He won't gossip, but he does act as a channel of information. Moisés is knowledgeable about the native desert plants, he appreciates that I have kept most of my lot in its natural state, and he often takes a minute or two to teach me the Spanish names of the plants: *ciruela de monte, palo adan,* and *pitahaya agria*.

I told Moisés about the injured burro, told him I was worried about her, and I asked him what he thought I should do.

Moisés, who is a kind and patient young man, considered the problem for a moment. "I have seen this injured burro too," he said. "When I get back to La Playa, I will call the animal authority."

La Playa, the next village west from us, is about five miles away. Moisés was born and raised there. La Playa used to be a small fishing village, but the government recently built a new marina there. Instead of sheltering small fishing *pangas* along the sandy beach, it now harbors the pleasure yachts of multimillionaires like Paul Allen, Greg Norman, and Carlos Slim. Even a small slip costs $1700 per month, which is more than most Mexicans earn in a month. Big developers have moved in, trying to snatch up property where the fishermen have lived for generations, but many of the old Mexican families are refusing to sell. Some of the houses in town have hand-painted signs posted out front that read, "This property is not for sale!" Moisés told me his own father refused an offer of about $500,000 for his marina-view lot.

Los Cabos is changing rapidly—too rapidly for many people, including me. But change will come, and much of it is good for people like Moisés who make their living providing services to the gringos who move here. Sometimes I have to remind myself that I am just a guest in this country.

"But Moisés," I said, "do you think the animal authority will drive all the way out here to Zacatitos for an injured burro?"

Moisés shrugged. "We can try."

"Well," I said, "In the meantime, if you see this injured burro, please let me know."

November 23

I drove out the East Cape road at dawn to get a feeling for this storm they say is coming. I don't have a lot of experience with hurricanes, but I know they can do funny things. I've heard stories of surfers during hurricane season riding big waves at Los Frailes, a place on the far East Cape that almost never gets surf of any size. Our typical swell angle is around 200 to 220 degrees (roughly the direction of New Zealand). But hurricanes that hug the Mexican coastline can produce swell angles of 170 degrees. Or they can produce swell angles of 250 degrees—nearly due west. I wasn't sure what would happen with this hurricane, but if it produced big surf, I didn't want to miss it.

But there were almost no waves at all. The hurricane had been 750 miles off the tip of Baja for three days now, spewing out winds of 130 miles per hour and moving in a direction that should have been ideal. Yet all we got were little 3-foot dribblers, unusual only in their odd approach angle. I was disappointed, yet I must admit I was also impressed. Imagine the horrendous winds, blowing for days, that are required to generate even head-high surf.

On the way back to Zacatitos, I spent a couple of hours driving up and down the arroyos, looking for the injured jenny. I was thinking that if she wasn't anywhere to be found in Zacatitos, she must be somewhere out in the desert. But the desert is huge, and the task of finding a wandering burro out there is nearly hopeless.

Something about this injured burro is affecting me in ways I don't understand. From our terrace at home we can see for nearly a mile in every direction. Every evening I sit there, watching for her. I dreamed about her last night too—a disturbing dream that woke me up and left me unsettled the rest of the night.

November 24, Thanksgiving Day

This morning I found myself trying to explain the meaning of Thanksgiving to the truck driver who had come to fill the propane tank at our house. He said he didn't speak English, so I tried to tell him in Spanish about the English *peregrinos* and the *Indios* and about giving *gracias a Dios* for *un buen cosecha*. He listened politely, but I could see he wasn't following a word of it. Finally, though, when I mentioned *pavo*, his face lit up in a big smile and he said in decent English,

"Oh, I know! That's when you try to eat a whole turkey in one day! We did that once when I was a little boy living in Phoenix. In Mexico we call that *Día Pavo*." Turkey Day.

It's not uncommon to meet Mexicans in Baja who have been deported from the United States after having lived there a decade or more, working at minimum wage, paying taxes, and raising a family. I've known young Mexicans who were born in the U.S. but because their parents never got them a birth certificate, they were deported to Mexico years later, even though they were obviously more American than Mexican. I rarely hear such Mexicans openly complain about their treatment in the U.S.—at least not in front of a gringo—but it's not difficult to imagine the bitterness, anger, and rejection they must feel.

In contrast, I am constantly amazed by the tolerance and generosity with which the Mexican people receive their American guests. In the forty-five years I've been coming to Mexico, I've never heard a Mexican speak so much as an unkind word to me. Almost every day, I am the recipient of their kindness, humor, and hospitality. And for that I am thankful.

November 25

Today we had dark clouds at dawn, and the air was colder and smelled like rain. This has nothing to do with Hurricane Kenneth, which has already fallen apart. This new weather pattern is what Mexicans call *el norte*, the remnants of a large storm that has moved down from Canada and the U.S. Most often these storms bring little rain, but this time everybody is hoping we get at least some moisture.

Better than most places in Baja, Los Cabos can survive a long drought because of the Sierra de la Laguna, which captures clouds moving in any direction and wrings them of whatever moisture they carry. The Lagunas, which we can see from our terrace, are steep, rugged peaks that rise abruptly from the Pacific. The highest is Picacho de la Laguna, which is greater than 7,000 feet in elevation. Along the eastern slope of the Lagunas, large, sandy arroyos, some almost a kilometer wide, channel runoff from the mountains to the south and east. Porous aquifers deep below the arroyos store much of the water, but some always manages to flow into the ocean at the beautiful, lush, and tropical *estero* just east of San José, which is a refuge for a profusion of birds and other wildlife.

The largest of the arroyos, Arroyo San José, is the reason the mission and pueblo of San José were built where they are. Even in the seventeenth century, the Spanish sailors were aware that that they could find fresh water there. The Spanish galleons would anchor off the coast, row in on small launches carrying wooden casks, and replenish their water supplies before heading off across the Pacific to the Philippines or south to Peru.

Today, around noon, rain began to fall—lightly at first, then in squalls—and Claudia and I started thinking it might be a good idea to head into San José to buy groceries. When it rains hard, the arroyos, which are dry for months at a time, can become raging torrents that are impassable for days. We had no idea whether this was going to be that kind of storm, but if it were, we needed to stock up on supplies.

So we drove into town and ran our normal errands: returned a case of empty Pacifico bottles and bought a case of filled ones, bought groceries at the Mega (our favorite supermarket), and got gas at the Pemex in La Choya.

It was still raining when we got to the Pemex, but only lightly, so I got out of the truck to speak with the attendant, who looked bored. We chatted awhile, then he eyed my mud-splattered four-wheel-drive truck and asked, "Tiene un casa a Cabo Pulmo?"

"No," I replied. "Zacatitos."

"Ah, that's very beautiful, Zacatitos. Sometimes I ride my motorcycle out that way. How long have you lived there?"

"Five years," I replied.

And then the man paid me a very kind compliment, "So then, you are a *choyero!*"

La choya (sometimes spelled *la cholla*) is a troublesome cactus that grows abundantly in Baja. When you walk through the desert, pieces of it break off and stick tenaciously to your shoes and pants. The bony longhorn cattle that roam these hills try to eat pieces of *la choya*, but it usually sticks to their faces, and they end up wearing it like bovine jewelry for the rest of their miserable lives. It's a god-awful plant, but it's also so ubiquitous in Los Cabos that it has become a symbol for the place. So people considered locals are called *choyeros*.

In the U.S., Latino families who have lived in the country for three generations are still called Mexicans, regardless of what their birth certificate says—many of them never were Mexican at all, but Guatemalan or Salvadoran. But this man hadn't asked me for my birth certificate, passport, or my visa. He didn't mind that I spoke his language imperfectly. As far as he was concerned, I had lived here long enough to be called a *choyero*.

As we were leaving San José, driving across the new concrete bridge on the north end of the *estero*, the rain began to let up. The sky was still dark, though, and we knew more rain would likely follow. The arroyo feeding into the *estero* had been dry for months, but in the late afternoon light we could see that the arroyo was flowing again. And then, suddenly, there was a white flash across our windshield, a great turmoil of feathers, and the sound of flapping wings. It took us a moment to understand. Then Claudia and I said at the same time, "Fish hawk!"

It had been an osprey, carrying in its talons a fish it had scooped from the *estero* below. The fish was so fat, the osprey struggled mightily to lift it into the air.

November 26

After spending most of the night awake, worrying about the injured burro, I set out early on the Rhino again to try to find her. The storm had dropped an inch of rain, though that still left us at only 25 percent of normal for the year. But I figured it would make a good day for tracking the burro, since the rain had erased several months of old tracks.

I drove slowly out the East Cape road until I cut two sets of fresh burro tracks heading up a small arroyo. I got out of the Rhino to study the tracks and saw that one of the burros was dragging a hoof through the sand. I knew it had to be her and that I had at least some hope now of catching up with her. Yet, the malformed track was proof that her leg hadn't healed.

My plan, if I could find the injured burro, was to offer her water in a bucket. I knew she wouldn't refuse. Then, as she was drinking, I would slip a rope around her neck. If she didn't resist, I would tie a loose bowline, and I would have her. By tying the other end of the rope to the Rhino, I could very slowly lead her back to our house, where I could hold her inside our fence, feed her and, hopefully, get a vet from San José to come out and examine her leg.

I got back in the Rhino and followed the tracks for nearly a mile, until the arroyo narrowed. Then the tracks separated and disappeared into a thicket of *palo adan* and *la choya* much too thick to follow even on foot.

Then I realized that the rain from the day before would make it more difficult to track this burro, not easier, as I had first thought. During a drought, burros must stay close to a known source of water, which in Zacatitos was where the arroyo emptied into the ocean. But now, pools of water stood almost everywhere, the native plants were already leafing out, and the desert was beginning to green, giving the burros a much bigger territory in which to roam.

November 28

I spent all morning driving around the desert looking for the injured burro, but I found nothing.

East Cape Burros

December:

Heap of Bones

December 1

I was beginning to think I would never see the injured burro again, that she had wandered into the desert, where she was suffering a long and painful death, and that I had failed in my resolution to help this poor creature. Then, this morning at 7:00 a.m., as we were going out for our morning walk, we saw the jenny collapsed on the road right in front of our gate. She lay on her side, too weak to get up. Her eyes were unfocused and rolling around in the sockets, and her legs were trembling uncontrollably.

I said to Claudia, "She's in terrible pain. We can't let this go on any longer."

Claudia agreed.

The young jack was there too, still trying to draw milk from its mother, indifferent to her condition. I tried to shoo him away, and Kirra, seeing my intention, barked and nipped at him too.

It was time to end her suffering, but we had no way to do that humanely. Was I supposed to take a kitchen knife to her throat? I woke our nearest neighbors, Rock and Cindy, explained the situation, and told them we were going to San José to find a vet to euthanize the burro. They agreed to keep the jack away from her until we got back and to try to get her to drink some water. Claudia snapped photos of the burro with her Iphone, then we hurried into town.

The vet, who has an office at a feed store on the edge of town, listened sadly to our story and looked at our pitiful pictures. Then he asked, "Do you own this burro?"

"No," I replied. "All the burros on the East Cape are wild."

The vet shook his head no. "That is not correct. All the burros have an owner. If I come and kill the burro, a rancher or somebody else will claim the burro as his own. They will demand money from you and probably from me too."

I knew he was right. One of our neighbors in Zacatitos had paid to euthanize a horse that had been hit by a car, and later on, two different ranchers demanded money from him for killing their horse. I could see how a cow, and maybe even some of the horses, had owners, even though their owners did almost nothing to care for them. But everybody knew the burros had been wild in this desert for 300 years. And I told the vet so.

"Believe me, if you have this burro killed, you will be asking for trouble," he insisted.

"Okay, maybe, that's true," I said. "But we aren't going to watch this burro suffer any longer. What can we do?"

The vet talked with his assistant in Spanish too rapid for me to follow. Then he said, "Perhaps you can talk to the police. They are the only ones who have the authority to kill the burro, if that's what needs to be done."

The police station in San José was a few blocks away. I parked down the street and walked to the station, leaving Claudia in our truck. Police stations in Mexico can be strange places. Many Mexicans say that whatever problem you have, getting the police involved will only make it worse. Some

Mexicans will not enter a police station for any reason at all if they can avoid it. But what choice did I have?

There was an air of chaos and tension inside the station that made me feel uneasy. The place was dark and noisy, and everybody except me was wearing a bulletproof vest. After asking around and being sent from one desk to another, I was directed to a senior officer whose badge identified him as a *comandante*. He listened to my story, then nodded and said maybe he could help.

The *comandante* led me through a labyrinth of dim hallways to the office of the chief of police. The door was open, but inside a tense discussion was taking place. The *comandante* removed his hat as a courtesy before entering, so I did the same. When the *comandante* explained to the chief that I had a problem with an injured burro in Zacatitos, the chief became so furious he couldn't even speak. I started to show him the photos Claudia had taken, but he refused to look at them. The *comandante* took my elbow, and we retreated without saying another word.

I thought that would be the end of it, but to my surprise, out in the hall, the *comandante* said, "Okay, here's what we can do. Many years ago, when I lived on a ranch, sometimes we would shoot an animal that is suffering. I know sometimes this is the best thing to do. If we come to Zacatitos and look at this burro, and if, maybe—just maybe—we decide that it needs to be shot, what will you do with the burro then?"

"I will go see Tomás," I said. "He has a backhoe. We will dig a hole in the arroyo, and we will bury the burro."

"Good. And who will pay for this?" he asked.

"I will pay for it," I said.

"Okay, then. That's good too." He paused for a moment to finish thinking the matter through. "There is just one more formality."

I pictured the stack of paperwork that must be hand typed and stamped before any official matter can proceed in Mexico. I also wondered if this was when I would be asked to pay the *mordida*. "And what is that?" I asked.

The *comandante* paused, clearly embarrassed to have to tell me this. He pointed a finger at my chest and said, "You must pay for the bullet!"

Now I was certain this was the *mordida*. But again, what choice did I have? "And how much does a bullet cost?" I asked.

The *comandante* sensed my suspicion. "You must understand," he explained, "that the department requires us to pay for our own bullets. Each and every one."

"That's okay," I said. "How much will the bullet cost?"

He thought for a moment. "Perhaps twenty pesos." About a buck fifty.

"That's not a problem," I said.

The *comandante* introduced me to a younger officer passing rapidly down the hallway, and the younger officer said he happened to be going to Zacatitos that very morning. The *comandante* explained the situation with the suffering burro, then instructed the younger officer on the correct procedure for dispatching a burro—with a shot "through the back of the head, not between the eyes like in the cowboy movies."

I thanked the *comandante* for his help, then I asked the younger officer what time he could come to Zacatitos. "I will leave here in one hour," he replied.

"Okay," I said, and I gave him a map to our house. "The burro is lying at our front gate."

When Claudia and I arrived home, we were surprised to find the police truck already parked out front—for some reason the officer had hurried on ahead of us. The jenny, which hadn't moved since we'd left that morning, was already dead, and blood flowed from its head into the dirt. The jack was braying fifty feet away, still intent on trying to draw milk from its mother's teats.

The officer, who was sweating heavily in his bulletproof

vest, asked me to sign his logbook, which I did. Then I thanked him and asked, "Do I pay for the bullet now?"

"Yes, of course," he replied. "How much did the *comandante* say it would cost?"

"Twenty pesos."

"Very well," he nodded. "I assure you the burro died quickly, without suffering. But it required two bullets."

As soon as the police truck left, I drove down to Tomás's compound. Tomás lives in La Choya but operates his business here in Zacatitos. In addition to his backhoe (called *la máquina* in Mexico), he owns a dump truck. But the gate to Tomás's compound was locked, and he was nowhere to be seen. I left a message in Spanish on his gate saying, "Please come to my house with the machine. I have a dead burro.... Esteban."

Then I drove home, and we waited and waited, while the dead burro lay there in the hot afternoon sun.

It took less than an hour for the first buzzards to arrive. They're amazingly efficient. They fly crosswind until they cut a scent, then they turn and follow it upwind to its source. Within a few hours, there were fifteen or more of them. They began pecking at the dead burro's eyes, and then at the belly, and soon they had entrails dragged across the road. And still the young jack refused to leave. Several times he tried to chase the buzzards off the carcass, and he never stopped trying to draw milk.

I drove back to Tomás's lot three times, but each time my note was still posted on his locked gate. I tried calling his cellphone, but there was no answer.

Just before dark, the jack wandered off three hundred yards or so from the carcass. Perhaps he was thirsty. He was accustomed to going anywhere he liked and having his mother follow. When he realized she wasn't coming, he gave out the saddest, longest bray I've ever heard. Then he started walking slowly back toward the carcass.

I knew it was time for the jack to go find a life of its own, so I ordered Kirra to chase him away. Kirra, who'd been waiting eagerly for that order, immediately dashed after him. But the jack stood his ground and tried to butt Kirra. Then he turned around and tried to kick her. Kirra looked back to me for further instructions. I ordered her to heel.

The jack put his head down and slowly retraced his steps to his mother's side, where he stood vigil all night long.

December 2

I was up at first light, made coffee, then drove down to Tomás's lot. To my relief, the gate was open, and his son Edgar was there warming up the backhoe. "Buenos dias," I said. "Did you see my note?"

"Yes," he nodded. "Give me five minutes and I will come."

Edgar followed me with *la máquina* back up the hill to the dead burro. Then he shut off the engine and climbed down to examine the carcass. I explained that a policeman had shot the burro, at my request, but now it was my responsibility to have it buried.

Edgar looked surprised. "You want to bury it? Why not take it out in the arroyo and let the animals eat it."

He was right, of course. If you walk up any of these desert arroyos, you eventually come upon a heap of bones where some poor beast has died and the remains have been gnawed on by other creatures until not even a morsel of cartilage remains. Even the bones are consumed eventually. But I had assumed responsibility for this burro. I had tried to relieve its suffering, mostly failed, and now it had become something like family to me. "No," I said. "This burro was my friend. I want to give her a good grave."

Edgar shrugged—nothing a gringo might say or do surprises him anymore. He climbed back onto *la máquina* and scooped up the carcass with his bucket. I used a shovel to gather up pieces of entrails the buzzards had scattered about, and I put them in the bucket too. "Where do you want to take it?" Edgar asked.

"I don't know. Someplace where there's good sand to dig a hole. Maybe the big arroyo on the other side of the mountain?"

"No," he decided. "I know a better place. Let's take it to the burro cemetery."

"Perfect. I'll follow you."

As we drove down the windy road, the smell of the carcass was so putrid, Edgar and I had to cover our noses with our shirts.

Edgar led me to a sandy flat, hidden by a mesquite thicket, not far out of town. He pointed to a spot under a tall *cardon* cactus and said, "A burro is buried there." Then he pointed to another mound where I could see the dirt had more recently been disturbed. "And another burro is buried there."

"Good," I said.

The soil was soft and even a bit moist a few feet below the surface, and in less than five minutes Edgar had dug a hole six feet deep, four feet wide, and eight feet long. It was more than adequate. I gave him the thumbs-up, and in another minute the grave was covered.

December 3

Before breakfast José came by with another load of water, and I went out to tell him about my experience with the burro. José said he'd seen that injured burro while driving out the East Cape road many times, and he'd been worried about it too. He thanked me for ending its suffering and especially for seeing that it was buried properly.

"What I don't understand," I said, "is why, with ten thousand hectares to roam, this burro came to my gate to die."

José nodded and said, without hesitation but great certainty, "God sent the burro to you."

December 5

Last June, not long before we set out on our pilgrimage to Mount Rushmore, I had one of my worst surfing injuries in many years. I was surfing at Nine Palms on a day when the surf was in the 10-foot range. It was late in the morning, I was getting tired, and surface conditions were beginning to get rough. I dropped into one of the biggest waves of the day, thinking it would be my last and I would ride it all the way to shore. I took a high line on the wave, trying to get as much speed as I could, when suddenly the crest lurched forward erratically. I had already planted my front foot in preparation for a cutback, and as my body was pitched forward, my left knee was wrenched severely. I felt the knee pop, so I immediately bellied out on my board and rode the whitewater to the beach.

I knew right away I had torn the medial collateral ligament—a common injury in football when a player gets blocked or tackled from the side—and I knew it might be very slow to heal. The knee was unstable—it collapsed under me when I tried to walk on it—and I made the difficult decision to stay out of the water for at least a week. But I got on my weight bench that same day and began doing leg extensions to strengthen the quad muscles. In a few days, I could feel the knee getting stronger and more stable, and I was able to surf the rest of that season without any more problems. But I learned an important lesson: anybody who wants to surf in his fifties or sixties had better get serious about a strength and exercise program.

So today I started my winter fitness program, which will include weight training to regain some of the muscle mass we all lose as we get older, and a daily stretching regimen.

Also, for an aerobics workout, I will do hill running in intervals of sixty seconds, followed by thirty seconds of recovery, which simulates the pattern of paddling and rest that is essential for surfing.

A lot of the aches and pains many surfers go through come from paddling, which is not a natural body motion. A paddler lying on a surfboard has to lift his arms higher than a swimmer, without the rolling torso motion that assists swimmers. Even worse, a paddler lies on his rib cage, which impedes chest expansion for breathing and causes all sorts of unexpected difficulties. I've found I can treat most of my surfing injuries through a combination of deep massage, naproxen, and stretching.

Tennis balls, I have learned, are wonderfully effective tools for deep massage to relieve knots, adhesions, and tight muscles when it's difficult or impossible to reach them by hand. During surf season, I spend half an hour every day lying on the terrace rolling around on a tennis ball. Kirra, who thinks I'm inviting her to play, tries to steal the ball from me and, failing that, she rolls around in imitation, or perhaps mockery, of my contortions.

A lot of surfers I know practice yoga, which accomplishes about the same thing as stretching. But I've always thought of yoga as an ancient and obsolete form of stretching with a lot of silly religious dogma thrown in. I prefer to think in terms of muscle groups, and to focus directly on my problem areas. My approach does nothing to improve my karma, though, and I'll probably have to suffer through several more reincarnations because of it.

My generation has benefitted greatly from the health and medical advances of the twentieth century. Our understanding of physical fitness has evolved far beyond the torture regimens imposed by our high school coaches. Now we have scientific programs for aerobics, strength training, and nutrition, and failing those, we have anti-inflammatory medicines, arthroscopic surgery, and joint replacements. As a result, a lot of us in our sixties, and even seventies, are still in decent shape—not out of personal virtue but from having been born at the right time. Younger surfers who are waiting impatiently for the graybeards of my generation to die off so they can have more waves to themselves might be disappointed.

Sometimes I wonder where this fascination for surfing comes from and why I work so hard for a chance at one more season. One friend who is in his seventies and still surfs, told me, "After fifty years of this, you'd think you'd finally get enough. But then another wave comes along, and it's different than any other wave you ever saw, and you feel like a little kid again."

I don't have a philosophical explanation for why I do this. I don't think I surf for any reason other than pure elation. I don't need to break any records or beat anybody to a finish line, and I don't care if I have an audience watching me or not. But if there has to be some advantage to surfing, some profit or long-term gain, I would say that surfing teaches you to be aware of your body and it inspires you to stay in the best physical condition you can.

December 9

Last night the temperature dropped to 54 degrees, which is cold for Los Cabos. The wind has been blowing too, which made it seem even colder. This is about as close as we get to winter here.

I drove to San Lucas this morning to renew my visa and was amused to see how the tourists were wearing shorts and flip-flops, while the Mexicans were dressed as if it might snow any minute. One Mexican woman, who was wearing fur-lined boots and a ski jacket, asked me how I could stand this cold without more clothing.

The stores all over Los Cabos are putting up their Christmas decorations: firs and pines withering in the desert heat, snow from a can, plastic models of a fat man in a red suit, and a tinseled sleigh pulled by flying reindeer. Sometimes Mexicans think they're missing out on something by living in such a paradise. They would like to see it snow just once in Los Cabos so they could find out why gringos make such a fuss about it. Meanwhile, the Los Cabos airport is growing more crowded every day, as hordes of *norteamericanos* flee the dark miseries of a northern winter and the manic hell of a Christmas they have created for themselves.

By noon the temperature was back in the high 80s, and it felt like summer again.

December 11

Those born-again Christian surfers in San Diego County like to say that Jesus loves surfers, and it must be true because today we received a 5-foot swell so out of character for this season that it had to be a gift from heaven. Fireman Tom and Rod were already on it when I got to Punta Espina at 7:00 a.m., and even though the tide was a bit too high, we still had our fun for a while.

I read online that Southern California has been hit hard by Santa Ana winds lately. That hot weather pattern sometimes sweeps all the way down the Gulf of California, bringing a gusty east wind with it. Out in the water, we can see that east wind coming—the purple line begins far out at sea and gradually creeps in like gangrene. Sometimes the east wind will back off again after it starts, but not often, and not today.

I had been hoping the cooler water would mean the end of jellyfish season, but it turned out not to be so. I developed terrible welts on my arms and legs, and I know I'll be itching in my sleep for the next few days.

December 14

The architect who built our house, Francisco Gómez Best, stopped by today to give us our *manifestación*, which is a legal document establishing the cost basis of our house for tax purposes. I have been pestering Francisco for this document ever since he finished our house. I figured he would have problems completing the document because he didn't have receipts for all the labor and materials, but he assured me it would all come out okay in the end. And Francisco was right—as he almost always is.

In Mexico the architect who designs your house is often the contractor who builds it as well. Some architects here are classically trained and have lofty career ambitions, which can become expensive for the homeowner, as the architect's creative notions crowd out the homeowner's needs. Other architects learn about building by doing every stage of the work with their own hands, and they are often more attuned to the practical side of the business. Fortunately for us, Francisco is that kind of architect.

When I first began searching for a builder for our house, I hired and fired three architects before I happened to meet Francisco, almost by chance. Though he already had twenty years' building experience when I met him, he had never built a house for a gringo. But he wanted that opportunity, because he knew that was where the real money was to be made. Before he moved to San José, Francisco had worked on skyscrapers in Mexico City, where his father is an architect. His maternal grandfather had come from England, but he had forbidden his children and grandchildren to speak English at home. Francisco's mother, however, taught him English on the sly, and it has served him well.

Francisco was fascinated to learn that we had moved to Baja for the surfing—like many local Mexicans, he has trouble understanding how exceptional the surfing here is. Francisco, who has a wiry, athletic build, has been the amateur tennis champion of Los Cabos for the past eleven years. Every year the tennis tournament is held on Thanksgiving weekend, and the prize for first place is always a frozen turkey. (Mexicans find this hilarious, but I'm not sure I get the joke.) So knowing he was a great athlete, I tried to talk Francisco into going surfing with me. "No, thank you," he said. "I tried surfing once about fifteen years ago. The waves were huge! Higher than my head! I started paddling for one wave, and the next thing I knew, I was bent backwards looking at the bottom of my feet!"

"That's impossible," I said. "Nobody can bend backwards and look at the bottom of their feet."

"Exactly! That's why I will never go surfing again!"

Like almost every Mexican I have ever met, Francisco drives like a maniac. The week I met him he destroyed the transmission in his truck by driving too fast on a rocky road. Before we had signed any agreement on building our house, or even got to know each other very well, Francisco asked me if he could borrow $1500 to have his transmission repaired. I figured he was testing me, to find out what sort of gringo I was. So I tested him too, by loaning him the money, which I think surprised him a great deal. And we were both happy with the results. He got his transmission repaired, and I deducted $1500 from his first paycheck. Throughout the construction process, we never had a disagreement over money, and we never had a reason to doubt one another's honesty or goodwill.

Besides being a master builder, and knowing practically every good craftsman in every construction trade in Los Cabos, Francisco has excellent taste and judgment. The house he built for us is a huge improvement over the original plans, which were drawn by me and the three architects I fired. Sometimes Francisco made changes to the plans without discussing them with me beforehand, which could have led to disaster but never did. Claudia and I were delighted with every change he made, and we soon learned to let him do almost as he pleased. The result is a house we like very much and Francisco adores. "Sometimes when I drive through Zacatitos," he once told me, "I catch a glimpse of your house up on the hill, and a piece of my heart jumps out and lives there for a few moments. That is my dream house."

But getting Francisco to complete our paperwork at the end of the project was another matter. Every few months I would ask him about it again. "I know Mexicans can ignore these things," I said, "but I'm a guest in this country. I have to observe the laws or the Mexican government can throw me out. I cannot afford to ignore this *trámite*."

Francisco would smile and say, "You worry too much. This is not a problem. Just a formality. You'll see."

Maybe, I thought, but I withheld the bonus I had promised him, and even though we never spoke of it, he knew he wouldn't see that bonus until I had the *manifestación* in my hands.

Mexicans routinely ignore government laws and regulations. This, I suppose, comes from a long tradition of bad government. Half the property tax in Los Cabos goes unpaid every year, even though the tax is absurdly cheap. (We pay less than $50 per year for our property tax, while our oldest son in San Diego pays more than $500 per month for his.) I insisted, however, that Francisco complete our *manifestación* so it could be officially registered, and neither I nor my heirs would have to unravel a snarl of Mexican paperwork years down the road. I know Mexican bureaucracies can be impossible, but my attitude from the start was that we would learn about Mexico and its culture by dealing with the government as honestly as we could.

This, of course, was another bit of gringo foolishness. Mexicans have the wisdom to understand that with a dysfunctional government, in which it is impossible to fulfill all the requirements of the law, there must be a backdoor solution for every bureaucratic dilemma. I had no idea what they were, but Francisco did. And to my amazement, he finally produced an officially stamped document that declared I had spent a sum of money that, as it turned out, was fairly close to the amount I actually paid.

"This is a miracle!" I said. "I never thought I would see this paper!"

"It's nothing," Francisco said, dismissing it with a wave of his hand. "And by the way, can I ask you now about my bonus?"

December 20

The waves today are about 1 foot high. Maybe after Christmas, when the big winter north swells begin arriving on the west side of the peninsula, we can head over there. Meanwhile, like surfers everywhere, I use the down time to make repairs around the house, tidy up the yard, and so forth.

Almost all my jellyfish welts have disappeared now. The self-inflicted wounds from my nightly itching attacks are healing, and some of the scabs are falling off too.

December 21

Today is the winter solstice, the day of the longest shadows and the fewest hours of light. The native shamans of Baja were able to predict this day with crude calendars they made by marking the shadows of light on cave walls. Old World celebrations of Christmas, of course, were based originally on pagan observations of this day. And for people like us, who rely on photovoltaics for our electricity, this is an important day as well.

After we had finished building our house, we mounted 2,000 watts of solar panels on the flat roof where they could receive full sunlight; we faced the panels due south, and we tilted them at 23 degrees, which is the latitude of Zacatitos and therefore the angle of the sun at noon on the spring and fall equinoxes. Throughout the fall, as the days grow shorter and shorter, the minutes for charging our battery bank become fewer and fewer. Because the nights are also growing longer and longer in the fall, there's an increasing need for lights. And because this is the holiday season, we have more guests, and each person adds more demand on lights, water pump, refrigerator, dishwasher, computers, and so on. With a little conservation, we get through this month without any real inconvenience, but like primitive people all over the world, we celebrate this day as the turning point of the year. Days begin to grow longer, nights shorter, and storage batteries fuller.

From here on, things can only get better.

December 22

The surf forecaster on *Surfing Magazine*'s Swellwatch has predicted a possible small swell arriving a few days before Christmas. I'm skeptical, yet I've learned to trust this particular forecaster, Austin Gendron. Once last spring he predicted the arrival of a swell before the storm producing the swell had even left the continent of Antarctica. By my estimation, that's some pretty slick prognosticating.

Gendron's forecasts don't specifically include the tip of Baja, but we extrapolate his projections for mainland Mexico to the East Cape. Waves travel across the open ocean at about 20 to 25 miles per hour, or roughly 600 miles per day; therefore, any south swell striking the coast of mainland Mexico can be expected to arrive on the tip of Baja something like eighteen to twenty-four hours later. If we throw out any swell angle less than 170 degrees, or greater than 230 degrees, since they won't strike this coastline anyway, we can have a pretty accurate forecast for the East Cape based on Gendron's predictions.

Like most surfers, I have mixed feelings about modern surf forecasts. On the one hand, surfers now can do a surf check without even getting out of bed, and in Southern California alone that must save one oil tanker of gasoline per year. But on the other hand, surfers in California, Texas, or Florida can look at the same forecasts for Baja that we're looking at and know with great precision when a juicy swell will hit Los Cabos. With a few more mouse clicks, they can make their plane, car, and hotel rental reservations and be sitting in the water next to me on the morning the swell arrives.

Still, surf forecasters don't create surf, they just predict its arrival. Most of the web-based forecasts are free, which means they're making their money by getting a piece of that hotel and car rental action. Their temptation to exaggerate and inflate the forecasts must be great. Hopefully, they'll continue to call it wrong just often enough to keep the surf tourists frustrated. At any rate, nothing will ever be more accurate than the old-fashioned dawn surf patrol.

So, this morning, with nothing better to do, Claudia and I drove out the East Cape to have a look for ourselves. I could see by the time we got to Shipwreck, though, that the projected swell wasn't going to amount to much. There were clean, organized swell lines, but the waves weren't more than 3 feet high.

You never know, though. Sometimes, depending on the swell angle, waves gets bigger as you move farther east and clear the wave shadow created by Cabo San Lucas. So we decided to continue on to Punta Espina.

As we pulled up to the beach at Punta Espina, the cove was nearly flat. I shut off the engine, and we got out of the Rhino to sit and enjoy the sunrise. And then suddenly, the entire shoreline erupted into a white froth and hundreds—probably thousands—of silver and blue sardines flung themselves onto the beach in a frenzied act of mass suicide. We had never seen anything like that before, and we watched in amazement as one surge after another of crazed sardines raced to the edge of the water and then kept going, flipping and thrashing to get just a foot or two farther onto the sand. And then we saw behind them a school of perhaps a hundred jack crevalles, which the Mexicans call *toros*, all about the size of a football, herding the sardines into a corner of the cove where it was impossible for them to escape in any other way than to take to land. Every fifteen seconds or so, a 1-foot wave would wash up the beach, capture all the struggling sardines that hadn't reached higher land, and drag them back into the water. Then the cove became a silvery boil again as *toros* gobbled up sardines until their bellies were bloated.

Two of the *panga* fishermen ran down to the beach with fishing poles and shiny, homemade lures and began casting into the ball of fish. As soon as they caught one of the *toros*, they would jerk the hook out of its mouth, fling the fish behind them, and cast again. They pulled out *toros* one after another, and their children ran behind, stuffing the fish into plastic buckets. In ten minutes the two fishermen must have caught thirty fish.

One of the fishermen, seeing the look on our faces, laughed and handed his pole to Claudia, who cast into the boil and soon caught a *toro* of her own.

Then it was over. The remaining *toros* swam away, their morning hunt an outrageous success. A few dozen exhausted sardines still flopped about on the sand, so the children went around with their buckets and gathered them up too, to be used later that morning as bait.

December 24

Our son Kyle is here visiting us during his Christmas break. Kyle loves to surf, but unfortunately we don't have rideable waves right now, and, like most college kids, when he has nothing better to do he likes to drink beer. What can I say? I was the same at his age and have changed little since. But Kyle has also inherited from me the restless need to be outdoors and moving about that I inherited from my father. In another age they called that wanderlust, nowadays they might call it attention deficit disorder, but both terms are slanderous. Some people have an urgent need to be out in the real world, doing real things. It's a habit I think ought to be encouraged.

After two days of gusty wind and high clouds, this morning the sky sparkled with a purity of light that I've never seen anyplace other than Baja. So Kyle and I climbed in the Rhino, with Kyle behind the wheel, and we headed off to the other side of Punta Gorda.

We followed a narrow track down the big arroyo that flows through old Rancho Zacatitos, until we arrived at a long stretch of white beach that is rarely visited. Kyle shut off the engine, and we sat for a while watching a cluster of dark birds out at sea picking on a floating carcass—without binoculars we couldn't identify either the scavenger or the scavenged. Then we got out and walked back toward the rocky point. We poked among the tide pools, marveling at the abundance of life. Hundreds of black crabs scrambled over the rocks and scattered in every direction as we approached. The shore-break was so steep, even the small waves cracked with surprising ferocity, and we had to keep watch between sets and flee for our lives when the biggest waves struck.

Punta Gorda from a distance looks like a sturdy landmark, something for boats at sea to take comfort in, but up close it becomes a confused gnarl of rock, with gray granite pushing up through yellowed limestone. The face of the point is pockmarked with small caves eroded by wind and sea, and whole sections slough off from time to time. In some places the beach is littered with mounds of shiny black cobblestones that have spent an eternity being heaved into the ocean only to be spit out again. In other places great swirls of sand, untouched by human footprints, have been left by the highest tides.

Up against the bluff, we found logs of *palo chino* and mango washed down in floods from the hills above Miraflores, then swept along the cape until they became entangled in the rocks. Most were so riddled by termites they crumbled in our fingers like rotten paper, but some were fresh enough that fragments of bark still clung to their trunks.

One of the things I love most about this cape is the sense that nature isn't half finished with it. It has been burnt by the heat of summer, pounded by heavy surf, desiccated by drought, shaken by earthquakes, washed by rains, and then swept clean by hurricane winds. And that was just in the last year!

As we walked back to the Rhino, Kyle said to me, "Even though the sky is clear today, it feels colder."

"It is," I said. "Last night the temperature on our terrace dropped to fifteen degrees."

"Fifteen? No way. It wasn't that cold!"

"I mean Celsius. That's like fifty-nine degrees Fahrenheit."

Kyle, who survived four semesters of calculus, thought that over for a moment, then said, "How do you convert Celsius to Fahrenheit in your head, anyway?"

Most of us who have lived in Mexico for a while can convert currency and mileage in our heads without thinking about it. But converting temperature isn't so easy. The Canadians, who grew up using the sensible metric system, always know what the Mexicans mean when they talk about temperature, while we *estadounidenses* are stuck trying to do conversions on our fingers and toes. Sometimes this can cause problems for us. One woman in Zacatitos baked a batch of brownies at 350 degrees, forgetting that her new oven was calibrated in Celsius, and that 350 degrees Fahrenheit is 662 degrees Celsius.

The formula for conversion is Celsius X 1.8, + 32 = Fahrenheit, but I can never do that in my head. So I told Kyle, "What I do is remember that twenty Celsius is sixty-eight Fahrenheit, and every five degrees more or less Celsius is nine degrees Fahrenheit. So twenty-five Celsius, for example, is seventy-seven Fahrenheit."

Kyle just laughed at me. "Thanks," he said. "I'll use my cellphone."

December 25

This morning on our terrace it was 10 degrees Celsius (that's 52 degrees Fahrenheit), which is about as cold as the air temperature ever gets here. I read in the local newspaper, *La Tribuna*, that the state secretary of health has issued an exhortation that people be extremely cautious with the harsh weather we're having here in Baja California Sur. The article included a photo of two stylish young Mexicans wearing thick overcoats and wool scarves. The secretary emphasized that this warning should be heeded especially by the sick and elderly. Three days ago I turned 63, which I suppose must be considered elderly, so I put on my only jacket and wore it around the house until about 11:00 a.m., when the temperature had reached almost 80 again. By then I was sweating profusely and just couldn't stand it any longer, so I disregarded the secretary's advice and went back to my normal surf trunks and flip-flops.

Claudia and I have a house full of family and friends visiting for the holidays, and we invited them all to go along on our morning walk. Kirra was thrilled to have a full herd, and she worked hard to keep them all under control, circling back time and again to nip at the heels of the stragglers and warn them to keep moving along. On the way home, though, half the herd chose to follow Claudia to the farmer's market in front of Zac's Bar and Grill. Because Kirra can get unbearably bossy in unruly crowds, I insisted that she follow me and my part of the herd back home. Kirra was disturbed to see the herd split like this—a serious violation of sheepdog ethics—and she tried to drop out of my sight so she could double back and pick up her strays. Back home I caught her twice trying to slink off to Zac's, but eventually I gave up and let her do what she had to do. Twenty minutes later she came prancing up the arroyo, marching the wayward half of the herd in front of her.

Not everybody in Zacatitos has a high opinion of Kirra. They object to her name, which they say makes her sound like a movie star. They say she's bossy and has a bad habit of nipping at the fingers of people she thinks are noncompliant—both of which are true. But we have no use for a fawning lap dog that will welcome every salesman and thief who might come around. Kirra might suffer from compulsive herding disorder, which can be annoying. But you have to admire her work ethic and her determination to complete the tasks she assigns to herself.

Later in the afternoon, after we and our guests had enjoyed several bottles of wine, we discovered what we thought must be a Christmas miracle. A few days earlier, I had noticed a watermark on the exterior block wall below our kitchen; at first I thought it was caused by the nightly dew. Then, as the watermark grew, and didn't evaporate during the day, I began to suspect faulty plumbing. It was no emergency, and I decided I would wait until after the holidays to investigate it further. But after three days, the watermark had gradually grown until it had taken on the image of the Virgin Mary, with an aura of pure white surrounding her angelic face.

In Mexico, where these events occur more often than they do elsewhere, they are called *apariciónes*, or *fantasmas*. The most famous was the appearance of the Virgin Mary to a

Mexican peasant in 1531, which is now celebrated by an icon known as Our Lady of Guadalupe. But there are hundreds of other examples: religious statues cry tears of blood; a fish caught in the ocean recites verses from the Bible; a driver who falls asleep at the wheel wakes to find an angel's hands steering for him; birds in the desert speak the German of the old Jesuit missionaries; clouds at Christmas take the form of the nativity scene; and distant mountains become a pregnant virgin in repose.

A few years ago I read in the *Los Angeles Times* about a man who discovered the image of Jesus in a pancake he was cooking for breakfast. A photo accompanied the story, but I failed to recognize the apparition the man spoke of—due, no doubt, to my lack of faith. Our neighbors have a dog with a birthmark on its belly in the shape of the Baja peninsula, or so they say—I've never been able to see that one, either. The fact that I am able to discern the image of the Virgin Mary on our wall, and the fact that this incident has occurred at Christmas, might be evidence that I am beginning to make some spiritual progress, though probably too late in life to do me any good.

December 31

All last night the wind was dead calm, which is unusual here. In the quiet, even the slightest sounds were carried a long way. We heard the lonesome bellowing of a cow coming all the way from Las Tres Nietas, the three peaks west of town where the old Rancho Zacatitos used to be. We heard the sound of Mexican music coming from a car radio at Punta Gorda, more than a mile away. But most curious of all, we heard a slapping sound coming from the direction of the ocean. The whales are beginning to arrive for the season; we see their plumes and sometimes hear them pounding their tails in the water, but this sound was different—not as loud, but much more frequent, like children clapping their hands.

At breakfast we could still hear the sound, yet we still had no idea what it might be.

On our morning walk, as soon as the arroyo we follow every morning opened onto the beach, we saw many, many silvery bat rays flying four or five out of the water and spinning a few joyful revolutions in the air before slapping back to the surface. All of them flew from west to east, which we assumed was their direction of travel. During the twenty minutes or so we spent walking the beach, we must have seen several hundred bat rays performing this aerial maneuver, though we still have no idea why they were doing it or what it achieved.

All our Christmas guests have gone home now, and the house is quiet again. The watermark on our stucco wall has dried out, and the mysterious apparition has disappeared, except for a slight white residue that bears no resemblance at all to the Virgin Mary, so far as I can tell.

Fireman Tom

January:

Nostalgic Hibernation

January 2

Miracles can happen in December, hope sometimes begins in late February, but nothing of any significance ever happens to an East Cape surfer during the month of January. This is another problem, you see, with a chronicle. Blank periods, when there is nothing to report, are bound to happen. Biographers can blur their way through years, or even decades. Novelists can hop around in time irresponsibly, or invent more falsehoods to fill their gaps. Poets can become ever more vague and abstract until nobody has any idea what they're talking about. But an honest chronicler must find some other cheap literary ploy to deal with his dead time. I have chosen nostalgic reminiscence. I realize I'm flirting with fiction here, since nostalgia is nothing more than a way for us to make our peace with the past by forgetting the unpleasant parts and lying to ourselves about the rest. I apologize for that, but I see no other choice.

Therefore, I have decided to devote January to explaining how Claudia and I arrived at Zacatitos. To maintain the pretense of a chronicle, I will record my remembrances as daily entries. I advise hardcore surfers reading this account to skip ahead to February.

When I started surfing, at age fourteen, I was the most frustrated and improbable surfer in California. Because, you see, I grew up in the San Joaquin Valley. It's taken me years to publicly admit that fact, but yes, I started out as a surfer who lived in the raisin capital of the world, 200 miles from the ocean.

Not long after I was born, my father, who worked as a microbiologist for the Veteran's Administration and was a major in the Army Reserve, accepted a job at the new VA hospital in Fresno, where he went on to spend most of his career studying valley fever, a potentially deadly fungal infection of the lungs. At that time, researchers believed the only places in the world where these fungal spores were found naturally in the soil were the San Joaquin Valley and the Soviet Union. People who have grown up in the San Joaquin Valley typically have a resistance to the disease, but it can be devastating to immigrants, particularly those who work with the soil.

I was nearly sixty years old before I grew cynical enough to ask myself why the U.S. military, which never funded medical research that didn't yield a direct benefit to the troops, would be interested in a disease that was killing mostly Mexican immigrant farmworkers. My father knew the answer to that question, but by then he was already in his nineties and had reached a state of dementia that made it impossible for him to answer. My own conclusion, however, is that the U.S. military was worried about the Soviet Union developing a biological weapon based on the valley fever fungus, and they were trying to develop an effective treatment and immunization in case American troops ever needed it. But it's possible the U.S. military was trying to develop a biological weapon of its own.

At any rate, because of valley fever, I grew up trapped deep in America's fruit basket. Most of my early schoolmates were from families of Dust Bowl Okies who had migrated to the San Joaquin Valley in the thirties, which is why people sometimes tell me I speak with a bit of an Oklahoma drawl. I suppose you could call me an Okie once removed.

January 3

I first became aware of surfing in the early sixties, about the same time everybody else did, when a group of Southern California adventure seekers, like Flippy Hoffman, Buzzy Trent, and Pat Curren, moved to the north shore of Oahu and began riding the faces of 20-foot giants that looked like something out of a child's nightmare. When photographs of these half-crazed daredevils began to appear in newspapers all over the world, people were shocked, horrified, and even offended by such foolishness. But some of us were fascinated too.

In the San Joaquin Valley we played football and baseball and wrestled. Sports for us were dirty, smelly, sometimes bloody, and often painful. We were tough and didn't expect athletics to be something you necessarily enjoyed—although that could happen if you were able to inflict more pain on your opponent than he could inflict on you. It had never occurred to me that a sport could be beautiful. All I'd seen of surfing so far were photos in surf magazines. But I thought that other than the nude female body (something else I knew about only from magazines), surfing was the most photogenic thing I had ever seen.

My surfing hero from that era was Mike Doyle, a tall, powerfully-built Malibu regular who had grown up in Inglewood, just a mile from the L.A. airport. Doyle hadn't been among the very first of those California crazies to invade Oahu, but he hadn't been far behind them, either, and after just one season on the North Shore, he was considered one of the top big-wave riders in the world.

In May of 1964 Doyle represented the U.S. at a world

surfing contest held at Manly Beach, Australia, where he finished second to Midget Farrelly. Some people said later that Doyle had been the best surfer that day, but the politics of nationalism demanded that an Australian surfer win a surf contest in Australian waters. It makes no difference, because the surf that day was small, and the idea of selecting a world champion in such conditions is ridiculous. At any rate, at just 23, Doyle became an American hero, something like an Olympic champion, and during the sixties Doyle became, in the opinion of his peers, the greatest surfer in the world.

So even though I'd never surfed, I had a surf hero. On my bedroom wall in Fresno, I had a color poster of Doyle at Sunset Beach; he was wearing orange trunks and was coming to his feet at the lip of a huge wave that was terrifying and eerily beautiful. I couldn't imagine why anybody would risk his life doing such a thing, yet I knew my life would be wasted if I couldn't attempt it myself. I loved the water and was a good swimmer. I knew nothing about the ocean, but I was eager to learn. The only problem was that I still lived a three-hour drive from the coast.

January 5

It wasn't until 1963 that I got my first chance to surf. My family spent a weekend at Santa Cruz, where I rented a surfboard on the boardwalk and tried my luck at Cowells Beach, the place where just about every gremmie on the central coast rides his first wave.

The first time I paddled out at Cowells, it seemed almost presumptuous to think I could do what my heroes did. Fortunately, Cowells is one of the most forgiving breaks on the West Coast. The waves wrap around a large point, where a high cliff shelters them from the wind, and they roll to the beach in long, lazy lines. The truth is, almost anybody can learn to surf at Cowells, even on their first try.

Like all beginners, I pearled the nose of my board on the first few waves I paddled into. But I'd read about this, I knew it was likely to happen, and I knew how to correct it. Within an hour or so, I was catching waves and, somehow, angling my thick slug of a rental board down the line. I was absolutely enthralled by the sensation of speed and the pure beauty of surfing, but I was puzzled too, and remember thinking, "What am I doing here? Human beings don't belong on waves!"

Knowing that I could learn how to surf filled me with joy and confidence. It was one of the greatest things that ever happened to me. I knew that no matter how bored I was with the San Joaquin Valley, how much I hated those gray winter days and long suffocating summers, there was an ocean out there somewhere. There were waves breaking on a beach. There were people having fun on this planet, and I could too.

I was aware from the start that there was something revolutionary about this sport. It had the power to warp old values, change the way you looked at the world, maybe even send you flying off on a wild tangent. But I was ready for that.

January 6

I was fortunate to have several good friends in Fresno who were as eager to learn how to surf as I was. After we turned sixteen and got our driver's licenses, we would get up at five o'clock on a wintery Saturday morning, drive three hours or so to Santa Cruz, surf all day long, then drive back home in the dark.

Santa Cruz in those days was a sleepy little retirement town of white cottages bathed in golden sunlight. The boardwalk closed in winter, and most of the residents went to sleep right after the sun went down. Surfers were the only thing moving in town after eight o'clock. My friends and I would pool our pocket change for gas and cruise between Steamer

Lane and Pleasure Point, looking for girls or, failing that, somebody willing to buy us beer.

If the weather was rainy or cold, we would rent a cheap motel room for the night. But more often we would sleep at the state park. We would surf again early Sunday morning, then head home that afternoon. I'm not sure why our parents let us go on these surf safaris at such a young age. But it was a different time, and parents still thought it was good for teenagers to learn by making their own mistakes. And we learned a lot.

On one of our trips coming back from Santa Cruz, near Los Banos, I was lying in the back of my friend Brian's Chevy Nomad, staring out the rear window. Suddenly, I saw our boards break loose from the racks and go sailing into the pale winter sky. I was intrigued by how the air currents lifted them higher and how they twirled and spun. It was a beautiful thing to see. Brian stopped the car, and we ran into the field where our boards had landed. Fortunately, the field had just been plowed and was wet from a recent rain. Amazingly, our boards were hardly damaged. That was one big advantage to those old longboards—they had thick wooden stringers and were very heavily glassed. It was hard to break one of those things. But it also hurt like hell to get hit by one.

The summer before our junior year in high school, Brian and I got a job knocking almonds. This is work in which you rise before dawn to beat the scorching heat, drag thick canvas tarps through the dusty almond orchards, and arrange the tarps in a circle around the base of a tree. Then you take an eight-pound rubber mallet and beat on the base of the tree for ten minutes or so until all the almonds fall to the ground. You do this in 100-degree heat for eight hours a day and get paid minimum wage.

Every day that summer, as we toiled under those miserable conditions, Brian and I promised ourselves that before school started in September, we would make a surfari to Santa Cruz, and that would somehow justify our brutish labor. We fantasized about the cool ocean waters, how we would surf all day long, eat hamburgers and onion rings on the boardwalk at night, and meet blonde girls in bikinis who would rendezvous with us back at the campground that night.

We fulfilled our dream too, Brian and I—for one-half of one day. While we were surfing at a place called Privates, just west of Pleasure Point, some jackass broke the wind wing on Brian's car, reached into the glove compartment, and stole all our hard-earned money. They even took the belt off my pants. We had to scrounge under the car seat for change to buy enough gas to get home.

Living in the San Joaquin Valley, it was impossible for us to get enough water time to become good at surfing. In the summer we tried wake surfing behind a boat on Millerton Lake, and that was better than nothing, but the lake was twenty miles away, and none of us had regular access to a boat.

And then we invented what might be called an early form of tow-in surfing. The San Joaquin Valley is blessed with an abundance of irrigation canals. My friends and I discovered that it was possible to run a nylon rope from a car bumper and, driving on the dirt maintenance road alongside a canal, pull a surfboard, with surfer, through the water. The summer before our senior year, we practiced this ditch surfing every day for hours at a time, learning to switch stances, walk the nose, and crank power turns that sprayed a wall of water six feet high. It wasn't truly surfing, but we considered it a pretty good substitute for the San Joaquin Valley.

Finally, one cold October evening just before dusk, an irrigation-district employee caught us. He angrily showed us how the wake from our surfboards was eroding the banks of the canal and warned us never to do it again. We ignored his warnings, of course, but he was on the lookout for us now. The very next day he caught us ditch surfing again and called a deputy sheriff. The driver of our tow vehicle was issued a citation, and we were told that if we were caught there again, our vehicle would be impounded.

So our glorious days of ditch surfing were over. To our disappointment, the sport we had invented never attracted the attention we always thought it deserved.

January 9

My first job out of high school, in the magical summer of 1967, was working as a busboy at the Yosemite Lodge cafeteria, in Yosemite Valley. I was a backpacker, rock climber, and backcountry skier by then, and I knew that the opportunities for wilderness adventure in Yosemite were among the finest in the world, which is why I took the job. But my pay as a busboy that summer was only $1.10 per hour, and my employer, Curry Company, took out 35 cents per hour for room and board. The room was a rat-infested canvas tent with a wooden floor, shared with four other employees; the shower was a fungal dungeon shared with leering old pervert cooks; and the board was whatever the cafeteria customers had refused to eat—usually some coagulated noodle casserole. So my net pay was 75 cents per hour, which, even in 1967, wasn't much. To make matters worse, busboys had to work a triple-split shift—breakfast, lunch, and dinner—which meant our workday lasted fourteen hours, six days a week. That didn't leave a lot of time for wilderness adventure.

By late August, it had dawned on me that I had been little more than an indentured servant that summer, and I felt frustrated and used. My first year of college would start in just three more weeks, and if I didn't get out and see something of the world, my summer would be wasted. I had two good friends working at the lodge—Luke and David—who were itching with the same wanderlust I had, and together we came up with a plan. We pooled our money and paid $50 dollars for a 1952 Chevrolet station wagon with a good six-cylinder engine but a bad differential. By making a few phones calls, we found a junkyard in the foothills that would sell us a used differential for $10. Luke was a good mechanic, and with my assistance he swapped the differential on our day off.

The last week in August, the three of us gave Curry Company our two-week notice. Our supervisor at the cafeteria— an earnest career man who slept with the waitresses—tried to talk us out of making such a foolish mistake, explaining it was company policy that anybody who quit before Labor Day would never work for Curry Company again.

One of the last things we did before leaving Yosemite Valley was hang about a hundred lodgepole pinecones around the body of our car, hooking them onto pieces of baling wire and jamming them into cracks along the decorative molding, like Christmas tree decorations. I can't explain why we did this, except to say again that it was the summer of 1967, and there were a lot of things going on that couldn't be easily explained. Finally, we loaded two surfboards onto the roof of our station wagon and set off for Mazatlán, Mexico, a distance of nearly 1500 miles, one way.

Once we got below the border, Luke insisted on doing all the driving. He was restless by nature and said he felt more comfortable behind the wheel. David and I took turns riding up front, where one of us navigated and kept Luke company, while the other napped in back. Every now and then we would stop at a roadside stand to buy fresh tamales wrapped in corn husks. The vendors kept galvanized tubs filled with ice, and for ten cents you could plunge a hand into the tub and pull out a dripping bottle of Coca-Cola, which for some reason tasted better than the American version. The weather was so hot and muggy, we wore nothing but our surf trunks, and still we could wipe a hand across our chests like a squeegee and fling off drops of sweat.

David, who was Mexican American, had never been to

Mexico before, and this journey had a special meaning for him that went far beyond the surf adventure it was for Luke and me. He had grown up speaking Spanish at home, but he kept telling us he wasn't sure if the Mexicans would be able to understand him or not. He was very worried about it. When he first saw that the roadside vendors could understand him perfectly, and he could understand them, he became so emotional he nearly cried.

Being from the San Joaquin Valley, I had grown up with Mexican Americans. Almost half the people in Fresno—the half who weren't Okies—had Hispanic roots. Yet, aside from my teammates on our high school wrestling and football teams, I had very few friends who were Mexican. To me, I'm ashamed to admit, Mexicans were people who wore pointed shoes, considered cockfighting a sport, fought with switchblade knives, used far too much hair ointment, and had a lot of bad luck with cars. Although I grew up hearing Spanish almost every day, I had never bothered to learn a single word of it. Those students in my high school who planned on going to college studied French—I can't imagine why. My French teachers always talked about how beautiful the French language was, but to me it always sounded nasal and whiny, like a distant cow mooing. At my high school only Mexicans studied Spanish, and we assumed that was because they already spoke the language and were assured of getting a good grade.

It wasn't until I heard David speaking Spanish with the roadside vendors that I really started listening to the language. And I came to the conclusion that Spanish is very expressive—more lyrical than English and more handsome than French—and I decided I was going to learn to speak it, if I could. David gave me my first informal lessons in Spanish as we drove down through the sweltering Sonoran Desert in our 1952 Chevrolet wagon with a hundred pinecones dancing at our sides.

Everywhere in the countryside, farmers were burning their fields, and the air smelled like smoke. The people still lived on small family farms, in homes that were humble but clean. Men still wore white pants of homespun cotton and *huaraches*, women wore hand-embroidered dresses, and children ran naked. Every town of any size—Guaymas, Hermosillo, Ciudad Obregón—had a monumental statue of some Mexican hero standing proudly in the middle of the main intersection; the message was supposed to be one of national pride, but to a young American it felt oppressive and totalitarian. On the outskirts of every village, women were washing clothes in the river and laying them out on the rocks to dry. It was easy to see the people were poor, but it wasn't like the demoralizing poverty I had seen among Mexican migrant farmworkers in the San Joaquin Valley.

Somewhere along the way, our car developed a carburetion problem. The engine purred along like it would run forever, and then all of a sudden it would sputter and stall. This was a terrifying thing on a Mexican highway, where a large truck is always crowding your tail, and the road has few turnouts. When the car would start to spurt, Luke would force it off the road wherever he could. We would get out and wait twenty minutes or so, then get back in and find that the car would run perfectly—until the whole thing happened again fifty miles farther down the road. Luke said it wasn't anything to worry about. We would be in Mazatlán in twenty-four hours if we drove straight through. "You can't stay awake that long," I said. "You have to sleep sometime."

"I'll let you know if I get tired," he replied. But he never did.

The farther south we drove, the closer we came to Mexico's tropical zone, where the summer storms begin. Crossing the desert at night, we saw lightning in the distant mountains that looked like nothing I'd ever seen before—heavenly explosions in a pulse-like rhythm that went on for hours at a time. For me Mexico didn't look and feel like another country; it was like another planet.

When we finally got to Mazatlan, we found that we could rent a good room, on a street just off the *malecón*, for a few dollars per night. Because this was hurricane season, just about the only tourists in town were surfers, and there weren't even very many of those. To save money, we stopped eating in restaurants; David would go to the market every day and come home with a shopping bag full of fresh tortillas, smoked tuna, avocadoes, tomatoes, bananas, papayas, and tart little pineapple empanadas.

In late afternoon, by lying outside under the shade in the ocean breeze, we found the climate to be tolerable. But at night, as soon as the sun went down, the ocean breezes stopped blowing, the heat radiated off the streets and block walls, the humidity fell over the town like a hot towel, and we could scarcely breathe.

Every morning we surfed at a reef break in town called Cannons; the place was never crowded. The board I had brought was an old brown 10-foot log that had been dinged and patched so many times it looked like some mutant vegetable that had grown out of the ground—easily the ugliest board I have ever seen. But it rode well enough, and at that stage in my development as a surfer, it didn't matter that its design was at least ten years out of date. I was thrilled with the clear water and the beautiful colors of the sand and palms. The waves were only about shoulder high, but the surface conditions were excellent. Luke and I surfed several hours together every morning. David didn't surf, and even though Luke and I offered to loan him our boards, he insisted he didn't want to learn.

The biggest problem at Mazatlán was that the rocky bottom was covered with thousands of spiny urchins. I had seen urchins in California but never like this. I tried my best to stay away from them, but eventually I lost my board (this was before the era of surf leashes), and during the long swim in, I stepped on urchins with both feet. They were so sharp, I didn't realize at first that I'd been stuck. But when I reached the beach, I discovered I had half a dozen broken spines embedded in each foot. At first I was amused. This was real adventure! But in another day or so, my puncture wounds became very painful. Urchin spines are brittle, and if you try to pull them out with tweezers, they usually break off. I found it impossible to get even one of them out. None of us knew what to do.

David, who was quickly making friends with people all over town, came back to our hotel room with a new folk remedy every day. "My friend Emilio tells me he stepped on urchins once as a child, and he doesn't recall exactly, but he thinks his mother dissolved them with vinegar."

Vinegar, we discovered, does not dissolve urchins.

"Now Emilio says he thinks it might have been lemon juice his mother used."

Lemon juice does not dissolve urchins.

"Ricardo tells me he gets urchins all the time, and he takes them out by melting paraffin and pouring it over the wounds. He says after the paraffin hardens, the spines will pull right out."

Paraffin does not remove urchins.

Finally, I took a razor blade and sliced off the thick callus on my heel to expose the ends of the spines. But when I tried to grab them with tweezers, the spines broke off again, this time even deeper. Not long after this crude and bloody surgery, my feet became so painful I could hardly walk, and I spent our last two or three days lying on the beach watching Luke surf.

January 10

All the way home, our car's carburetion problem steadily

grew worse. Driving across the desert flats wasn't so bad, but climbing a long steep hill, just when the engine needed the most gas, the engine would sputter, and the car would lurch violently. More than once the engine stalled near the top of a hill, with a long line of impatient truck drivers behind us. My mechanical skills at that time were limited, so I was no help. David's mechanical knowledge was even worse—he simply made the sign of the cross over and over again with great fervor. Luke finally said, "We have to do something about this or we're going to get ourselves killed."

At the next town, we stopped at a Pemex, and with David translating, Luke explained our problem to a young attendant. The man nodded, told Luke to open the hood and, with just a screwdriver, removed the float bowl on the side of the carburetor. He drained the gas into a Coke bottle, then held the bottle up to the light and showed us tiny filaments floating in the gas. "These," he said with a laugh, "are tobacco. Somebody has put a cigarette in your tank."

"So what can we do?" Luke asked. "Drain the whole tank?"

Without even bothering to explain it to us, the attendant went next door to an auto parts store, came back with a small inline filter, cut our rubber gas line where it went into the fuel pump, and spliced in the new filter. The repair didn't take five minutes.

After we had thanked and paid the attendant and were about to leave, he asked us, "What are these things hanging from the side of your car?"

"These are pinecones," David explained. "From Yosemite."

The attendant touched one lightly. "I have never seen anything like this."

"Would you like to have one?" David asked.

"Very much," he nodded.

We gladly gave him three.

At the El Centro border crossing, the American customs agents took one look at our ragged appearance and ordered us to pull into the full inspection area. Though I didn't know it at the time, marijuana smuggling was already a big business in Mexico, and Mazatlán was the center of the action. Two bleary-eyed surfers, and one Mexican American who spoke fluent Spanish, must have triggered the customs agents' warning bell. The agents tore our car apart, removed the door panels, ripped open the roof lining, searched under the body panels with flashlights, and questioned each of us separately about where we'd been, what we had been doing in Mexico, and what we had brought back with us. But the only thing we had to declare was a fuel filter and three pairs of *huaraches*. One frustrated agent finally took me aside and said, "You seem like a nice kid. Let me give you a bit of advice. Mexico is a disgusting place. Don't ... you ... ever ... go back there again!"

In the end, all the customs agents confiscated were our remaining pinecones, suspecting they were some exotic drug they hadn't encountered before.

By the time I reached home, my sea urchin spines had begun to fester, and with a little encouragement, they began to pop out. In the years since, I have suffered from sea urchins many times, but I have never found a better treatment than to leave them alone until they're ready to come out on their own.

January 11

During the late sixties and early seventies, when surfing was going through an awkward transition from the longboard era to the modern shortboard era, I stopped surfing entirely. I hadn't lost my interest in the sport, but I was going to college all winter and working hard all summer, and I simply didn't have the time or money for it. I still read the surf magazines whenever I could get my hands on them, and in 1969 I was delighted to see that my old surf hero, Mike Doyle, had won the Duke Kahanamoku Classic, which at that time was the most prestigious event in surfing—the equivalent of a world championship. Doyle was almost thirty by then—some younger surfers were already calling him "the old man of surfing,"—and after that season he never competed in professional contests again.

After college, with a useless degree in English literature tucked away in my mother's dresser drawer, I holed up in a little shack in the Sierra Nevada for nine months to teach myself how to write. You would think I might have picked up the fundamentals of writing while earning my English degree, but somehow I had avoided that. So I lived the life of a hermit, scribbling pages every day, stopping only to shove a piece of split oak into my wood stove.

By spring of that year, 1974, tired of the cold, sick of sitting inside all day, and ready again for human companionship, I decided it was time for another trip to Mexico. I drove to Mexicali, where I boarded a train to Tepic; from there I took a bus to the little beach town of San Blas.

There were a handful of gringo surfers in San Blas at that time, and early one morning I went with them to Matachín Bay, where I watched them ride surfboards smaller and more agile than any I'd seen before. On one hand, I longed to be out there with these new wave warriors, but on the other hand I wondered if my chance to become a true surfer had passed me by.

After leaving San Blas, I started buying second-class bus tickets that took me in random patterns up and down the heart of Mexico. I had no plan other than to see the country: Guadalajara, Mexico City, Acapulco, Oaxaca, and all the way to Mérida. Along the way, I saw a five-year-old boy, who was selling candy on the street, bribe a policeman with a penny's worth of gum. I saw, in a small farm town called Tomátlan, gaudily painted prostitutes patrolling the streets at dusk—if you looked closely, you could see they were actually young men in drag. I saw a pregnant Indian woman trudging along a remote highway with a baby at each breast. And once again, something about Mexico overwhelmed me—the colors of the landscape, the taste of fresh fruit bought on the street, the smell of diesel fumes and burning garbage, the vibrant energy of every dusty little town, and the optimism and generosity of the people. When I left this time, I knew Mexico would play a part in my future. I knew I would be back.

January 12

For several summers during and after college, I worked on a backcountry trail crew at Sequoia National Park. A friend who worked there with me, Tim Stubbs, was from a little beach town in north San Diego County called Encinitas. So on my way back from Mexico, I stopped there to see him.

Tim, who was studying botany at San Diego State, lived in a run-down triplex on Third Street, just around the corner from Moonlight Beach. He surfed every evening at dusk, riding one of the fat little fishes that were popular with surfers at that time. Tim and his neighbors, who were all surfers too, made horrible-tasting beer in his bathtub and had a communal garden in a vacant lot behind the triplex. With Tim's expertise as a master gardener, he and his friends produced more food than they could eat, at practically no cost.

North County in those days was about as close to paradise as anything I'd ever seen. The towns of Cardiff, Encinitas, and Leucadia were just rural villages strung along the Coast Highway. The only industries in North County were flower farms and ornamental nurseries. But the surfing along that stretch of coastline, between La Jolla and San Onofre, was undoubtedly the best in the continental United States. The weather was perfect twelve months out of the year, the rent was cheap, the coffee shops were even cheaper, and beautiful young women from all over California flocked there to enjoy the laid-back beach lifestyle.

So once I'd had a chance to check out Encinitas, I thought maybe I didn't need to get back to my summer job just yet. Tim allowed me to sleep on his couch for a few days, and I spent my time writing a feature story about Tim and his clan of communal surfers. I submitted the story to a new San Diego weekly called the *San Diego Reader*, then I forgot about it.

One evening, while we were working in the communal garden, a young woman drove up the alley in a red Volkswagen bug, parked in front of the garden, and got out with her three-year-old son. She was wearing bell-bottom pants and a Mexican peasant blouse. She knew everybody at the triplex except me and had stopped by to kill a little time before going to work. I thought she was the most beautiful woman I'd ever seen in my life: tall and thin, with long dark hair, amber eyes, and luminous skin. She had an engaging personality and a funny way of flirting that some guys found intimidating. Tim told me her name was Claudia, she was only nineteen years old, and she worked as a waitress at a local coffee shop that was popular with surfers. Her hyperactive little boy, who had shoulder-length hair, was named John; his father had been killed in a logging accident a couple of years after John had been born.

Claudia took no notice of me at all, which was a good thing, because if she had spoken to me at the time I would not have found the courage to reply to her.

On the day before I had to leave, I happened to walk by a newsstand on the Coast Highway. I saw that the latest edition of the *Reader* was out, so I picked up a copy and, to my astonishment, saw that the story on the cover was my own.

I quickly got on the phone with the *Reader*'s young editor, Paul Krueger. He offered to pay me $300 for the feature story and asked if I could write more like it. I explained that I had a summer job that I had to get back to, but I would return to Encinitas in the fall. "Good," Paul said. "Call us when you get back."

January 14

So in the fall of 1974, I moved to Encinitas, rented a room near Moonlight Beach where I could hear the waves cracking at night, and began writing feature stories full-time for the *San Diego Reader*. I could go anywhere I liked in San Diego and Imperial counties, poke my nose into all sorts of things that were none of my business, and then write any kind of story I wanted, as long as it was honest and fair. I ridiculed pompous Marine Corps generals with impunity and glorified drunks who lived on the beach and made their living selling blood. I interviewed broke-down drug-addicted surfers who had been cult heroes just a few years earlier. I climbed El Picacho del Diablo, the highest peak in Baja California, by myself, and got paid for it. I wandered remote Baja canyons where Indian artifacts lay untouched, just as the natives had left them. I once lost a couple of hundred dollars while researching a story on poker parlors and had my gambling losses reimbursed by the *Reader*. There were people my age in North County making a lot more money than I was, some had nice offices and impressive job titles, but nobody I knew was having more fun.

I got to know Claudia little by little, and every time I saw her she impressed me more—always funnier, livelier, more beautiful. A local newspaper columnist wrote a paragraph about how she had dumped a five-gallon bucket of blue cheese dressing over the head of an obnoxious supervisor at the restaurant where she worked. That got her fired, of course, but she became a North County working-class heroine. Then she got a better job as a cocktail waitress at La Costa Spa, which was a glittery hangout for mob bosses, movie stars, and professional athletes. Claudia had a young son to support, and at La Costa she made great tips She could be quick-witted and charming with the high rollers, and she looked fantastic in the pink miniskirt they made her wear.

As soon as I got settled in Encinitas, I bought a new surfboard—a standard 9'0"—and I began teaching myself how to surf all over again. Except, these were real waves now, not irrigation canals, and I had all the water time I wanted. I started out that fall at a little break north of Beacons, where I could practice by myself. I spent many a fall evening there, surfing until it was too dark to see. When winter came, and the powerful north swells began rolling down from the Gulf of Alaska, I bought a full-length wetsuit and moved two miles south to Swami's, one of the finest point breaks in North America. I got called a cowboy, a kook, and a dozen other worse things, but by the end of that winter I could hold my own in double-overhead surf, take off as deep as anybody, and make sure I got at least my fair share of waves.

January 17

Anybody who had the good fortune to live in Encinitas in those days will tell you there was a sweetness to the place that is hard to imagine today and will never be recaptured again. In the years since, I've made surf trips to Hawaii, Australia, Peru, and many other so-called surf havens. But I've never seen any place that filled me with as much joy as North County did in those days.

One of the great pleasures of living in Encinitas back in the seventies was going to La Paloma to watch surf movies. The theater, on the corner of D Street and the Coast Highway, is a gorgeous old Spanish-style building. Except for the mission at San Luis Rey, La Paloma is probably the most beautiful building in North County. And in those days it was the perfect place to watch surf movies. I saw several of the great classics there: *Five Summer Stories*, *Morning of the Earth*, and *Big Wednesday*.

The audience at La Paloma included some of the most knowledgeable young surfers in the U.S. They appreciated footage of great surfing, and they wouldn't tolerate Hollywood hype. They could be very vocal in hooting for their heroes, like Gerry Lopez and Reno Abellira, or pooh-poohing any footage that bordered on travelogue filler. Almost everybody smuggled a quart of beer inside, and the place often reeked of marijuana. But the best thing of all about La Paloma was the seating. Rather than the standard, folding theater seats, La Paloma had long, padded, purple, velvet-covered benches, where you could stretch out with your girlfriend and even lie down if you liked.

Many years later, while I was surfing on the East Cape, I happened to meet the man who had owned La Paloma back in those days. I told him what fond memories I had of the place, and I mentioned the great seating. He said to me, "You wouldn't believe how many young people come up to me and say, 'I heard you used to own La Paloma. I just wanted to tell you my parents told me that was where I was conceived.'"

January 18

I once walked out of Juanita's Taco Shop, on the Coast Highway in Leucadia, with a carne asada burrito in my hand, sat cross-legged on the highway, and finished the entire burrito before a single car came by. I wouldn't even try to cross that intersection today on foot for fear of getting hit. What happened to Encinitas, of course, is the same thing that happened to all of coastal Southern California. It was such a wonderful place to live that everybody in the world wanted to live there. And they kept coming and coming, until almost all the reasons for living there were ruined. Subdivisions were subdivided into more subdivisions, the houses became newer but uglier, all open space was put to its highest economic use, and the entire coastline from Scripps Pier to Camp Pendleton was turned into the same sort of nightmare that drove people out of Los Angeles and Orange counties in the seventies and eighties.

January 19

Throughout the seventies and eighties, I continued writing feature stories for the *San Diego Reader*. During that time, I happened to meet Mike Doyle through a common friend, and we quickly became surf buddies. He had already built his house in San José del Cabo by then, but he spent most of his time in Encinitas, where he could stay involved with the surf and ski industry and therefore make a living. During this period he developed the soft surfboard and the first single ski, which is considered by many to have been the prototype of the modern snowboard.

During surf season, Doyle would give me a wake-up call about five in the morning; then he would pick me up in his van and we would drive to Cardiff Reef or Swami's. Doyle rarely tried to coach me in a direct way, yet I learned a lot about surfing from being around him. He taught me the importance of getting in the water during those first couple of hours after sunrise. He taught me to pay attention to the tide and the wind. Sometimes he would point out the surfers in the water he thought had special talent and I should pay attention to. And he taught me not to be intimidated by the overly-aggressive surfers in the water. We talked a lot about surfboard design and function, and he kept me supplied with good boards too. Doyle had a hundred surf buddies in North County who were more experienced than I was, but he chose to surf with me every day because my enthusiasm reminded him of his early days, before surfing became a profession for him. While so many of his old surf buddies had grown cynical and bored, I was still stoked.

As I journalist, I interviewed interesting people every day, but I'd never met anybody who had seen so much of the world and could tell such stories as Doyle. Over time, he introduced me to many legends of surfing—Tom Morey, Dale Velzy, Mickey Muñoz, Nat Young, and Joey Cabell—all fascinating characters. Eventually, I suggested to Doyle that he and I write a book about his adventures, and he agreed. That was the beginning of our collaboration on *Morning Glass.*

January 20

In January of 1984, Doyle and I flew to Los Cabos to spend a week at his house on Gringo Hill and begin working on our book. Though I had already been to Mexico many times, and I had toured much of South America alone, I had never been to southern Baja. When I stepped off the plane, I said to Doyle, "This place is amazing—like Arizona with an ocean."

"Exactly!" he replied. A lot of people don't appreciate the desert, and he was pleased to see that I did.

There was no surf that time of year, so Doyle and I would go for a long swim every morning, climb the hill behind his house, or hop in his dune buggy and take a roaring tour of the East Cape. Every afternoon, we would sit on Doyle's terrace, turn on the tape recorder, and drink beer while he recounted his life's adventures. Anybody who has received a letter or email from Doyle knows that his spelling and punctuation are so atrocious that sometimes you can scarcely make out what he's trying to say. But even now, when I listen to those tapes we recorded on Gringo Hill so many years ago, I marvel at his natural storytelling ability.

January 23

Meanwhile, back in Encinitas, Claudia and I kept running into each other—at a friend's wedding, having an after-work drink at the Daily Double, or at the local mall. She had blossomed from the thin girl in the peasant blouse I had seen years earlier into a voluptuous young woman, and I thought she was more beautiful every time I saw her. By then she had gone back to school to become a computer programmer and had managed to buy a lovely little house just down the hill from Beacons. She was impressed that I worked for the *Reader* too, not understanding yet how poorly journalists are paid. Even if we were with our own dates, we would always latch on to each other and spend half an hour or so in intense conversation.

Claudia's son John had become an outstanding surfer by then and he competed in contests almost every weekend. Unlike some parents, Claudia encouraged her son to surf after school because she knew it kept him out of trouble. As she told me, "When John comes home from surfing, I know he's tired, clean, and hungry."

Claudia and I both knew there was something going on between us, but we weren't sure where it was headed. I had also bought a house a couple of blocks from Beacons, and the single life suited me fine. (Besides being a surfer's paradise in those days, North County was a bachelor's paradise as well.) Though I didn't realize it at the time, I understand now that I had avoided dating Claudia for so long because I was afraid she might be perfect for me. Eventually, though, I overcame my fears, asked Claudia out on our first real date, and she accepted.

Almost exactly one year later, we were driving back to Encinitas after getting married in Lake Tahoe, at Chapel of the Bells. It hadn't quite been a drive-through wedding, but the whole thing took no longer than it takes to order a Big

Mac and fries, and it cost about the same. Chapel of the Bells provided champagne in disposable plastic cups, which Claudia has kept all these years as if they were priceless family heirlooms. We still think it was the ideal way to get married—quick, cheap, and painless.

As we drove home through the Mojave Desert, Claudia and I were discussing our future life together, and I said, "You know, my only reservation about marrying you was that you had been single and independent for so long, I was worried you might not like taking orders from somebody else."

"Yeah, I know," she said. "I was thinking the same thing about you."

January 24

After starting married life so late, Claudia and I both had some adjusting to do. I sold my house on Hermes, and we lived in her house on Daphne St., which was a bit closer to the beach. Claudia's son John, who was sixteen years old by then, was a good kid—certainly less troublesome than I had been at his age. We got along well enough, he and I, and we even surfed together now and then. He had developed into a much better surfer than I would ever be, though he didn't make fun of me, so far as I know.

One of the decisions Claudia and I had to make was whether we wanted to stay in North County. Throughout the seventies and eighties, the place had grown much too rapidly, and it no longer felt the same to me. Years earlier I'd had a dream—actually a recurring nightmare—in which I saw the hillsides of north San Diego County, which had always been covered with flowers, converted into white condominiums that looked like skulls stacked one on top of another. And now that nightmare was coming true.

I had no intention of ever going back to the San Joaquin Valley, but I longed to be someplace where you didn't hear the sound of the freeway from your bedroom window at night and where we could afford to buy a piece of land large enough for a garden and fruit trees. With John ready to start college, I figured we might never get a better chance to move.

At first I was reluctant to mention these thoughts to Claudia, but when I finally confided to her what I was thinking, to my surprise she said, "I'm ready to move if you are."

January 26

All my life, I've struggled to balance my love of the mountains with my love of the ocean. I know many other surfers and skiers who have struggled with the same problem. That's why you see surfers here in Baja with Colorado license plates, and snowboarders from San Diego in Montana. With the exception of New Zealand, I don't suppose there's any place on earth where you can easily satisfy both desires. But central California comes close.

The house we built in Three Rivers, in the Sierra Nevada foothills, was on eight acres overlooking the Kaweah River, where we couldn't see another house. We planted our big garden and fruit trees, and every fall we would cut our own firewood. Every summer I would take our two young boys on long backpacking trips into the Sierra Nevada. They were too small to carry more than a sleeping bag, so I served as the beast of burden, carrying a pack that often weighed 70 pounds. In a week, we would cover fifty miles or more. During the winters, I would go on weeklong backcountry ski trips in the Sierra Nevada with my mountain buddies, telemarking 5,000 foot descents in untracked powder, and sometimes even getting paid for doing backcountry snow surveys for the State of California.

During those years, Claudia always said she missed the ocean as much as I did, yet neither of us wanted anything to do with Southern California again. For a while we thought about moving to San Luis Obispo. Years earlier I had owned a small cabin at Cambria, which is one of the most beautiful places on the entire West Coast. But the water on the central coast is cold, the wind blows hard every day, and good surf breaks there are scarce.

January 30

In the spring of 2005, one of our sons was about to graduate from high school, the other wasn't far behind, and Claudia and I started thinking maybe it was time for another move. Doyle was living full-time in Baja then, making his living as an artist, but he and I had stayed in touch over the years, always finding time to surf and snowboard together. He came to Three Rivers late that winter, and we talked about the possibility of Claudia and me moving to Baja. He invited me to come down and spend a few days with him, so, with Claudia's approval, I took him up on the offer.

That May, Doyle and I spent several days surfing together on the East Cape with waves in the 8- to 10-foot range. Every evening at dusk, blissfully exhausted, we would drive back to his house on Gringo Hill, along the old, rugged beach road. I was intrigued to see a scattering of new homes along the route—when Doyle had first taken me out to the East Cape in the eighties, almost nobody lived there. But now the surf refugees, most of them from California, were starting to build a few simple but creative Mexican-style homes. Rather than waiting for the paved roads and power lines to arrive, they had leaped out into the desert, relying entirely on solar panels for electricity and four-wheel-drive vehicles to get them back and forth to town. And the homes weren't bunched together in subdivisions like they would be in the U.S. Photovoltaics had given people the freedom to spread out and live like human beings, instead of like bacteria trapped under glass. Surfers had finally begun to mutate outside the Petri dish of

Southern California. It was a lifestyle that made sense to me, and I started thinking I would like to be part of it.

Then one evening, as Doyle and I drove home along the beach route, we came to a cluster of homes lit up dramatically by the glow of the sunset. We had passed that way every day, but now it was as if I were seeing it for the first time, and I thought it looked like some imaginary place in a children's fairy tale book. I asked Doyle, "What do they call this place?"

"This is Zacatitos."

"I think maybe I could live here."

That evening Doyle called a realtor he knew, and the next day the three of us drove out to Zacatitos to look at lots. The third lot we looked at was on a hill with excellent views of the ocean to the south and the mountains and desert to the west. It was a large, flat lot, next to a beautiful arroyo where tall *palo blancos* grew. Because it was higher than most of the surrounding terrain, it picked up the cool ocean breezes. I thought it was perfect, and less than ten minutes after laying eyes on the property, I told the realtor, "I'll take this one."

That evening, back at Doyle's house on Gringo Hill, I called Claudia and said, "I think I found the place where we belong."

After I described the lot in Zacatitos to her, Claudia said, "That sounds wonderful. Buy it. I can't wait to see it."

February:

Ofertas to the Dead

February 1

Late this afternoon, we heard the shrill cry of German opera warbling across our little village, vibrating over the desert and echoing back off the surrounding hills. I'm not an opera fan; therefore, I'm not fit to judge the quality of this particular rendition, but my impression was that it was absolutely wretched music, as it was intended to be, since it was being applied as a form of punishment.

A hundred yards or so below our house, our neighbor Jack was holding band practice for his rock group, which he calls The Lost Dogs. The band consists of gringo men in their fifties and sixties, retired or on extended vacation, several of them surfers, living out their teenage rock fantasies once a week in Jack's garage. Every now and then the band plays publicly at Zac's Bar and Grill or at some private party here in town. When we first moved to Zacatitos, we dreaded The Lost Dogs' practice day because they knew only three or four songs, and even those they played in the crudest fashion. We probably heard them struggle through "House of the Rising Sun" and "Louie Louie" a hundred times. It is not my place to criticize the band's musical skill, but I believe it would be fair to say that their guitar playing was awkward and their singing flat. But they had loud amplifiers, they played with great enthusiasm, and it was obvious The Lost Dogs were having a lot of fun.

Claudia and I tried hard to be tolerant. Our attitude about the band's loud music was that everybody alive, including us, is doing something that irritates somebody; we just don't always know what it is. As long as our neighbors can tolerate our annoyances and oddities, we should at least try to do the same for them. To survive an hour or so of The Lost Dogs each week, Claudia and I would go indoors, shut the windows, and turn on our own music. When that failed, I would put on an old pair of ear mufflers I used to wear while running my chainsaw. Claudia would put on her earphones and practice her Spanish lessons. Kirra, oddly enough, didn't seem to mind The Lost Dogs at all.

Not everyone in Zacatitos weathered band practice as well as we did. Frank and Carrie, who live much closer to Jack's garage, couldn't find any remedy for the band's clumsy guitar and tone-deaf singing, and their frustration often flared out of control. From my terrace, I could see the drama play out below. After an hour or so of band practice, Frank would go to the edge of his property and begin shouting, "You guys are terrible! You should never be allowed to touch a guitar! For chrissake, turn that horrible crap down!"

And Jack would shout back something like, "I guess we're gonna have to move to a SMALL town!"

More than once these shouting matches came close to fisticuffs.

Sometimes on our morning walk, we would see Frank and Carrie, and we would stop to offer our sympathy. "They've got five or six old farts in that band," Frank would say, "so why don't they hold band practice in somebody else's garage? Why does it always have to be right next door to us?"

We didn't want to be drawn into a neighborhood feud, but

we tended to side with Frank and Carrie, on the theory that silence is like a common well: if somebody pollutes the water, everybody in town gets poisoned. At the same time, we know most of the members of the band, we like them personally, and we could see the dispute from their point of view too. If a rock and roll band, of any skill level, can't crank up the volume a bit when they're out in the desert of Baja, where can they? And if a group of frustrated musicians can't act out their rock fantasies by the time they're 60, when, in god's name, will they ever get a chance?

If a dispute like this occurred in the U.S., the disgruntled neighbors would probably call the police. Most likely the police would talk to both parties and try to reach a compromise; if they couldn't, the police might issue a warning for disturbance of the peace. If that didn't settle the matter, one of the parties would break out his arsenal of weapons, open fire on his neighbors, somebody would end up shot, and the matter would be finished. But here in Baja, there are no police who would respond to a gringo's complaint of loud music, and nobody is allowed to own a gun. So here neighbors must find another way to settle their disputes.

Last year sometime, The Lost Dogs added a lead guitarist and singer, Josh, who is a surfer from Colorado. Josh didn't begin to surf until he was in his fifties, but he pursued the sport with a remarkable passion and energy. Many mornings on my way out to the East Cape, I would see Josh at La Fortuna, attacking the reef break there with a persistence and dedication that I found inspiring. Josh has now developed as a surfer beyond the level of beginner to what I would call intermediate, a very impressive accomplishment for somebody his age. And Josh is a much better musician than a surfer. In my judgment he's an excellent guitarist, and a good singer. After he joined The Lost Dogs, their playing improved considerably. Perhaps more important, though, somehow Josh, who is calm and thoughtful, convinced the band to turn down their amplifiers a notch or two.

Even Frank and Carrie agree that things have gotten better since Josh joined the band. After a few bars of each song now, we can at least identify the tune. And instead of cursing the flat vocalists, we're able to bend their efforts around in our imaginations enough to see what their intentions might be.

Today, though, after an hour or so of band practice, Frank's patience had frayed to the point that he couldn't take it anymore. But instead of shouting at the band again or threatening violence, Frank turned two large amplifiers of his own toward Jack's garage, put on a CD of German opera, and blasted The Lost Dogs with the shrillest warning this corner of the Baja peninsula has ever heard. And the effect was remarkable. Apparently, it's impossible to play rock music against the tempo of German opera, and eventually The Lost Dogs were forced to abandon band practice for the day.

After a few more minutes of opera, when Frank was certain he had achieved full compliance and inflicted a fair measure of punishment, he turned off his amplifiers too. Nobody got shot, nobody got knifed, and nobody went to jail.

February 3

The daytime temperatures have returned to the mid-80s, and we're back to wearing surf trunks again as soon as we get out of bed in the morning. The wind has been calm, the sea is glassy, every day is gorgeous, and tourist season is in full swing, which makes the Mexicans happy and fills them with the energy of purpose.

Tourism, which provides about a third of Mexico's gross domestic product, is a good match for this country, where the people are warm and gracious by nature and always eager for work. Also, tourism doesn't require any special talent other than a tolerance for strangers, though it helps if you know how to fish, pilot a boat, cook, or drive a taxi. Although the big investors will always control the large hotels, car rentals, and golf courses, almost anybody here can find some way to earn a share of the tourist dollars. The tourist industry in Baja has reminded the people of the value of their country's natural resources—the ocean, the deserts, the fish, and the wildlife—and they understand that if they don't protect these assets, tourists will not come.

Driving around San José today, we saw lots of sunburned, fleshy-looking tourists with hangovers and bad tattoos. Some looked as though they were ready to dive for the sidewalk at the first sound of gunshots. These are our countrymen, our *compadres*, so to speak, though sometimes we can hardly recognize them.

At the counter of a pharmacy, I saw a young, skinny *turista* who looked as if she hadn't slept in days. She had a mound of medications piled in front of her, and she was shouting at the clerk in English, "What about downers? Seconal? Percodan? Vicodin? You have anything like that?"

In the supermarket parking lot, a foul-tempered gringo was berating a Mexican man who refused to wash his car for ten pesos—about 75 cents. "I guess you aren't that hungry yet, are you?" he shouted.

A polite but bewildered young woman came up to me and said, "Excuse me. You look like somebody who might live around here. We're from Wisconsin. Can you tell me what there is to do?" Her faced was flushed like somebody approaching sunstroke, even though it was a fairly cool morning for Los Cabos, and she squinted hard against the light.

I couldn't think of anything that might compete with ice fishing or a farm-equipment show, so I said, "We mostly surf. You can take a lesson over at Costa Azul, if you'd like to give it a try. If you like fishing, you can drive out to La Playita and rent a *panga* for the day. Or, you could go snorkeling at Chileno Bay—you'd be amazed at the variety of fish."

She listened politely but skeptically, and I got the feeling she might have been happier if she'd saved her money for Super Bowl tickets this year.

February 7

No surf yet on the East Cape, and the forecasts show nothing on the horizon. I would gladly drive the 60 miles to Todos Santos if there were any surf on the Pacific side, but except for one big swell after Christmas, there hasn't been much on that side, either. Every few days I take out the SUP and cruise up and down the coast. It makes a good workout, but it sure as hell ain't surfing.

Sometimes I think I might buy a small aluminum boat so I can go fishing when the surf is flat like this. The fishing for tuna, wahoo, and dorado here is world famous. The problem with that idea, though, is that the open-water fishing is best after the water starts to warm up again, in May and June, and by then we have plenty of surf. I could always forget about the open-water fishing, though, and focus on the red snapper and rock bass that stay closer to shore.

February 9

Today Claudia and I completed our annual two-week treatment of fluorouracil, a topical ointment that destroys precancerous sun lesions. In the U.S. we used to have to go to our physician for a prescription, then pay for the little tube of medication at the pharmacy, and one treatment would end up costing us $500. In Mexico, where it's marketed as Efudex, we buy it over the counter at a fraction of the cost. For Claudia, who has olive skin, the ointment has little effect; but for me it can be quite dramatic. My entire face is broken out in raw, painful scabs that make it hard for me to laugh, or even smile. But it's better than getting skin cancer, and I know that in just three or four days all the dead skin will have peeled off, and I won't look any worse than I did before.

A few days ago I asked our friend and neighbor Dr. Lynn, a retired dermatologist who uses fluorouracil himself every winter, what would happen if everybody who loves outdoor sports used fluorouracil once a year. "Oh," he said, "their rate of skin cancer would be dramatically reduced."

I have tried to get my surf buddies to use fluorouracil. Some will, some won't. Surfers who spend hundreds of dollars every month on worthless nutritional supplements, with no proven benefit, won't use a product that has been proven to destroy pre-cancerous lesions. I hate to sound like some carnival barker hawking the latest miracle cure, but this stuff really does work.

February 12

A little 3-foot swell arrived last night. It didn't look like much at first light, but it was better than nothing, so we drove out to the East Cape, where I surfed alone for a couple of hours.

The odd thing about small surf is that in some ways it's more difficult to ride than head-high surf. Bigger waves provide more energy to work with, they're easier to catch, and the steeper drop makes it easier to get to your feet because the board is angled and falling away from you. Today, though, all I really wanted to do was paddle around enough to give my weak shoulders some work.

Later in the afternoon, back at home, we saw our first pair of hooded orioles this year. These beautiful black and yellow birds live in Baja year-around, but we don't see them near our house until late winter, when they build their nests in our coco palms by shredding long fibers from the fronds, then weaving the still-attached fibers into sturdy pouch-like nests. When the wind blows, the nests are thrashed violently back and forth, but deep in their pouches the baby birds are snug and secure. The swaying fronds must have a soothing effect on the young birds that they crave all their lives—maybe like being rocked to sleep in a rocking chair—because I've seen the adult birds land on palm fronds in a stiff wind and ride the fronds for no apparent reason other than the pure pleasure of it, very much like surfers.

February 14

I heard today that our surf buddy Howard Benedict has died from complications of dementia. Howard was a well-known surfer from Encinitas, where he had a dental practice for thirty years—a lot of surfers I know went to him for their dental work. Howard was also a world-renowned blue-water diver and spear fisherman, respected for his knowledge and experience in the ocean. He even made his own beautifully crafted spearguns out of wood. Without the aid of air tanks, Howard would descend to a depth where he knew he would find fish, then wait calmly for the wahoo, marlin, or sea bass to swim by. Somewhere I have a photo of him posing with a sea bass he speared that looks bigger than he is.

In 2002, when he was in his late fifties, Howard had a terrible accident while tow-in surfing off Todos Santos Island, on the coast of northern Baja. The waves that day were said to have been in the 50-foot range, but Howard wasn't afraid of huge surf because of his experience in deep water and his ability to hold his breath much longer than the average person. Howard took off too late on a gigantic wave that day and got absolutely crushed. They say he disappeared for several minutes. Guys on jet skis tried frantically to locate him in the whitewater, but the surf was so rough they couldn't. When they finally found Howard, he was unconscious, washed up in the channel. Nobody knew what happened to him during the time he disappeared, but a long period of oxygen deprivation was likely involved.

After that day, Howard began having blackout spells and other serious neurological problems, and the symptoms gradually worsened.

I surfed with Howard on the East Cape in 2005, after his accident. We talked for a long time during the lulls, and he seemed fine to me—calm, well-spoken, and good humored. He still surfed well too. And then last year, another surfer told me Howard had been diagnosed with advanced dementia. He was living in a full-care facility, and his prognosis was not good.

I suspect that one gigantic wave at Todos Santos Island is what killed our friend Howard. But it took him ten years to die.

February 17

There's still a little south swell here today, but rather than drive all the way to the East Cape to ride mushy surf, I took my son Jens's bodyboard and fins down to a little reef break close by.

Jens suffered a serious brachial plexus injury in his right arm when he was eight years old. The nerves were permanently damaged, and in spite of several surgeries, he never recovered full strength in that arm. But Jens, who in May will graduate from college, loves the ocean and always wanted to surf, even when he was a kid, and even after his injury. So we bought him a bodyboard, Doyle gave him a good set of swim fins, and every time I went surfing, Jens came along and rode his bodyboard, using the strong muscles in his legs to propel himself into the waves. Jens became a good bodyboarder too. He's perfectly comfortable being in the ocean, he swims as well with one arm as most people do with two, and he's not afraid of big surf. We surf together often at Punta

Espina when he's here on his Christmas and Easter breaks, and he's usually right there next to me in the lineup, dropping in on overhead waves.

I've always considered the bodyboard a work of genius— its brilliance being its simplicity and functionality. What looks like a crude slab of foam is in fact the perfect hydrodynamic solution for getting the world's clumsiest mammal into the ocean. Given a few eons of time, it might even change the course of human evolution by persuading us to abandon land altogether and follow the example of our freer and more intelligent cousins, the dolphins and whales. At the very least, the bodyboard has encouraged millions of human beings to trudge down to the water's edge and give surfing a try.

While it's true that riding a bodyboard is surfing simplified, it's every bit as fun as riding a surfboard. The buoyancy of the foam compensates for the blubber some humans lack. Lying in a prone but arched position on a bodyboard, our fragile spines, which were never designed to stand upright, are at ease again. And on a bodyboard, close to the surface of the wave, feeling the speed with our hands, and trailing our legs like the tailfins they were meant to be, it's almost as if we're an animal that belongs in the ocean, naked, weightless, and free.

Around 1990 Mike Doyle took me to Orange County to meet his old friend Tom Morey, the inventor of the Boogie Board, which is what Morey called his first foam bodyboard. For me it was like meeting a beatnik Leonardo da Vinci, barefoot and unshaven, tinkering around in his garage. Morey had quit his job as an aeronautics engineer in Washington State and was back working on several new prototype bodyboards, which he was eager to show us. He had a lot of restless energy that day, and every now and then he would step into his soundproof room and bang away on his drum set for a few minutes, as if that were the only way he could dislodge a thought stuck in his crowded brain. He was especially obsessed, on that day, with the idea of using the energy from sunlight to power interplanetary flight, and he tried to explain to us how it might be possible, though without success.

After riding just a few waves this morning, my thighs were so exhausted from kicking, I knew I was through. But I wasn't ready to go in, so I paddled outside the breakers, where I could bob around like a piece of shark bait and let the swells pass under me. Sometimes it's a great pleasure just to be in the ocean, with no plan, purpose, or ambition whatsoever.

February 19

I've gotten into the habit, on Sunday mornings when there's no surf, of taking the Rhino out to Flippy's Point and paddling around on my SUP. Usually, I'm the only person there.

The point is named after the renowned Flippy Hoffman, who had a house on the bluff here before he died of pulmonary fibrosis in 2010 at the age of 80. I knew Flippy a little, talked with him several times, but only in the last couple years of his life, when he could scarcely breathe. Mostly I knew Flippy by his reputation.

Flippy and his brother Walter were pioneers of surfing on Oahu's North Shore. Flippy surfed huge waves at Kaena Point long before tow-in surfing was invented. Later, he was among the first to surf mainland Mexico. His adventures while diving and sailing around the world are beyond legendary—almost mythological. Phil Edwards, who was considered the greatest surfer in the world throughout the late fifties and early sixties, used to say that Flippy Hoffman was his hero. But by the time I got to know Flippy, he had suffered at least seven bouts with the bends, or nitrogen narcosis, and he could barely walk.

One surfer who knew Flippy much better than I did told

me that the reason Flippy had gotten the bends so many times was that he thought his body was indestructible. He refused to believe the laws of physics applied to him. And even at the end, Flippy believed his body's failure was only temporary. To his old surf buddies, he would say, "You gotta—*gasp, gasp, gasp*—figure out a way to—*gasp, gasp, gasp*—get me back—*gasp, gasp, gasp*—into the water."

The first time I saw Flippy in person was just a few years ago at Punta Espina, which he told me later was one of his favorite places to surf. He had a long, white paddleboard with a rope attached around the rails so he could hold on. Dick, who lived on the point, and a few other surfers carried Flippy down to the shorebreak, placed him on that board, and shoved him out through the waves. Then Flippy was on his own. The surf was about 5 feet that day and pumping. Flippy paddled out a hundred yards or so, somehow managed to get that big board turned around, and caught a wave. He rode the shoulder on his belly until, eventually, he caught a rail and got tossed ten feet from his board. He floundered around a bit—one of the greatest watermen ever, struggling to keep his head above water—but he was eventually able to dog paddle back to his board, grab the rope handle, and pull himself on. I watched Flippy ride a dozen or more waves that way. Usually, he was able to get back to his board, but sometimes not. One of his friends was always close by, pretending not to watch, and if Flippy got in trouble they would quickly paddle over and give him a hand. I thought what Flippy was doing was one of the craziest things I'd ever seen. But to Flippy it was no big deal. He was just playing in the water, having fun, like a kid learning to swim in a wading pool.

I know Flippy was no saint. People who knew him better than I did say he could be stubborn and willful. But the person I got to know in his last few years was an inspiration to me, for his courage, his childlike enthusiasm, his passion for the ocean, and his joy for life.

Every now and then there are rideable waves at Flippy's Point, but it's a fickle place, and I've seen it break decently there only once or twice. It needs a special combination of swell direction and tide—or something. I've never figured the place out. But I'd heard that Flippy used to surf there, and one time at a potluck dinner at Fireman Tom's house, I asked Flippy what that point needed to break with good, rideable surf. Flippy smiled, apparently glad that I'd asked; he sucked in a big gulp of air and said, "I'll tell you what it needs—" And just then somebody yelled, "Food's ready!" Flippy lost his train of thought, and I never got to hear his answer.

Later that afternoon, as Claudia and I drove home from the potluck, a red Polaris ATV roared past us on the left, lurching up and down like a bronco and throwing clouds of dust. Flippy, who was riding on the passenger side, was holding on to the roll bar with one hand and dangling his emaciated body out as far as it would go, apparently just for the reckless hell of it. He laughed at the expression on my face; then he leaned back and waved goodbye. And that was the last time I ever saw him.

February 23

None of the surf forecasts show anything from the southern hemisphere headed our way yet. But this is still February. March is when the season usually starts.

I'm not proud to say this, but I often become poor company during long lulls like the one we've been in. I become quiet, withdrawn, less spontaneous and communicative. It's not that I become sad or depressed; it's that I feel sensory deprived, flat—bored, really. I realize this raises disturbing questions about the addictive nature of surfing. But I don't feel the need to apologize to anybody for my desire to feel alive. I chose this addiction and, like Flippy, I know I'll be cured of it soon enough.

February 29

While running errands in San José today, I saw two things that disturbed me and one that gave me hope.

First, while standing in line at the pharmacy, I saw an older American man in front of me who had what appeared to be a basal cell carcinoma on the side of his face. The cancer apparently hadn't been treated, and I wondered if I should ask the man if he was even aware he had it. But the thing was almost the size of a pinto bean, oddly shaped, and purplish brown, and I assumed he had to know it was there. So I said nothing.

Skin cancers here in southern Baja are very common. We all know people who have been afflicted with them. Most of the gringos who move here learn to take the sensible precautions, eventually. But it's an odd thing. Some people have a hard time giving up their sun-worshipping habits, even though they can see the damage it's causing. It's almost as if sunbathing is a kind of compulsion for them.

Tourists are different. They don't know any better, never having lived in a tropical place. They come here to lie in the sun, and most are sunburned after the first two days. They wear their ultraviolet damage proudly, almost like new clothes or tattoos, and can't wait to show off their radiant glow to their pallid friend's back home.

We all have the skin we were born with, and there's not much we can do about it. If people of northern European descent keep migrating toward the equator—and they seem determined to do just that—then the best thing they can do is somehow try to pass on darker genes to their children. Because I can tell you, they aren't going to survive in the tropics. In the long run, light-skinned people might be an anomaly, just nature's capricious experiment, fun and amusing—like a teenage girl dying her hair platinum blonde—but doomed to extinction.

The second disturbing thing I saw in town today was at the grocery store. I was in the soap isle looking for a glycerin-based soap that might help my dry skin during surf season. In addition to the many American brands of soap, there were dozens of Mexican brands as well—many of them traditional folk concoctions. Some were crudely shaped and reminded me of the lye soap my grandmother used to make in a tub using animal fat and ash. But one brand caught my eye because it was advertised to be a *piel blanqueadura*, or skin whitener. It was the cheapest bar of soap on the shelf, which I assumed meant it was targeted for the poorest Mexicans, who are usually Indians. At first I laughed, because the idea of a product for lightening the color of a person's skin was so clearly fraudulent that it struck me as funny. Then it occurred to me that this soap wouldn't be on the shelf if there weren't customers who bought it. And the idea of some Indian woman buying a product to make her beautiful bronze skin one shade whiter made me feel sick.

Later on, though, driving back to Zacatitos, I saw something that renewed my faith in Mexico and filled me with glee. A blocklayer was trying to transport a big wheelbarrow to his job site, but the wheelbarrow was too big to fit inside his battered little hatchback. So the man turned the wheelbarrow around, opened the back of the hatchback, and lashed the wheelbarrow handles to the backseat. Then he drove off with the wheelbarrow following behind him like a trailer.

Viva Mexico!

José Delivering Water

March:

False Apparitions

March 1

On our morning walk today we found the surf to be about as flat at it ever gets—like a lake, with perfectly shaped six-inch waves lapping the shore. The surf was so quiet you could hear the swishing sand.

We've been doing this hourlong morning walk now, with minor variations, almost every day for five years. We run into different neighbors, and we stop and chat with them, the way life in a small village is meant to be. For Kirra, the morning walk provides a social life too. She has never been good at making friends with other dogs, so like anxious parents, we encourage her to try. Kirra has two white eyes, which they say is intimidating to sheep but probably looks odd to other dogs. Lately, though, I've begun to wonder about another possible cause for Kirra's social problems. When dogs we don't know approach us on the beach, they usually raise their tails high in the air and wag them as a signal of their friendly intentions. Kirra does the same thing, except she doesn't have a tail. She shakes her fanny like a mambo dancer, but without that tail in the air, her message isn't getting across. So other dogs instinctively treat her with suspicion.

Docking Aussie's tails is traditional and usually done at

birth, or shortly thereafter. They say it has a purpose, that horses and mules will grab a threatening dog's tail in their mouth and shake the dog vigorously until its dead. I've seen photos of mules doing just that. But then again, Aussies are a sub-breed of the border collie, whose tails aren't normally docked. And even if docking a dog's tail did serve a reasonable purpose, wouldn't the ability for a dog to make friends with other dogs be more important?

I know it's probably impossible, if not crazy, but if I could I would make Kirra a prosthetic tail so she could make friends more easily.

Claudia uses our morning walks for collecting shells, which sounds like a harmless habit if you visit the beach only once in a while, but it gets to be a real problem when you go there every day, even if you put only one or two shells in your pocket at a time. I've seen her pick up a shell, recognize it as one she rejected on a previous day, and throw it away. At home we have buckets, baskets, and bowls filled with shells, and still she brings home more. I've tried to get Claudia to practice the "catch and release" method of shell collecting, which works well for fishermen who would rather catch a fish than eat one, but Claudia won't accept this suggestion.

Today Claudia said, "It seems like there used to be a lot more shells on the beach. Where'd they all go?"

"I think you've already got them all," I replied.

When our boys were little and we took them to the beach, we would let them collect all the shells they wanted. Before we left, I would put the boys in the car, fasten their seat belts, then very quietly go behind the car, where they couldn't see me, and pour out their bucket of shells. By the time we got home, they had forgotten all about them. Claudia doesn't know it yet, but every now and then I take a handful of shells from her buckets at home, slip them into my pockets, and release them when I get to the beach. Somebody has to be the parent.

March 4

Sometimes while we're driving around the East Cape, we see Mexican sheepdogs guarding their flocks of goats. The dogs take their work seriously, never leaving the herd or taking their eyes off the goats for even a second. When Kirra sees these dogs at work, she watches longingly from the truck window, and she whimpers for us to let her out so she can pursue what she knows should be her purpose in life.

A new group of burros arrived in the neighborhood. I don't know where they came from, but I know I've never seen them before. They're much darker than the cream-colored band we usually see; in fact, they're almost black. Always the opportunists, the burros soon discovered that the little yellow grass inside our fenced yard hadn't been grazed yet, and they come around every day to see if I've left the front gate open.

Kirra knows the burros can be treacherous. Once, a baby burro, which looked like a furry little rocking horse you would buy for your child, acted as if it wanted to make friends with Kirra, prancing toward her playfully and lowering its head to sniff her. Kirra fell for this ploy by wagging her fanny and allowing the baby burro to come near. As soon as Kirra was within reach, the little burro turned around and tried to kick her in the head. Luckily, the blow glanced off Kirra's shoulder, but she got the message. She stalked away without glancing back and has never trusted burros again.

Today three of these black burros discovered that I'd finally left the front gate open just a crack, and they quietly filed into the yard. Kirra lay on her belly and watched them calmly from inside the garage until every one of them had been lured into her trap. She waited patiently, carefully studying them, and relishing her good fortune. I was upstairs and unaware that the burros had gotten into the yard until I heard them stripping low-hanging fronds off the coco palms. When I came downstairs to see what was going on, Kirra was sniffing the burros' fascinating odors, but she still hadn't made her move.

As soon as I said, "Kirra, get the burros!" she roared after them. But instead of herding them directly out the gate, she boxed them together into a corner of the fence, where she could yap and cuss at them until she had them worked into a frenzy. I moved to one side of the fence to block the burros' rear escape, while Kirra began pushing the whole group toward the front gate. I followed behind Kirra and off to one side, acting as a silent though inept member of her pack. Once the burros began moving in the right direction, they were done for. They kicked and brayed in protest, but they knew the game was over. Soon Kirra had them all marching obediently out the gate.

A rancher friend of mine who owned several Aussies back in California once told me, "No wonder cowboys can't find work anymore. One good Australian shepherd can do more than ten cowboys, and you don't have to listen to the dog recite poetry!"

March 12

The Christmas miracle of the Virgin Mary that had appeared on our block wall turned out to be a false apparition. After soberer inspection, it became clear that the watermark was caused by a leaking PVC drainage pipe. I proved this by taking a hammer to the block wall and smashing the apparition to pieces.

I'm no better than a half-assed plumber myself. I know nothing about block work and even less about stucco repair. So I hired Moisés to help me repair the damage. Like most Mexicans, Moisés is an expert in all cement work, which they must teach in elementary school here. I figured I could pay him to do the labor and, if he didn't mind having me watch, I might learn how to do some basic block repair myself. Plus, I could practice my Spanish.

My theory about learning Spanish is that you can study grammar and verb conjugations all you want, but eventually you have to be willing to make a complete fool out of yourself and begin speaking to any Mexican who is willing to listen. It's amazing how many gringos here won't do that, and after twenty years they can't utter a complete sentence in Spanish.

So today, while I was watching Moisés work, I was babbling on about fish luggage, when he stopped, struggled to conceal a smile, and said, "That is not correct Spanish. I think you mean to say 'fishing equipment.'"

Okay, no harm done, and now I will never mistake *equipaje* with *equipo* again.

After Moisés had finished excavating my crude demolition work, he carefully opened the wall more with a hammer and chisel. He found exactly where the water leak was coming from, and he assured me that it would be a simple matter to repair it. The only problem was that the working space was so small, it was impossible to get even a hacksaw blade in there to cut the broken PVC pipe.

"Do you have any old wire?" Moisés asked.

I went to the garage and came back with a piece of electrical wire. "No," Moisés said. "This is what we call *cable*. I need a piece of old rusted *alambre*."

I thought for a moment but had to tell him, no, I didn't have any old rusted wire. So Moisés excused himself and walked up the road a ways. In a couple of minutes he came back with a piece of the rusted construction wire that can be found lying all over Mexico. He fed one end behind the pipe, then pulled both ends of the wire back and forth until it had sawed through the PVC. It didn't take thirty seconds.

I had to laugh at seeing such a simple and effective solution, and Moisés smiled modestly too.

Once, when our house in Zacatitos was being built, my architect Francisco and I were standing on the rooftop, watching the workers below as they laid a sewer line to the septic tank. We could see they lacked a coupling needed to connect the two final pieces of PVC, so I said to Francisco, "Well, I can run into town and buy a coupling. It'll only take thirty minutes."

"No, that isn't necessary," he said with a grin. "Just watch."

The workers twisted a piece of newspaper around the end of one pipe and lit the newspaper with a cigarette lighter. After the newspaper had burned for a few seconds, the end of the PVC pipe was soft enough that the workers could force the end of the other pipe into it. By the time it had cooled, the connection was more snug than it would have been with a proper coupling. Francisco smiled proudly and said, "I love my country!"

After Moisés had finished sawing the pipe, he said to me, "The *norteamericanos* in Zacatitos are always telling me how surprised they are to see how Mexicans are able to fix anything that breaks." He glanced at me shyly to see if I agreed.

"Absolutely," I nodded.

"It's not like that in the United States?"

"Maybe a long time ago," I said. "Not anymore. Now when something breaks, most *norteamericanos* throw it away and buy a new one."

The idea caused Moisés discomfort. "In Mexico we don't have that option. Maybe that's why we learn how to fix everything."

I thought for a moment to see if I could come up with a term for that Mexican mechanical ingenuity that I admire so much. But I wanted to say it in Spanish. So I said, "The Mexican people have what I call *la inteligencia de necesidad.*"

Moisés stopped what he was doing, gave me a pat on the

back, and said, "Your Spanish is getting better already."

March 13

The surf forecasts have been calling for a south swell to arrive today, so I slapped myself out of my winter sloth and made the predawn drive to the East Cape to have a look. There were surfers from all over the East Cape out looking too, as well as guys I knew from San José, and even as far as Pescadero and Todos Santos. In addition, I saw rental cars with surfboards stacked on top and filled with surfers from California who had flown down for this first spring swell. I even saw an old yellow school bus with young surfers who had driven all the way from British Columbia.

I stopped on the bluff overlooking Shipwreck, where I saw by first light that the swell hadn't arrived yet. These modern surf forecasts are amazingly accurate in every respect except the precise arrival time. I watched and waited for fifteen minutes, just in case I was seeing a long lull between sets. I was about to head home when I saw something that surprised me: two tiny dolphins, one following the other, leaping out of the water playfully as they made their way east across the cove. At first I wondered if they might be *vaquitas*, whose normal range is far to the north in the Gulf of California, but later I realized I was wrong. At any rate, the endangered *vaquita* is a porpoise, not a dolphin. What I had seen were most likely short-beaked common dolphins.

On my way back to Zacatitos, I came across something else that surprised me—a wild horse caught in a barbed-wire fence. As near as I could tell, the small horse had tried to step through the loose strands of wire and tripped; as it fell, one leg had gotten caught between the strands, and as the horse somersaulted forward, the strands twisted tightly around the fetlock, making it impossible for the horse to escape. The horse was lying head down on a steep embankment, and by the time I got there it had struggled so long it was exhausted. I know I couldn't have been the first person to come along and find the horse in this desperate situation, but apparently I was the first to stop.

There are wild horses running all over the Baja peninsula. Supposedly, they belong to somebody, but I rarely see a brand on them. Usually, the horses look healthy, considering they forage in this harsh desert, but with the extended drought we're in, many of them are starting to look desperately malnourished.

I had a pair of wire cutters in my tool kit. (In a land of barbed-wire fences and locked gates, wire cutters are better than a master key. In case wire cutters can't get the job done, I carry bolt cutters as well.) I climbed up the bank and carefully approached the horse. It didn't struggle, just looked up at me with passive brown eyes. I don't believe that look was trust, but rather an acceptance that I was going to do whatever I wanted and there was nothing it could do to stop me. I reached down slowly, so as not to startle the horse, and with one snip it was free. The horse immediately slid a foot or two down the steep slope, but it was so thoroughly exhausted, it still couldn't right itself. I climbed a little higher up the embankment, grabbed both of the horse's rear fetlocks, and with the aid of gravity, spun it around 180 degrees. Then, with a roll of the head and a toss of the shoulders, the horse came to its feet. It had bleeding lacerations on its lower leg, but as it walked away, I saw with relief that it wasn't limping badly.

March 14

The first south swell of the season arrived today—just one day late. And what a beautiful thing it was to see. There were powerful, head-high waves stacking up at Punta Espina, sometimes five or six to a set. With an outgoing tide, a building swell, and not a wisp of wind, conditions were almost perfect.

I was the first surfer on it, right after sunrise. Nathan, a surfer from San José, watched me skeptically from his truck for thirty minutes or so, then paddled out to join me. I was on my new 90" Kies, which I hadn't touched in four months, and I was feeling a bit tentative. On the first wave, I laid too hard into a bottom turn and caught the rail, then corrected too hard and squirreled my way down the line just ahead of the breaking wave. As I started paddling back out, I heard a wheezing sound coming from my lungs and felt a sharp cramp between my shoulder blades.

During the lulls between sets, Nathan and I complained to each other about what poor shape we were in. "My arms feel heavy, my shoulders ache, and I feel like puking," I said.

"I know," Nathan said. "I feel the same way. At the end of last season I was feeling great. Now I have to start all over again."

I thought I was staying in decent shape all these months, but the truth is, it's easy to lie to yourself. That long winter idle always takes its toll, and laziness becomes a habit. The amount of physical and mental energy necessary to surf at even a marginal level is enormous, and it can't be faked. After you get pummeled a few times, you know you aren't fooling anyone.

But surfing is its own training program. Paddling for a couple of minutes after riding a wave, then waiting a few minutes for the next wave and repeating the process over again, is just about the perfect form of interval training. After ten days or so—if I can survive that long—I should be okay.

Though I was feeling tired and wobbly, I stayed out in the water for three hours, and even then the conditions were so good I would have stayed longer if I could have paddled another stroke.

Back on the beach, I went through the ritual a tropical

surfer should perform to avoid the ailments and irritations that come with surfing in warm water: drink as much fresh water as soon as possible to ward off dehydration; remove wet trunks immediately; dry all body parts and apply Desitin to the crotch and armpits to avoid rash; irrigate the ears with a vinegar-and-alcohol solution to prevent swimmer's ear; and smear any open cuts with antibiotic ointment to guard against staph infection. Warm water produces more bacteria than cold water, and to all those little microscopic beasties, human flesh is a luscious treat.

March 15

I was out early again this morning. The swell was still pumping, though we could see some loss of energy. Yesterday the waves were thick and moving fast, and if you got hit by one while paddling out, it wrenched the board out of your hands and knocked you end over end. Today the waves were thinner and more playful.

Some of the younger surfers today were teasing me for wearing a hat in the water. "In California a surfer with a hat might be considered a kook," I lectured them, "but in Baja any surfer without a hat on his head is a damned fool." Everybody learns this for himself sooner or later—hopefully, before they get skin cancer. Same thing with wearing a shirt. Even with a rash guard that is supposed to block UV rays, I've gotten sunburned on the chest and back before 10:00 a.m. "This tropical sun is no joke in any season," I warned my naive young friends, "and this ain't winter anymore!"

Wearing sunglasses in the water is a different thing—more a matter of personal preference—but I often choose to wear them too. Surfing in the morning here means you're staring directly into the sun much of the time, and that's hard on the eyes. A couple of years ago our surf buddy Tom McKray had to have cataracts removed from both eyes. His doctor told him, "We can't know for sure why you got cataracts, but too much UV light could be a contributing factor. You should probably think about quitting surfing."

Tom (we sometimes call him Ten O'clock Tom for his habit of showing up around mid morning) is a stylish long-boarder who was on the Hobie surf team in the sixties and hasn't stopped surfing since. He said, "Doc, I'd rather go blind than quit surfing."

"Well, then, at least start wearing sunglasses," the doctor advised.

So Tom started wearing Sea Specs, which are sunglasses made for water sports, and one day last year Tom let me try them out. I liked the sunglasses so much I bought a pair for myself, and I've been wearing them ever since. I apply Rain-X to the lenses so the water will bead off them, but they still pick up sunscreen and salt crust, and sometimes they fog up. So when it's time to catch a wave, I slip the sunglasses down around my neck so my vision is clear when I need it to be. The result is that even after three hours in the water, my eyes don't hurt, they don't sting later at night, and the next morning, when I'm ready to surf again, my eyes don't feel dry and burnt.

A surfer my age needs an edge, even if it's just psycho-logical. I might be the most heavily accessorized surfer on the East Cape, and I get teased for it by younger guys all the time. But I don't care. I'm slathered in sunscreen, zinc oxide, Desitin, and Rain-X, and their teasing rolls off me like water.

March 17

That first real swell has all but disappeared now. I drove out to Punta Espina anyway, hoping the surf might look better once I got out that way. It didn't, but that's okay. My aching body can use a couple days' rest.

Just as I was getting ready to leave the beach, one of the

blue and white Mexican fishing *pangas* appeared on the horizon, coming back with the morning's catch. The families of the fishermen emerged from their beach *palapas* and hurried to the shore to see what the men were bringing in.

The *panga* paused outside the surf line and waited for the last wave of the set. Then the pilot gunned his big Honda motor, the other fishermen in the boat grabbed their hats and tucked down low, and they raced directly toward the beach at full speed. With perfect timing, they rode the broken wave high onto the beach, and the boat's momentum carried it a few feet higher.

The women and children ran to the *panga*, and I knew by their squealing, and the fishermen's laughter, that the men had brought back something special. So I wandered closer to have a better look.

By the time I got there, they had already rolled out of the boat a seven-foot bull shark. The ugly beast was bleeding from its mouth, and I assumed it was dead, so I reached down to lift its snout and inspect its teeth. As soon as I touched it, the shark rolled up one eye and stared at me scornfully, as if to say, "I should have eaten you while I had the chance."

After almost fifty years of surfing, I've never seen a shark in the water, though I've seen them from boats many times. Mike Doyle told me that back in the days when he was windsurfing, he used to break his fins on hammerheads all the time. Yet Doyle has never seen a shark while surfing here either.

The fact is, sharks of all kinds have been overfished in Mexican waters. The Chinese pay well for just the fins, which they serve at weddings and other celebrations as shark-fin soup. The practice of taking the sharks for their fins is illegal, but apparently the *panga* fishermen, who struggle to feed their families, have a hard time resisting easy money like that.

I asked the *panga* owner, an older, animated, gap-toothed fellow wearing a cowboy hat, if he sees a lot of sharks in these waters.

"Many, many sharks," he nodded. Then he wagged one arthritic finger at me and said, "And not far out either. There are sharks right here, where you are every day. Maybe you don't see them, but I do!"

I must have squirmed, because the other fishermen laughed, and some of the women and children giggled too.

March 19

The forecast was calling for a new swell to arrive yesterday, but it never showed. Thinking it might be late, I listened for it all last night, but again, nothing. Most likely there is a south swell out there somewhere, but its angle is too far from the west to reach us here.

I'm disappointed, but all I can do is what surfers always do—wait.

March 21

I drove to La Fortuna this morning, hoping, almost superstitiously, that making the effort of an old-fashioned surf check might somehow cause surf to appear. Of course I was disappointed. On the drive home, I passed by one of the little ranches tucked back in the mesquite. I could barely see the place from the road, but I could smell the wonderful aroma of food cooking. One of the places has a pack of dogs that likes to chase passing cars. For some reason they prefer to chase gringo rather than Mexican cars, though how they know the difference, I don't know—perhaps the sound of the muffler. At any rate, they always go mad over the Rhino— perhaps because it has no doors or windshield and they can make eye contact with the driver. The dogs aren't vicious, really, they just enjoy having something to chase. It's great sport for them. But chasing cars is a dangerous habit for dogs, especially in Mexico, where I've seen drivers swerve to hit them. Once I saw a dog here bite the tire of a slow moving car and get flipped in a complete circle before it could let go. So I've been thinking of ways I could teach these dogs not to chase the Rhino without actually hurting them.

The pack of dogs was led by one young, yellow male who enjoyed the chase more than the others. Some of the dogs made only a half-hearted attempt to catch up with me, then dropped back to sit in the dirt and scratch their fleas while they watched the spectacle play out. But this yellow male wouldn't give up. He chased me for a hundred yards or more, until he was even with me, prancing almost sideways at full speed so he could look directly in my eyes while he barked. So I slowed down just a bit, leaned out of the Rhino, lowered my head until I was almost even with him, and I said, "Ar! Ar! Ar! Ar! Ar!"

The dog immediately stopped, sat down with a look of shock and confusion on his face, then slowly turned to rejoin his pack.

March 25

No surf at all last week—extremely frustrating. Then late yesterday afternoon a new swell began to appear. At dusk the swell was showing size, but it was coming slightly from the southeast, a very unusual angle that favors surf spots farther out on the East Cape. All night long I could hear the swell increasing in power, so this morning we got up early and drove all the way to Punta Perfecta, several miles east of Zacatitos.

A true point break, Punta Perfecta is remote and difficult to access. You either have to trespass, leave your vehicle where it's vulnerable to break-ins, or walk a long ways on the beach. Perfecta holds a big swell well, though, and it breaks in long, straight lines. I've seen Punta Perfecta breaking at 12-foot, from the point to almost as far as I could see. But the place is finicky about swell direction, and if it isn't just right, it does what we saw it do today, which is to break in several disconnected sections. Disappointed, Claudia and I retreated to Nine Palms.

Nine Palms is a remarkable break, and it would be one of my favorites if it weren't for the fact that it can be seen from the East Cape road, and surfers flying down from California find it easily. The beach was populated with rental cars by the time we arrived, and there were probably twenty surfers in the water. The surface was still glassy, but I was afraid the wind was going to blow early.

The set waves were 8 to 10 feet high at the outside break, 300 yards from shore, and as I paddled out I could see they were thick and powerful. Sometimes an 8-foot wave is so thin you can see clear through it, and when it hits you, it feels like being sprayed with a water hose. But these waves, at the front of this new swell, were heavy grinders, pushing a lot of water. And I knew that getting hit by one of them would feel like getting hit by a truck. So I played it cautiously, sitting outside, and watching a perfectly good set roll under me while I caught my breath.

Most of the surfers in the water were sitting inside of the main peak. They were all good surfers and much younger than me. I don't mean to be dismissive, but nearly all of them were grossly undergunned for a wave like that. Little 6-foot boards are good for a fast, hollow wave like Shipwreck; they're agile and can be easily pushed under breaking surf. But they're nearly useless in heavy surf. It wasn't my problem, and I wouldn't have cared, except that the shortboarders were congregating like flotsam just inside the takeoff zone. They couldn't paddle into the waves before they broke, so they were trying to catch them in the whitewater and accelerate into the open wave. Somebody like me, who was taking

off farther outside, had to weave through them at top speed.
I consider that one of the most dangerous situations in surfing. The person already riding the wave isn't likely to get
hurt, but the shortboarder sitting inside could get killed.

The only other surfer sitting on the far outside was Ryan,
another South Dakota surf refugee, who lives in San José.
Ryan knows Nine Palms well and surfs it better than anybody
I know. So I watched how he went about his business: where
he lined up, which waves he let pass by, and which waves he
took. Before I even tried for a wave, I had watched him ride
three clean, very fast, 10-foot waves with the style and ease
of a master, which he is. After he'd paddled back out from
his last wave, I said to Ryan, "I'm not used to so many guys
sitting on the inside like that. It makes me nervous. I'm afraid
I'm going to hit somebody."

Ryan, who looks as if he could play a pirate in the movies,
scowled and said, "Ah, they'll get outta your way. Most of
'em!"

Finally, I lined up a sizable peak—probably 10-foot. As I
came to my feet, the crowd miraculously parted, and I rode
that screamer nearly to the beach. It was easily the best wave
I'd had since last October, and with my heart still pounding,
I paddled back out for another.

Ryan was still sitting outside, studying the horizon with a
skeptical expression. "Here it comes," he said.

I thought he meant the next set, but then I looked and saw
the dark purple line. That east wind was already stirring up
the surface farther out, and it was moving in quickly.

"I think it's gonna blow like hell today," Ryan said. "So,
unfortunately, I think I'm finished here." He took the very
next wave, rode it to the beach, and all of a sudden I was sitting way out there by myself.

I wasn't ready to quit so soon, wind or no wind—not on
the first big swell of the season—and I caught one more thick
lunker. Within ten minutes, though, whitecaps were showing

all around me, and the faces of the waves were gnarled and ugly. Now the shortboarders had no chance at all—in fact, most of them had already given up and gone in. I struggled into one more big wave, but just as I was coming to my feet, my board hit a lurching bump, and I was launched four feet into the air. I dropped to my belly, held on, and rode the whitewater the rest of the way to the beach.

Sometimes it can be so frustrating to come so close to having a great day, then having it snatched away like that.

March 26

Today was everything yesterday should have been. I went to Punta Espina early, where the biggest sets were a solid 8 feet but much cleaner than the day before. Jeff King and I had it to ourselves for an hour or so. Jeff has lost nearly twenty pounds since I saw him last. He's down to maybe 210 now and looking more fit than I've seen him in some time. We sat together between sets and reminisced about surfing in north San Diego County back in the seventies and eighties.

Jeff told me he'd been watching me paddle, he thought I was rolling too much from side to side, and he showed me how that was breaking my plane and costing me paddling efficiency. Some surfers, especially older guys, don't like to be coached in the water. They view it as a way to undermine another surfer's confidence, in a sport where self-reliance and independent judgment mean everything. Sometimes I feel that way too. But Jeff is one of the strongest paddlers I've ever seen, he understands the mechanics of surfing, and he teaches them well. So I took what he said to heart, and paddling more smoothly is something I'll be working on this spring.

A little later Fireman Tom paddled out on his SUP. He said he was feeling stiff and out of shape, but Tom has more patience than I have. He waited outside, then snatched a clean 10-footer and rode it 400 yards to the beach—probably the best ride anybody got all day.

Around nine o'clock, the late sleepers started showing up, and after a while the point began to get crowded. Spring break has arrived, and we're starting to see lots of vacationers. Because this community is private and has a locked entrance, we don't usually get invaded by many California surfers. But the gringos who live here invite their friends to come and surf with them, and sometimes that causes resentment. I've seen good friends nearly come to blows here over the slightest violation of surf etiquette.

The funny thing is, anybody who wants to surf alone in Baja can find plenty of places to do that. But not many surfers truly want to surf alone. Having friends, or even friendly strangers, to share the experience with somehow makes it more gratifying. And it can be fun, too, watching newcomers experience this place for the first time.

When I first showed up at Punta Espina, I was considered the outsider, and sometimes I felt ostracized by the same people who are complaining now about somebody else. My role model in those days was Fireman Tom, because he always tried to make everybody feel welcome. There have been many times when somebody said or did something in the water that infuriated me, but I kept my mouth shut because I knew that's what Tom would do.

March 27

We have a dying swell today, much weaker than yesterday, with long lulls sometimes lasting twenty minutes or more. The high point of my day was finding that Mike and Annie Doyle are back after spending their winter snowboarding in Aspen—I hadn't seen them in weeks—and we surfed together for a couple of hours.

Annie is always fun to surf with because she's so enthusiastic. And she's aggressive. She takes off as deep as any of the guys, and she has the athletic ability to handle almost anything. To see that in such a tiny frame is surprising—shocking, really—but she gets away with it because her strength-to-weight ratio is extremely high. Annie is built like a barracuda—one lean strap of muscle.

Doyle went in twice to switch surfboards, then came back out a third time on his SUP. He never did look comfortable, and he finally resigned himself to sitting on the beach. After a couple of hours, I went in to join him.

When I first started surfing with Doyle back in the eighties, competitive surfing had already evolved into the shortboard era, which favored surfers who were shorter and lighter. Most of the fluidity and grace of longboarding had been replaced by an aggressive, dysfunctional, hacking style that was hard for some of us to watch. More than once, in smaller surf, I saw younger guys who had never heard of Mike Doyle mock the clean and expressive style that had made him the best surfer of his generation. But at Swami's, on a double-overhead day, when power and experience mattered, Doyle, even in his forties and fifties, was almost always the best surfer in the water.

Now Doyle has reached the point where age becomes a factor. He doesn't like to talk about the many injuries he has accumulated. I believe this is because in his youth he competed against the best surfers in the world, and he knew it wasn't wise to advertise his weaknesses. Even today Doyle rarely talks about the effects of growing old, but he doesn't pretend he's a kid anymore either. He seems to have made his peace with age. He's still often the strongest paddler in the water. With those broad shoulders, freakishly long arms, and big hands, god obviously meant this boy of Polish-Irish ancestry to become a surfer. Sometimes I notice he has a little difficulty coming to his feet after catching a wave—not unusual for older surfers—but once he's in control of his board, he surfs with the same power and grace he always had.

Much of the pride Doyle once had in his own ability he has transferred to his wife Annie now. He watches and coaches her every minute they're surfing together. "I never had a wife or girlfriend who went out in the water with me every day, did the same things I like to do, and was just as eager to get up tomorrow and do it all again," he said. "Until I met Annie."

After a while Annie came in, and I figured she was through for the day. But Doyle said, "No, she's not finished yet. Just watch. She's got to rummage around for food." Because Annie has no body fat but burns an enormous number of calories, she's like a little hamster that has to eat its weight in food every day.

And sure enough, Annie went straight to Jeff King's truck and rifled through the glove box. "Jeff's a sugar freak," she said. "I know he's got a candy bar hidden in here somewhere."

March 30

At dawn the waves were only about shoulder high, but the size built slowly all morning. By ten o'clock, the tide was low and getting lower, the wind was down to almost nothing, and the water had warmed up a degree or two. All in all, conditions looked beautiful.

These south swells come with long lulls between sets, and sometimes we like to gather in little packs and shoot the bull while we're waiting. Men, especially as they get older, have a tendency to become isolated. But these morning sessions give us a social life in a neutral setting. The women in the water are always welcome to join us too, of course, and sometimes they do. But then women tend to have better social lives anyway, and they don't care much for our gruff manners and crude humor.

One of the guys said, "This is my first day without a wetsuit, and now I'm freezing my balls off."

A woman within earshot replied, "I'm not!"

A little later, a group of us were talking about how long we've been married. We were surprised to find that many of us have been with our wives at least twenty-five years. One guy said, "My wife told me she'll have me for another twenty-five years if I'll start doing the dishes."

"So what did you tell her?"

"Nothing, yet. I'm still trying to decide if I'm ready for that big a commitment."

Jeff, who's been married to his high school sweetheart for more than thirty-two years, said, "Geez, you guys sound like you're talking about doing federal time."

Then another guy said, "I've been married twenty-five years too—if you count all three wives."

The humpback whales are starting to migrate north. There are many different species of whales in these waters, but the humpbacks are the easiest to identify. When they jump out of the water, they arc to the side and lift one huge pectoral fin into the air. They make an enormous splash when they hit, and the sound can be heard for at least a mile, with a few seconds' delay. Often we hear the humpbacks splashing before we even realize they're approaching. Today we watched an adult whale pass less than a hundred yards from us, followed by three small whales imitating the adult's leaps and splashes. I've read that females have only one calf per year. Were the small whales from the same mother over several years? Or were they unrelated calves playing together? Or was there another mother nearby that we couldn't see?

Punta Espina

April:

Descansos

April 2

Yesterday we had one more day of overhead surf, then the swell began to fall apart. I was hoping for one more big session, but Claudia told me I had already surfed myself to a frazzle. Even though I've doubled my calorie consumption in the past two weeks, I've already lost several pounds. Surfing hard every day is the best weight-loss program I have ever seen. And the most fun.

Now that the water is starting to warm, the jellyfish are back. I have stings on my legs and feet, but a new tight-fitting rash guard has kept most of them off my upper body.

This is the beginning of *Semana Santa*, or Easter week, and many Mexicans are on vacation. For families here in Los Cabos, one of the most popular vacations has become camping on the East Cape.

When I first came to Mexico in the sixties, camping by Mexicans was almost unheard of. The notion of voluntarily reverting to primitive living conditions, after working so hard to gain the few conveniences you had, must have looked to most Mexicans like gringo foolishness. The increasing popularity of camping in Mexico today, I believe, is one more sign of a rapidly growing middle class.

While it's true that no people on earth work harder than Mexicans, it's also true that nobody knows how to have more fun than a Mexican family on vacation. I love watching them: adolescent girls holding hands and walking on the beach with their cousins, boys with hand lines surf fishing with their fathers, grandmothers in long dresses frolicking in the surf, men underneath the family car repairing something while Grandpa in a cowboy hat leans under the hood to offer his advice, brown babies in diapers smearing their faces with watermelon.

You rarely see Mexicans going on vacation with Mom and Dad in the front seat of the family car and two kids in the back, like you do in the U.S. When Mexicans go on vacation, they take the entire extended family, which means at least three generations, including all living grandparents, aunts and uncles, cousins and nephews and, of course, the children. They move in caravans, and if everybody can't fit in the family cars, they ride in the back of pickups. When they set up the family compound on the beach, it's an entire subdivision of tents centered around a communal kitchen with a stove big enough to serve a restaurant. And if there isn't enough room for everybody to sleep in the tents, then the kids curl up at night with their cousins in thick woolen blankets on the beach.

Just a generation ago, Mexican families were much bigger than American families. But that's not true anymore. Mexican women discovered birth control, and today the average Mexican family is about the same size as the average American family. Mexican families still appear large, though, because the bonds in an extended Mexican family are strong. We *norteamericanos* might be able to tolerate our relatives for a few hours on Thanksgiving Day—as long as we strictly avoid any talk of politics, divorce, teen pregnancy, financial shenanigans, drug problems, marital infidelities, or legal embarrassments. But Mexicans are able to suffer the foolishness of their cousins and in-laws every weekend.

During *Semana Santa*, Mexican families produce mountains of baby diapers, cantaloupe rinds, cardboard boxes, plastic soda bottles, and aluminum cans. The first year I lived here, much of that garbage was left on the beach. Fireman Tom organized a cleanup at Punta Espina that year, and some of us gave up a morning of good surf to comb the beach dragging plastic bags behind us. The next year, however, the municipal government in Los Cabos announced in the local paper that they would send a garbage truck out the East Cape road the day after Easter Sunday. The Mexican campers organized their own beach cleanup, scoured the beach for garbage, and left enormous heaps of plastic bags stacked neatly alongside the road. Trash collection is another middle-class concept but one the Mexican people are taking to as well.

Today on the beach east of Zacatitos, I watched a clever grandmother collect four long pieces of driftwood, dig holes in the sand with her hands, bury the poles firmly, then tie the corners of an old sheet to all four posts. She had shade for her infant grandchildren in less than five minutes.

April 3

Lots of our neighbors in Zacatitos are serious fishermen, especially the Canadians and Oregonians. It might be too cold to surf much in the Northwest, but those northerners know their way around a rough ocean in a small craft. They go out every morning at dawn in open aluminum or fiberglass boats and work the Gorda Banks. Sometimes Claudia and I, on our morning walk, help them launch their boats.

One of our neighbors, Don, is a good fisherman who refuses to eat the fish he catches. "I'll start eating fish when it starts tasting like hamburger," he says. That's fine with us because he's always giving us his red snapper, sierra, and wahoo. Once he gave us a yellow-fin tuna that must have weighed fifteen pounds. I filleted it, and Claudia smoked big chunks of it on our barbecue, using mesquite she gathered in the arroyo below our house. The flavor was wonderful.

Yesterday, one of our neighborhood fishermen was pushing off from shore with a load of visiting relatives when the boat was struck by a big wave and flipped over. They lost all their expensive fishing gear, but fortunately nobody was hurt. With a little luck, maybe some of that gear will wash in later with the surf.

I used to fly-fish in my backpacking days, but I've never taken the time to learn much about ocean fishing. I suppose someday, when I get too old to surf, I'll take it up. I've been saying the same thing about golf, but every time somebody invites me to join him on one of the many local courses, I beg off, saying I don't have any lime green pants or a shirt with that little alligator on it.

I'm beginning to think my fishing days might not be too far away, though, because I find myself fantasizing about what sort of boat I'd like to get. I can't imagine myself in anything too big. I'm thinking a small aluminum boat with a little Honda motor might be the way to go. They're easy to launch and don't use a lot of fuel. But with the way these east winds kick up in the spring, I can see how being out on a small boat might be tricky. If that motor won't start, a fisherman could get blown miles to the west. I've heard several stories of fishermen who had to spend a night out on the water before somebody rescued them.

The other day while we were surfing at Punta Espina, a big white yacht passed by, just a hundred feet outside the surf line, with two guys fishing off the stern. I suppose that boat was worth a few hundred thousand dollars. One of the surfers

I was with said, "I wonder if those guys ever figure out what fish costs them per pound?"

April 5

This morning I drove a couple of miles east of Zacatitos to get a good look at the surf. Just a month ago I would have called what I saw today decent surf, but now, after several days of excellent conditions, I consider these ragged leftovers not worth my time. And with the diminishing swell and high morning tides, I know conditions will get worse before they get better.

I drove back along the beach and noticed once again, at the mouth of almost every arroyo, a large mound of dark, chocolate-colored earth. I already knew what these mounds indicated, but I stopped at one anyway to poke through it for a few minutes. What I found were old pieces of charcoal, charred heaps of bone, broken shell and, occasionally, slick pink rock—maybe chert—that human hands had fashioned into crude cutting tools.

When the Spaniards first landed here in southern Baja, they believed they would find even more gold than they had plundered on the mainland. What they found instead were naked people squatting on shellfish mounds in the sun, weaving coiled baskets, hacking spear points from stone, and lashing together crude rafts to fish along this rocky shore.

Those people, the Pericú, are extinct today. They died in mass from smallpox and other European diseases not long after the Jesuit priests came to save their souls. Even modern anthropologists, who are supposed to know better, have described the Pericú as some of the most primitive people on the face of the earth, without so much as ceramic pottery and using the ancient atlatl for killing large game.

But what I see when I poke among these ancient Pericú shell mounds are the remains of a culture that lived in perfect abundance. They had an inexhaustible supply of food: fish, oysters, clams, mussels, and lobsters, as well as fruit of the *pitahaya* cactus and mesquite beans. They had no need to gallop naked across the desert chasing deer and sheep. They were never that hungry. The simplicity of their lifestyle was not a failure but an advantage. Their extreme isolation wasn't a curse but their security—at least for a very long time. And I find it ironic that today only rich tourists on vacation—and sometimes surfers like me—can afford to do what the Pericú did every day: fish, bask in the sun, eat shellfish, and play in the ocean with crude watercraft.

I wonder how many of us who think we long for the biblical Garden of Eden would be shocked and disgusted if we found ourselves in a place truly like that. My guess is that most of us would hop on the very next plane out of Eden and head straight for Las Vegas, or some other man-made hell.

April 8

With no surf and nothing better to do, I've been wondering if what I wrote a few days ago about the Pericú might be a lot of sentimental nonsense. It's easy to romanticize the lives of primitive people, as long as you don't have to live under such conditions yourself. Were their lives really as idyllic and carefree as we sometimes like to imagine? In the case of the Pericú, we are fortunate to have the record of a man who lived among them. The following is taken from *Observations in Lower Baja* by Johann Jakob Baegert, a Jesuit priest.

One could consider the California native as the poorest and most pitiable among Adam's children; yet, I wish to state with full assurance and without fear of contradiction that, as far as this earthly life is concerned, they are incomparably happier than those who live in Europe.... The California native sleeps as gently and as well on the hard soil under the

*open sky as a wealthy European spendthrift in his soft feath-
erbed behind a rich curtain in his gilded room....*

*The California natives seem to have nothing, and yet they
have at all times whatever they need and as much as they
need of it.... Therefore it is no miracle that hardly one among
them has gray hair, and then only very late in life, that they
always are in good spirits, and that they joke and laugh con-
tinually. This perpetual gaiety is a clear proof that they are
always contented, always joyful, which without doubt makes
for real happiness. That is what everyone in this world strives
and sighs for, each according to his position and ability, but
only very few achieve it....*

Baegert didn't always speak so kindly of the Baja natives.
He was often frustrated by their refusal to give up their primitive ways, accept Christianity, and behave like Europeans.
After all, he had come to save their souls but they preferred
being lost. But I have a feeling that in moments of perfect
clarity, Baegert understood the advantage of the Pericú ways.

April 10

Yesterday, just before dusk, we spied a coyote traveling
across the flat below our house. He was carrying something
white in his mouth, and he was holding it high, exactly the
way Kirra carries a prized bone or tennis ball. The sun had
already set, and in the dim light I couldn't make out what the
coyote was carrying, but my first guess was that it was a plastic bag of garbage he had stolen, perhaps from some construction site where the workers had left the remains of their lunch.
I grabbed the binoculars and focused on the coyote before he
disappeared into the brushy arroyo, and I clearly saw that it
was an animal he was carrying, not trash. The animal was
limp, as if it were dead or had at least given up. But what
desert animal, I wondered, was so completely white? Animals
here in the Baja desert are brownish gray so they can blend

in with the landscape. Seagulls, egrets, and some other seabirds are white, but we never see them this far from shore.

Then this morning, coming back from my morning surf check, I saw a group of local women gathered at the main crossroads in Zacatitos, where there's a weekly organic market. I stopped and asked one of the women if she knew of anybody in town who raises white rabbits.

"Oh, thank god, you found my daughter's bunny rabbit!" the woman said. "We bought it for her Easter present, but somehow it got out of the cage! I told her somebody would find it! She's going to be so happy!"

"Um, not exactly," I said. Then I explained in fairly blunt terms what we had seen the night before.

The poor woman broke into tears.

We have a large population of jackrabbits in Zacatitos, but they are fast and wary, and I imagine a coyote would have to work hard to catch one of them. But what a succulent treat that fat, dumb gringo rabbit must have been for him.

I felt bad for the woman, and especially for her daughter. But I must admit, I was happy for the coyote.

April 15

The past several days have been disappointing. A swell that should have arrived last week failed to show, and then another that should have arrived yesterday failed to show as well. What makes it even more frustrating is that the swells showed up on the computer models; they had been tracked by the surf forecasters, we had followed their progress daily, and they certainly produced waves somewhere. Just not here.

Surfing isn't like voodoo or Santería—at least not anymore. We aren't going to set our surfboards on fire and throw them over the cliffs, like we did back in the sixties, as an appeasement to the gods. We have satellites that take all the witchcraft and religion out of surf forecasting now. The problem over these last two weeks can be explained with high school physics. It really comes down to wave refraction. Because we live on the east tip of the peninsula, waves coming from an angle greater than 180 degrees must refract around the point to reach us. If the waves are coming from an angle greater than 230 degrees, they might never make it here. In other words, we sometimes find ourselves in a wave shadow—the darkest, gloomiest shadow a surfer can know.

And then, today, a minor miracle occurred. A swell nobody had predicted came out of nowhere to produce small but clean little waves. They were nothing at all like the 10-footers we rode in March—but with the low tides in the early morning, the 3-foot swell was jacking up to about chest high, and with scarcely any wind, we at least had something to play with.

April 16

The water is still cold—around 72 degrees—and I'm still wearing a full-length three-millimeter wetsuit, which makes me the subject of ridicule from my fellow surfers who apparently are hardier than me.

I don't know why some people tolerate cold water better than others. I have noticed, though, that many of my friends who never wear a wetsuit have adopted the whales' strategy for surviving in cold water—they add an extra layer or two of blubber—and I commend them for their resourcefulness. But skinny surfers need that layer of neoprene insulation or they might end up hypothermic. I'm neither very fat nor very thin, so theoretically I should be able to get by with a rash guard. But I can't. All I know is that I don't like being cold, and even with a wetsuit I sometimes still get the shivers.

Our friend Rick, an outstanding stand-up paddler who rarely wears anything but his surf trunks and tattoos, said,

"The water's seventy-two today! It almost never gets that warm in San Diego!"

"I know, but my body is still ninety-eight," I replied. "That means I'm giving up twenty-six degrees! If I do that long enough, I'm gonna freeze to death."

Due to my hypersensitivity to jellyfish and the fact that a full wetsuit provides better protection from jellyfish than anything else, I will wear my neoprene as long into the spring as I can.

Dawn, one of the daily regulars on the East Cape, told me, "Maybe you could wear a spandex suit for the jellyfish, like what the triathletes wear."

"I thought about wearing a full-body spandex suit," I admitted. "But they're pretty revealing, and I'm afraid my butt might not look good enough."

Dawn laughed—women consider such practical matters all the time—but the men in the water eyed me suspiciously. All-Day Ray spit and looked away, muttering, "You could always wear a pair of surf trunks over it, I suppose."

All-Day Ray acquired his nickname for his habit of surfing seven or eight hours at a time. He's one of the smoothest longboarders I ever saw, and, in my opinion, one of the best all-around surfers in this part of Baja. Ray's tall and lean, speaks with a gravelly voice, and sometimes reminds me of Clint Eastwood. "Another thing you might try," he said, "are Speedo Fastskins. They were banned by the Olympics because they were too fast, so maybe you can pick them up cheap. I've got a pair. I'll wear them one of these days so you can see for yourself."

April 17

The water was amazingly clear this morning. Sitting out on the point with a few other surfers, we watched as a panicked swarm of sardines raced through the water below us, then flew up in front of us, flashing silver and blue, followed by a big-finned fish we couldn't see well enough to identify. Instinctively, we all pulled our feet up out of the water, just in case that fish was attracted to white toes, as well.

Later on, during a long lull, Dawn asked All-Day Ray, "Ray, why doesn't your wife ever surf?" On the whole East Cape there are only a handful of female surfers, and I'm sure Dawn and the others sometimes long for female companionship.

"I can get her out on a stand-up sometimes," Ray said, "but that's about it. To tell you the truth, I'm glad she doesn't surf. I'm afraid she'll get hurt. She likes the lifestyle, though."

Then Dawn asked me why Claudia doesn't surf.

"I've tried to get her out here too, but she's always more concerned with what's happening under the water than what's happening on top of it," I said. "I think Claudia might be afraid of the ocean."

Dawn raised an interesting question: Why aren't there more female surfers? In California, where the ratio of female to male surfers is only perhaps 1 in 20, the reason often given is male aggression. There are too many surfers in California and not enough waves, and any surfer who isn't prepared to fight for position won't get his—or her—share. But here in Baja, where most waves go unridden, that isn't true.

At the risk of getting myself into trouble, I might speculate that there's a strength-to-weight issue involved. The most physically demanding part of surfing is paddling. Women ride surfboards as gracefully as men, but you can't ride a surfboard if you can't catch the wave. And that requires upper-body strength in proportion to body weight. Women might be at a disadvantage in that respect, but they can certainly overcome it by staying extra fit. The best female surfers I know are all lean and strong.

And then there's the tolerance for risk. Although surfing

isn't nearly as dangerous as some people suppose, there is an element of danger. Maybe male testosterone provides men with the willingness, or perhaps foolishness, to engage risk.

But then I have to ask myself, if I'm more comfortable with risk than Claudia, why can't she ever get me on a dance floor? The truth is, watching a large, dark object swim directly beneath my feet isn't nearly as terrifying as the thought of dancing in public.

April 18

I drove all the way to Punta Perfecta this morning looking for surf, but it was a waste of time and gas. The lingering swell we saw yesterday has faded now. On my way back I stopped at a large ficus, or fig tree, growing alongside the road. These beautiful white-barked trees are native to Baja, but on the East Cape they only grow along the arroyos where they can find water. Their exposed roots grow over and around rocks like melted wax and their thick canopies provide the only shade around. This particular ficus is a favorite of mine because it has been used by campers and vagrants for years; in a hollow of the trunk they have installed a kind of shrine or sanctuary, with votive candles, plaster statues, wooden crosses, and other religious articles. Perhaps the space had been intended exclusively as a *descanso* at one time, but in this desert the living require shade more than the dead, so the space is used as a shelter too. Articles of clothing were scattered about, blackened cookware, and ragged blankets. But what interested me the most were the faded *ofrendas*, or offerings, left behind for the dead: a pre-paid phone card, chewing gum, a vitamin pack still sealed in plastic, surf wax, a Dodgers baseball cap, a coupon for a Big Mac, dead marigolds, and other things.

Americans sometimes tell me they think the *descansos* are morbid, but Mexicans don't see them that way. *Descansos* are meant to honor the dead, but they are also meant to remind the living that death can come at any time. And sometimes the *ofrendas* are intended to make us laugh about death and, therefore, maybe fear it a little less.

April 19

I surfed this morning again with All-Day Ray, which is always a pleasure. So many great surfers have big egos, and they're in the habit of accepting praise, not giving it out. But Ray isn't like that. Today he said to me, "I remember when you first moved to the East Cape. We could all see you'd been out of the water awhile. Now I see you starting deeper and making it through sections you never would have made before. I just wanted to tell you, I think your surfing has really improved."

Ray has endured his share of crises in the past couple of years, with several friends and family members suffering from cancer. He's constantly reminding us to have our prostates checked, our colons scoped, our breasts X-rayed, and to cover our skin from the sun. Today, during a lull, Ray paddled over to me and said, "You know who I really miss out here?"

"Who's that?"

"I miss Dick. That was a bad deal, what happened to him."

"It was," I said. "And I miss Dick too."

Dick was a retired nursery owner from Encinitas who built the first house here at Punta Espina, and for several years he had the break mostly to himself. Dick was an experienced surfer, and a shrewd observer of the weather and tides. When I first started surfing here, I watched Dick carefully, trying to understand why he positioned himself where he did in the lineup, what size and shape of board he rode, and how he handled himself in different conditions. The guy knew a lot about surfing.

Dick was in excellent shape for a man his age, but he had one physical problem that gave him trouble: he often experienced severe pain in his lower back due to a herniated disc. Some days his back didn't bother him much, but other days he could stay out in the water only a few minutes; then he would ride a wave to the beach, lie down in the warm sand under his *palapa*, and spend the rest of the day reading or staring out to sea. While the rest of us were enjoying the day, Dick would be lying there, three hundred yards away, suffering stoically.

Sometimes after I'd come in, I'd sit and talk with Dick. He shared his knowledge of the ocean with me, and in return I offered him my experience with back problems—ten years earlier I had suffered from the same condition Dick had.

Like Dick, I had lived with sciatic pain for a long time— twenty years in my case. My own back pain gradually worsened until, by the time I was 53, I couldn't do much of anything except lie flat on my back. I couldn't sit in a chair or ride in a car comfortably, or do any exercise at all except pedal a reclining stationary bike. The pressure on my sciatic nerve was so severe that several doctors told me it would eventually lead to the paralysis of my leg if I didn't do something about it. I was fortunate, though. I found an experienced neurosurgeon at UCLA who was confident that he could help me, and a week later I submitted to his scalpel. From the moment I woke up from the anesthetic, I never experienced sciatic pain again.

Dick was encouraged to hear about my successful surgery. He asked me about it several times. I explained to him that the surgery took less than an hour, that I hadn't spent even one night in the hospital, and that the recovery period only took a few days. I showed Dick my scar, which is less than two inches long, and I gave him the name and phone number of my surgeon. But Dick was reluctant to undergo the procedure himself. I'm not sure why.

Finally, though, Dick came to the conclusion that his back wasn't going to get better on its own and if he wanted to continue surfing, he had to get it fixed. He flew to California and had the procedure done at a clinic in L.A. The surgery went fine, but the next day Dick died of an embolism.

An embolism is just a blood clot that finds its way to some part of the body. It's a fairly rare complication from surgery, but it's always a statistical possibility. If the clot makes it to the lungs or brain, it is very dangerous situation.

I'm not a superstitious person, and I don't believe in ghosts. Apparitions, though, are a different matter. I said to Ray, "You know, several times now, when I'm out here surfing by myself in the early morning, in the dim light, I think I can see somebody lying there in the sand under Dick's old *palapa*, where he always used to be. I know it's not him. It's just one of those Baja things. You see stuff you know isn't there. But it kind of gives me the spooks."

Ray nodded, said nothing, then paddled away.

April 21

We finally got some more overhead surf today. The tide was a bit too high in the early morning, making the waves difficult to paddle into, but every thirty minutes or so a larger set would push through. By then, most of us had paddled inside to ride the more consistent but smaller waves. When the dark lines of a bigger set loomed on the horizon, we had to sprint hard for the outside to avoid getting pounded.

I caught a couple of big, screaming-fast waves today— one of them probably the best I've ridden this month. I love working with the power of big surf. Sometimes in smaller surf I can't find the speed to crank a big power turn or slap one off the lip. In big surf, though, you need to be thinking ahead two or three moves to avoid getting crushed. The wave ahead is like an empty canvas that can be painted an infinite number of ways. The right strokes can create a thing of beauty, the wrong strokes an ugly or painful mistake. But the surfer's decisions have to be quick and spontaneous.

As I've grown older and more experienced, I've learned to stay high on big waves as long as possible. Rounded bottom turns waste energy and leave you down in the trough, depleted, when you need that speed to get down the line. Riding bigger waves is about managing energy wisely.

April 23

A lot of strangers were in the water today, and for a while things were getting a bit tense. As I was paddling back out after riding a wave, a woman on a SUP was riding the next wave in, and because she didn't appear to be in full control of that big clumsy board, I veered down wave and paddled hard to get by her. But instead of taking the line behind me, she drove even harder to pass in front of me. I had to angle quickly to avoid being run over, and I made a note to stay as far away from her as I possibly could. Five minutes later, she did the same thing to another surfer, except this time she ran over the nose of his board and her fin sliced six inches into the fiberglass and foam.

Punta Espina isn't a secret surf spot, though some people like to think it is. And it isn't really private, either—in Mexico all beaches are open to the public—though the access road to the point has a gate, and the gate is locked. The strangers who show up here are most often guests of somebody who lives on the point. They're usually here just a few days, then we might not see them again for a year. Some can surf well but most are out of shape, inexperienced, sunburned, jetlagged, or intimidated by big surf. Every now and then, conditions get crowded, and that sets some local surfers to grumbling. Who can blame them?

Sometimes we wonder if this place will end up ruined like

all our favorite surf spots in California. The way I look at it, of the young and adventurous surfers who would like to live here, few have the financial means to make the move. They come on vacation and see the advantages, but they can't figure out a way to pay for it. Mexico has strict laws forbidding foreigners from taking jobs from Mexican citizens. There are legal ways around that—incorporating in Mexico and opening a business, for example. But the financial opportunities in Mexico are fewer than they are up north. The median annual income is about one-third what it is in the U.S.

Some older surfers I know in California say they would love to retire here. After years of saving and planning, they have the money to build a house and get themselves comfortably through their retirement years. But their wives won't even consider it. They say Mexico is too dangerous, too third world, too Mexican. They don't even want to vacation here. After a lifetime of avoiding risk, their comfort zone is about the size of a condominium in Orange County.

My guess is that southern Baja will continue to be a favorite vacation destination for surfers but will never become a major retirement haven. The cultural and language barriers are too much for most people.

April 26

After doing the dawn surf check in Zacatitos, I didn't think the swell looked too promising, but I drove to Punta Espina anyway, then sat on the beach for thirty minutes, watching while conditions steadily improved. By the time I finally paddled out, the waves were about head-high, the surface remained glassy, and four of us had the place to ourselves for two hours—an absolutely beautiful morning of surfing.

When I got home, Claudia was out visiting her girlfriends, so I made my own lunch and shared it with Kirra on the terrace.

Then I got a call from my sister Deborah. She said, "I'm sorry to have to tell you this, but Dad passed away about thirty minutes ago."

Having a parent die only happens to you twice in a lifetime, and I suppose you will never know how you will react until it happens. To my surprise and confusion, I mostly felt happy for my father. I knew from having visited him last summer that he was ready to go. It was what he had wanted.

My father grew up on a ranch in the middle of Utah, where his family raised wheat, alfalfa, cattle, and sheep. From a poor and humble background, he became a research microbiologist, with seven children, twenty-one grandchildren, and thirty-seven great-grandchildren.

In the town where my father grew up, there were no swimming pools, lakes, or even swimming holes, other than the small creek that ran behind the farmhouse. So my father never learned to swim, which I know he regretted all his life. Although my father loved to see the ocean, the idea of entering it was unimaginable to him. To make sure his children never suffered from the embarrassment of not being able to swim, every summer he sent all seven of us to Red Cross swimming lessons. By the time I was eleven, I had completed all the courses available in our town, including the junior lifeguard course. Because you couldn't be certified until you were twelve, I had to wait until my birthday in December before the Red Cross would mail me the card.

The summer of my twelfth year, I completed the mile-long swimming course at Camp Chawanakee, at Shaver Lake, in the Sierra Nevada. My father rowed a boat in front of me the entire way. I already understood that there was hardly any limit to how far a person could swim. You just put your head down and stroked, and eventually you got to where you wanted to go. To my father, though, the idea of swimming a mile was outrageous, like some superhuman feat, and for months afterwards he told everybody he knew about what I'd done.

I don't think my father ever understood my love of surfing. Except for my first time on a surfboard at Santa Cruz, he never saw me surf. It wasn't the sport itself he objected to but the lifestyle, which in his imagination tended toward idleness, indulgence in godless pleasure, and the pursuit of scantily clad women, all of which had attracted me to the sport in the first place. In the world my father came from, the difference between fun and vice wasn't much. He warned me several times about the dangers of liquor, billiards, and playing cards, which never interested me but must have been the temptations he struggled with in his youth.

My father never stood in my way, though, when I took up surfing. He never prevented me from heading off with my friends for a weekend at Santa Cruz when I was 16, he never tried to stop me from driving to Mazatlán in a $50 car when I was 18, and he never said I was foolish or reckless when I retired to Mexico many years later, though plenty of other people did. Though he came from a conservative background, my father allowed me the freedom to live my life the way I wanted, and for that I love him dearly.

April 29

A powerful swell from the southwest is pounding the East Cape today, with waves 2 or 3 feet overhead at every break that can receive waves from that unusual angle. Many of the breaks look odd, though, with the takeoff point shifted in one direction or another. Some places like La Fortuna and Casa Morena are breaking bigger and with better form than I've ever seen there.

At Punta Espina, I struggled all morning on my 9'0". I couldn't paddle fast enough to catch the waves early—those thick grinders just rolled right under me. After I moved in a bit, I was catching the waves late, at a point where they wanted to jack up abruptly, so I got tossed a couple of times before I could get to my feet. I felt more like a rodeo cowboy than a surfer. Even when I made the drop and turned down the line, I was stuck too far back and had to watch helplessly as the wave closed out in front of me. Then I had to float in the foam, clutching my board, and coughing up saltwater, while the next three or four waves in the set pounded me.

Once, while I was bobbing around inside, I watched All-Day Ray catch a big wave at least a hundred feet deeper than the normal takeoff spot. Somehow, he was able to generate tremendous speed early on, and he took the highest line possible on a wave with a long, steep wall. He flew gracefully across sections that most of us would have considered impossible—an utterly terrifying yet beautiful thing to watch.

During a long lull, after I'd made it back outside, I said to Ray, "I don't know why, but I'm really struggling today. I can't seem to do anything right."

Ray said, "Well, you know as well as I do that surfing is mostly mental. Why don't you go in? Hit it hard again tomorrow."

"I would," I said, "except I hate to end the day like this. I'll have to lie awake all night thinking about how badly I screwed up."

I said to Nathan, another surfer nearby, "You know how it is when you blow a couple takeoffs, and you lose a little confidence, so you play it more cautiously on the next wave, and then that makes it worse, because instead of charging hard the way you know you should, you hold back a little bit, and that just screws everything up?"

Nathan raised one cynical eyebrow and gave me a crooked smile. "Oh, yeah, I know all about that. Maybe more than anybody."

I had chosen not to tell my surf buddies about the loss of my father, mostly because it had nothing to do with surfing.

I knew it would be difficult to explain that my father had been ready to die for a long time, that he had wanted this, and for that reason, I was happy for him. I thought I had already made my peace with my father's departure, and maybe I had, in a way. But now I found myself struggling with the realization that I would never see him again. Is that what they call grieving? I don't know.

For the past four years, everywhere we have traveled, I have carried along a bag containing my funeral clothes, in anticipation of this occasion. Now that it has come, I find myself wondering if I even want to go to my father's funeral, 2,000 miles away, in the mountains of northern Utah. What exactly is the point of a funeral, anyway? I've heard people say you go to a funeral to pay your respect for the dead, as if it were a debt we owe. But what use can a dead person possibly have for our respect? How does it help him?

Many years ago I failed to attend the funeral of a friend who had committed suicide. I was angry at him and not ready to forgive him for his selfish act. As a result, I have been haunted by his restless apparition all my life. That's the true purpose of a funeral, I believe—to give the living a chance to make their peace with ghosts. But my father was hoping to be released from this earth, and I know he won't be coming back. He has found his resting place. Mourning his passing would be hypocritical and counter to his true wishes. Or so it seems to me.

And then there was the distasteful matter of religion. My parents, and nearly all my extended family, are devout Mormons. I have been the black sheep since I was sixteen—about the same time I took up surfing. While my parents are going to their celestial kingdom, the highest rung of glory in the Mormon cosmology, I am headed for hell. Some of my Mormon friends and family suspect that I have moved to Mexico in preparation for my eternal reward, not understanding the paradise we have found here. I sometimes need to remind

them that it was Mexico that offered refuge to our polygamous ancestors when the United States government was trying to throw them into prison.

The last several times I've seen my mother, she has lectured me severely on the requirements I must fulfill if I wish
to see her in the hereafter. They include repentance from sins
too numerous to list, rebaptism, and a visit to the Mormon
temple, where I can have the secrets of nineteenth century
Masonry revealed to me and be issued the famous magic
Mormon underwear. My father, on the other hand, never
bothered with all that nonsense and always allowed me the
freedom to believe whatever I wished. But with him gone,
I'm afraid my mother's destroying angels will be unleashed
on me, and I'm not ready yet for her version of hell.

I haven't decided yet if I'm going to the funeral, but as of
right now I'm thinking I might let it pass. And I'm beginning
to feel guilty about that.

So you see, All-Day Ray was right. Surfing is mostly mental.

April 30

Ray has started wearing a white, hooded rash guard, and
today he wore his Speedo Fastskins—the full-body swimsuit
banned by the Olympics—which he thinks might be good
protection from the sun. "Some California surfers might think
they look silly," he said, "but I'm past caring what California
surfers think. I'm telling you, somehow we gotta figure out
how to keep this damned sun off us, or we're all gonna die
of skin cancer."

Almost every week we hear about surfers we know who
are being treated for some form of skin cancer. My personal
goal is to go the entire season without getting sunburned
once. Now that we're past the spring solstice and the sun is
seriously intense, I never stay in the water after ten o'clock.

Besides using sunscreen by the gallon, I'm also experimenting with extra-strength Desitin, which is 40 percent zinc oxide and can be purchased in a sixteen-ounce tub that will last all season. It's mixed with fish oil, which gives it an odd odor, but surprisingly, it doesn't feel greasy. Desitin offers excellent sun protection, it stays on the skin a long time, and it's good for jock itch too.

The surf was cleaner today, and I got in several great rides before the east wind arrived.

Casa Sorensen

All Day Ray

May:

Snakebit Dogs

May 4

The tides have not been in our favor lately, and things will get worse before they get better. It will be full moon in two days, and as surfers everywhere know, that means we'll have extreme high and low tides, plus a high tide every morning not long after dawn. Here on the East Cape, high tides don't hurt the surf too much if the waves are head high or bigger, but high tides smother medium-sized waves. The opposite is also true. Low tides can jack up a small wave and add a foot or two to its height. Most surfers here despise a high tide, but there's nothing we can do about it except wait for the slow gears of the earth and moon to grind around in our favor once again.

May 5

Until we moved to Baja, I thought Cinco de Mayo was as important a holiday in Mexico as it is in the U.S. It's true that the date marks an important victory the Mexicans won over the French at the Battle of Puebla in 1862. But in Mexico, every week—and practically every day—has a celebration of some sort or another, and the celebration for Cinco de Mayo doesn't amount to all that much. Last year, when we went to San Lucas to attend to a visa matter on Cinco de Mayo, the only establishment in town that was closed for the holiday was the U.S. consulate. Later, when I told our builder Francisco that Cinco de Mayo is widely celebrated in the U.S., he looked perplexed and asked, "Why?"

"I'm not sure," I said. "I think it's because we saw the Mexican Americans drinking beer and having fun. We got jealous and figured we could celebrate that day too."

Francisco nodded enthusiastically and said, "Of course, why not? We borrowed Halloween and Mother's Day from you!"

Two days ago, on May 3, the Mexicans celebrated Día de la Santa Cruz, or Day of the Holy Cross. As the story goes, a dead construction worker in Jerusalem was resurrected after touching the cross on which Jesus had been crucified—or something like that. In Mexico blocklayers take half the day off, and at all construction sites the workers mount a cross at the highest point of their labor in the belief that the cross protects them from injury. At one job site here in Zacatitos, I saw that the always-resourceful workers raised a crude cross made of PVC pipe.

Last night at dusk, the sky over the ocean grew dark with turbulent clouds, and we were treated to a spectacular lightning storm that lasted two hours. We turned off our lights and sat on the terrace to enjoy the show. The streaks of lightning appeared to be very close, but the clap of thunder didn't follow until several seconds later, so the center of the storm had to have been far out to sea. We hoped a little rain might follow, but it never came.

The desert plants are as dry as I've ever seen them. They aren't pretty to look at right now, all shriveled and gray. Grasshoppers are devouring the leaves on our *bugambilias*, since they and our coco palms are the only plants here getting water.

This drought is becoming serious now. The government says that many of the water wells are registering record lows, though that doesn't stop them from approving more hotels, condos, and golf courses. (One desert golf course uses as much water as 10,000 people.) The green fees are outrageously expensive, which might explain why the golf courses are empty most of the time—I don't know a single Mexican who plays. They say golf courses are a major selling point for new condo projects, but the developers can't even sell the condos they've already built.

One of my greatest worries for Los Cabos is that the development will continue in this desert paradise until it is no longer sustainable and the apparition collapses or dries up. Already, there's a large desalination plant near San Lucas, and there's talk of building more like it. But that's an expensive source of water, requiring a lot of energy, which, in this case, arrives in oil tankers from the mainland. The people of Mexico rely on their precious oil resources to provide revenue for expanding the country's infrastructure, and it's difficult to see how wasting those resources on keeping a few unused golf courses green provides much of a benefit. We gringos have no right criticizing the Mexicans for their foolish development projects, though, considering the disasters we have created in Southern California, Nevada, and Arizona.

NOAA has issued a report saying the long period of La Niña has likely ended and there is at least a fifty percent chance of El Niño conditions returning. If that's true—and I hope it is—we can expect more rainfall in the coming tropical storm season.

May 6

We have a beautiful new south swell today. The waves this

morning were well overhead, with an outgoing tide and glassy conditions. I surfed for a couple of hours after the sun came up; then around nine o'clock, Mike Doyle and Annie paddled out to join me. I hadn't seen them in a while, and I wanted to show off for them a bit. I dropped in very late on the peak of a large wave, survived a near-vertical freefall, with the lip of the wave breaking on my back, and was launched down the line like a stone out of a slingshot. It's not the sort of thing I can do with any regularity, but it certainly worked this time. As I flew past Doyle, he sat up on his board to watch, grinned, and covered his eyes with both hands as if what I had done was too terrifying to watch.

After I'd paddled back out, Doyle said, "That looked like something a pro would pull off."

"Thanks," I replied. It was the closest Doyle had ever come to complimenting my surfing. "So what happens now? Do the paychecks just start arriving in the mail?"

May 7

Around 11:30 this morning, we got a call on Skype saying Fireman Tom had just fallen off a ladder. He was hurt badly, bleeding from the head, and his wife Paula was pleading for help. Paula had first called Dr. Lynn, but he was on his way to the airport and suggested calling me, since he knew I had been trained as an EMT by the National Park Service some thirty-five years ago. It terrified me to think I might be the best-qualified person on the East Cape to help a badly injured person, but the truth is there are no fire stations out here, no medical clinics, and no ambulance services.

Claudia and I jumped in the truck and headed east as fast as we could go. Tom had been an EMT too, though one with far more experience than I ever had, so I was hoping that if he was conscious, he could give instructions until more help arrived.

We had driven four miles or so when we saw Tom and Paula's car coming rapidly toward us. We all stopped in the middle of the road, and I saw that Tom was sitting upright. Although his head was still bleeding, he had been well bandaged by his good neighbor Rod. I asked Tom and Paula if there was anything I could do to help or if they wanted me to ride along with them to the hospital in San José. "I was unconscious for a bit," Tom said, "but I think I'm okay now. The best thing is probably to just continue on to the hospital, get an X-ray and a CT scan as soon as possible."

I was relieved to hear that. Then, since Tom was conscious, and a fellow surfer, I said, "This swell looks like it's increased by a couple of feet since Claudia and I did our dawn surf check, and it's surprising to see how glassy the conditions are this late in the day. When we drove by Shipwreck just now, it looked about as good as it ever gets, and there were only three surfers out, which is pretty funny because there had been sixteen surfers in the water when we drove by there on Sunday when it wasn't nearly this good. I'm thinking maybe this would be a good day for an evening session. What do you think?"

Tom, with one hand still pressed against the bloody compress on his head, gave me a glance that reminded me of Jack Nicholson in *The Shining*, and I decided to drop the subject. "Good luck, then," I said. "We'll see you when you get back."

May 8

The word on Tom is that he had a CT scan at the hospital and everything looked fine. The doctors in San José made a small incision to drain a hematoma the size of a lemon on the side of his head, and for that reason, he spent the night in the hospital. He should be coming home later today.

I surfed for three hours this morning in nearly perfect conditions—overhead and glassy. For some reason, I was the only person out. I knew Tom's excuse, but where was everybody else?

Sometimes surfing alone almost feels like cheating. When you can always position yourself in the best spot and take every wave you want, it becomes surprisingly easy. Surfing in a crowd, so much energy is wasted trying to outsmart and out-position everybody else. Surfing by myself, I felt like a teenage kid starring in his own surf movie.

It's every surfer's dream to have his favorite surf spot all to himself at least once. In all the years I surfed Swami's, Cardiff Reef, Rincon, or Black's, I never had those places to myself, ever. Once I drove by Swami's at three o'clock in the morning, and there were at least five guys on it, all wearing headlamps. But now that I've surfed alone many times, I must admit that the experience lacks something. I find I miss the laughter and the camaraderie. I miss having somebody to tease me when I do something foolish and somebody to compliment me when I do something right.

By ten o'clock, the east wind had crept in and ruined the perfect conditions. I was tired anyway, so I took one last wave to the beach. As I walked back to the Rhino, I saw Mike Doyle and Jeff King sitting together under one of the driftwood *palapas*. I hadn't known they were there until then, which was a good thing because I usually surf poorly when I know one of those two guys is watching me.

"Nice session," Jeff said, struggling to suppress a grin. "We didn't even know that was you out there. Every now and then you almost looked like you knew what you were doing."

"We were saying you looked like somebody who used to be pretty good before he got old," Doyle added.

I almost appreciated that insult coming from Doyle, since that was exactly what he had become too. They were both teasing, of course, but their words still stung. I knew, though, they could be much harder on each other. I once heard Doyle describe Jeff as "the world's fattest vegetarian." And Jeff once introduced me at a party as "the guy who translated Mike Doyle's autobiography into English."

"You need to get a new spring suit," Jeff said. "That one you're wearing is way too big for you."

I made a feeble attempt to defend myself. "I guess I've lost a couple of pounds since the start of surf season. Does it really look that big?"

"We were just saying you looked like a baby with a full load in its diapers," Doyle replied.

Nothing can be more humiliating, even at my age, than to be ridiculed by your boyhood idol. In two minutes, I had gone from starring in my own surf movie to being a kook from the San Joaquin Valley once again.

And then this evening I received an email from Jeff. Attached was a photo he'd taken of me this morning with a telephoto lens. I was laying hard into a bottom turn, looking up at an overhead wave, it's face glistening like a jewel, and my fins spraying water into the sky. It was the best surfing photo anybody has ever taken of me.

Doyle was right, though—my spring suit looked soggy in the butt.

May 9

We had a fading swell today, and the east wind wrecked it early, but we still got in a decent session. While I was sitting out on the point between sets, two large sea lions passed by, headed west, not more than a hundred feet away. Sometimes passing sea lions will see us riding waves and loiter nearby, as if they understand we're playing and they want to join in. But these sea lions were swimming quickly, with a deep undulating motion like whales. I know their biggest enemy in these waters is the bull shark, so I turned toward the east and watched my back for a minute, just to make sure a big fin wasn't following the sea lions.

Later, I watched as a long line of brown pelicans smoothly and effortlessly rode the air currents along the face of a cresting wave. In aeronautics they call that "riding the ground effect," though in this case I suppose it should be called "the water effect." Birds get some lift gliding low over a calm sea, but they get additional lift from a wave, which pushes air in front of it like the windshield of a car. The pelicans glided three or four hundred yards—the full distance of the wave at Punta Espina—without flapping their wings even once.

Every now and then, one of the pelicans would spot a fish, veer erratically, and spear into the water with its beak. The movement was so sudden, the pelicans didn't have time to tuck in their wings, and the wings slapped the surface with an awkward motion. Because bird bones are hollow and very light, they aren't particularly strong, and for this reason the accident rate for pelicans is high. We find them dead or injured on the beach all the time.

I know the pelicans must fly to eat. I understand they're at work. They're hungry, and they're hunting for fish. But clearly they're surfing too, in a method and style so far advanced they make us, on our crude slabs of foam, look like primitive misfits. And you can't tell me those pelicans aren't having fun.

May 12

Today was the social event of every surf season—the potluck at Fireman Tom's house.

Tom and his wife Paula live on the bluff overlooking Punta Espina. The soil along that ridge has the consistency of sugar, and every time it rains, whole sections of it melt away. Their house appears to be built in a secure spot, but the arroyo below them is eroding like the badlands of Utah. So Tom and Paula have named their annual spring bash the "Sinkhole de Mayo."

Something like seventy-five people were in attendance, most of them surfers I've spent hundreds of hours with in the water. I had trouble recognizing some of them, though, as I'm sure they had trouble recognizing me. We all looked different without a wetsuit, hat, and thick coat of zinc oxide smeared across our faces—out of uniform, so to speak. The men were either taller or shorter than I had imagined; some of them I hadn't even known were bald. The women were even more difficult to recognize, with their makeup, dresses, and un-braided hair.

Tom had to repeat his story about falling off the ladder over and over, until he was sick of talking about it. Somebody suggested he make a video reenacting the accident and invite his guests to watch it as soon as they came through the front door. The only reason he'd been up on the ladder in the first place, he said, was that he was cleaning up his patio for the potluck and decided to wash off some bird shit that had accumulated on a metal pole. "The embarrassing thing is, when I was a firefighter I answered that call a hundred times," Tom said. "Some poor jackass is up on a ladder cleaning his rain gutter, he falls down and hits his head, and his wife calls the dispatcher screaming that her husband is dying. And here I go and do the same damned thing myself."

"Tom, after your accident I got on the internet and looked up some statistics," I said. "Last year something like 58 people in the U.S. were killed in surfing-related accidents—drownings, head injuries, whatever. But there were 355 ladder-related fatalities. So you would have been something like six times safer if you'd just gone surfing that day."

Tom nodded and said, "You're right. And the surf was really good that day too."

Actually, surfing is not nearly as dangerous as many people think. In my surfing career, I've had only three injuries, only one of those serious enough to be called potentially life threatening. Statistics in the U.S. show that both basketball and soccer are more dangerous than surfing and far more people die fishing every year. But then, I suppose alcohol must play some role there.

A study done in New Zealand (a nation with a lot of surfers) shows the injury rate per 1,000 participants of various sports and activities:

Aerobics 0.18
Cycling 0.46
Fishing 0.12
Golf 0.39
Home injuries 5.18
Jogging 0.17
Motorsports 2.40
Motor vehicles 3.09
Rugby 20.27
Skiing 4.22
Soccer 7.25
Surfing/bodyboarding 0.58
Swimming 0.13
Trampoline 0.17

So, according to these statistics, in New Zealand you're almost ten times more likely to be injured staying at home than surfing. And playing rugby is positively suicidal.

Our friend Dr. Lynn, a retired dermatologist, took a seat on the patio and held an informal skin-cancer clinic. He hadn't planned it that way, but this is what happens to him at every social occasion on the East Cape—wrinkled, sun-blistered gringos form a waiting line next to him, and he graciously inspects everybody's odd-looking growths. I always like to sit close by and watch him—not only because I learn so much but because I enjoy his cynical sense of humor. As a retired physician he wants fewer patients, not more, and can tell people what he really thinks.

One by one, the surfers filed by, and Dr. Lynn would say,

"I would call that a pre-cancerous lesion," and he would take a sip of wine. "Go to the pharmacy and buy a tube of Efudex… cost you about five hundred pesos, but at least in Mexico you don't need a prescription."

To another surfer he would say, "You'd better stop by my house and let me remove that little growth…. No? Not ready yet? Well, then wait until it becomes full-blown squamous cell and we'll try to remove it then."

When one stubborn natural-health nut told him about a growth on the back of his neck that he had been treating with sesame seed oil, Dr. Lynn shrugged and said, "That's wonderful. I guess you don't need my help then."

In his younger days, Dr. Lynn had been a surfer and marathon runner himself, so he understands the love of being outdoors. But his advice for surfers is this: "Wear a hat, wear a long-sleeved rash guard, use sunscreen and zinc oxide, and stay out of the sun after ten o'clock."

May 14

This morning around eleven, Kirra went down to the garage to drink from her water bucket. During the night a two-foot rattlesnake had found its way into the cool shelter of the garage and coiled itself between the water bucket and the wall. When Kirra poked her nose closer to investigate this new, odd-smelling creature, the rattlesnake bit her.

Claudia, who was working in her art studio downstairs, heard the snake rattling, but the noise was so amplified and distorted by the echo of the garage, she couldn't make out what it was. When she finally went to investigate, she saw the snake coiled behind the water bucket and saw Kirra bleeding from her snout, about halfway between the tip of her nose and her eyes.

Claudia ran upstairs to tell me what had happened and Kirra scampered up behind her, not sure what all the commotion was about. I could see blood oozing from the bite on Kirra's nose, so I sat her down on the stairs and squeezed the thin flesh where she had been bitten. A blob of wet blood— perhaps a tablespoonful—splattered onto the steps. It looked as though the snake's venom had pooled in the space between the skin and bone, and I hoped I had gotten most of it out.

It took me less than a minute to kill the snake with a shovel. My deal with rattlesnakes—or *cascabels*, as they are called in Baja—has always been live and let live. But this snake had violated that truce, and in my judgment it had to die. Then we put Kirra in the truck and quickly drove the ten miles to San José.

Our vet—the same man who had given me his advice on the injured burro—put Kirra on the stainless-steel examination table and took her vital signs, which he said were not too bad. Normally Kirra will not allow anybody but Claudia or me to touch her, but by now she was in some discomfort, her nose had begun to swell, she understood that she was in trouble, and she calmly submitted to this stranger.

Then the vet told us, "In Mexico we do not give antivenom to dogs. It is very expensive, and it would have to be flown in from San Diego. It would never arrive in time to help your dog."

"So what can we do?" I asked.

He gave me a few vials of antibiotics and the syringes, so I could give the injection to Kirra myself. "This is all we can do," he shrugged. "I don't believe the snakes in Baja are as venomous as the snakes you have up north, but we can't know that for certain. If she survives forty-eight hours, I think she will be all right."

We took Kirra back home, where she took her usual shady spot on the terrace. By now her face had swelled up to twice its normal size, and we were worried she might lose her airway. She put her chin down on the cool tile floor and watched us passively with her two pale eyes. Her expression was that of somebody resigned to a hard time, but she was calm—not at all agitated.

This incident is especially horrifying for Claudia and me because a few years earlier, back in California, we had lost another Australian shepherd—Sadie, Kirra's cousin—to a snakebite. Sadie, who was the most wonderful dog I'd ever owned, had been bitten on the chest, deep in the muscle, where the venom slowly worked its evil. She endured three surgeries, and we spent an entire month (plus a small fortune) trying to keep her alive. But, unfortunately, the venom continued to spread through her body, and eventually Sadie died of congestive heart failure.

The thought of watching Kirra go through the same slow, painful death was almost unbearable for Claudia and me.

May 15

I got up several times in the night to check on Kirra, who never moved from her place on the terrace. Once, I sat down in the moonlight and talked to her quietly for a few minutes. She had already heard the story about her marvelous cousin Sadie, and she wasn't interested in hearing it again, so I just told her we were doing all we could to help her. She didn't raise her head off the cool tile, but she looked up at me with her bloodshot eyes and let me know I had her trust.

Kirra appears to be breathing almost normally now, if a bit noisily. The swelling on her face hasn't gone down, but it isn't getting worse, either. I suspect I was able to squeeze most of the snake venom from her snout, and I'm hoping she'll be okay. But it's still too early to know.

May 16

Forty-eight hours after Kirra's snakebite, the swelling is completely gone. She has a bloody scab on her nose, but she acts as if nothing ever happened at all, and after breakfast she insisted on going along with us on our morning walk.

Making her morning rounds is Kirra's favorite part of the day. Even if we don't meet other dogs along the way, she sniffs every bush for news of the town dogs and leaves her own comments as well. We like to say that she's answering her morning p-mail. But this morning, when she poked her nose into a tangle of coral vine, I made a clicking sound with my tongue, in imitation of a rattlesnake. Kirra jumped about a foot in the air and three feet back, so at least we know she has learned something useful from her encounter with the *cascabel*.

May 17

We drove into San José this morning to buy groceries and run our weekly errands. When we got home, there were seven young golden eagles perched in the limbs of a big *cardon* cactus fifty feet from our house. We have never seen them here before; we have no idea where they came from or why they suddenly appeared out of nowhere. At first glance, we took them for buzzards, which are about the same size, but as we got closer, we knew by their color they had to be eagles. They must have been juveniles, because they had a few white flecks in their feathers and because mature eagles don't often flock together that way. If I had to guess, I would say the golden eagles were passing through this area, noticed our out-of-control population of jackrabbits, and decided to linger awhile.

Sometimes I wonder how I ever became a birdwatcher. I'm a bit concerned it's another sign of growing old, like taking afternoon naps or sprouting hair from your ears. During all my years working for the park service, I did my best to ignore birds—or at least I thought I did. I considered them less interesting than so many other things in the natural world, and bird watchers hopelessly dull. But later, when I started taking Claudia on backpacking trips with me, I found to my shame and embarrassment that I could name most of the birds we encountered. Somehow I had become an unwilling Audubonite, and now I find that I've completely changed my mind on the subject. For me, few things in the natural world are more interesting than birds.

Earlier this spring, a couple of rosy house finches started hanging around our terrace. At first there were three of them—two females and a male—but the male eventually rejected the polygamous opportunity before him, made up his mind between the two, and chased the other female away. I told Claudia, "I'd love to know how he made his decision. Did the winner seem like a better homemaker or better conversationalist or was she just better-looking?"

"Maybe he loved her," Claudia replied.

The finches tried to build a nest in the little round *palapa* on our roof, but I objected to cleaning up their poop every day, which was stained red by the boxthorn berries they feast on. I knew if I didn't put an end to their handiwork right away, I'd soon find myself climbing a ladder like Fireman Tom. So I destroyed the finches' nest, and after making several repeat attempts, they finally gave up and decided to build their home elsewhere.

Before long, though, the finches started coming around several times a day to drink from Kirra's water dish, which must be the only water available in the neighborhood. The finches would land on the guardrail and chatter aggressively at Kirra, trying to provoke a response from her. But Kirra is the survivor of a near-death experience; she has one eye on eternity now. She doesn't trouble herself with petty squabbling, and she completely ignored their provocations. As soon as the finches were sure they were safe, they would fly to her bowl, steal a couple of quick sips, then fly away.

May 18

This morning we took the beach route out to the East Cape. It takes a little longer than the washboard road and uses a bit more gas, but it's more scenic. The Rhino floats easily over the sand, where heavier vehicles would bog down, but every now and then I'll get it stuck, like I did today. Using an army trenching tool, I dug out the sand where the skid plates were hanging up, and in a few minutes we were on our way again.

Driving on the beach is controversial around here. It's not exactly legal, though the law is rarely, if ever, enforced. Sometimes arguments over driving on the beach can get become heated. A couple of years ago, here in Zacatitos, two gringas, both old enough to be grandmothers, got in a fistfight over this issue. Today, though, Claudia and I encountered our first turtle tracks of the year, which means we will restrict our beach driving for the rest of this spring and summer.

We surf with turtles on the East Cape almost every day. Often, when we're paddling out, we see their silhouettes through the face of a looming wave. Sometimes, when we're in the water waiting for a set, turtles pop up directly in front of us, which can be heart-stopping, even though they seem motivated by nothing more than curiosity. I've seen only the olive ridleys myself, but I know the Leatherbacks are here as well. Turtles spend a lot of time in the surf zone, eating algae and sea grass, and they also eat jellyfish, for which I am grateful. We rarely see turtles on the beach, though, except during nesting season, which begins now and extends through the early fall.

Turtles bury their eggs in the sand, just above the high-tide line, and their floundering tracks in the wet sand demonstrate how awkward they are on land and how hard they work to get to a place where they know their eggs will be safe. Turtles and turtle eggs have traditionally been a source of food for Mexicans. Nowadays turtles are officially protected by law, though the nests are still frequently looted for eggs, and back in the arroyos I have found campfires where humans have made a meal of mature turtles as well.

It's true that while turtles are on land they are vulnerable to being crushed under vehicle tires. And it's also true that vehicles on the beach allow poachers easy access to their nests. Perhaps for those reasons, vehicles should be prevented from driving on the beaches here, though I don't think that will ever happen.

In my opinion, the approach already being used by the Mexicans will have the best long-term success. A government-sanctioned environmental group, Campamento Tortuguero Don Mañuel Orantes, using private donations, employs one worker on the East Cape to protect the turtles. During nesting season, the worker drives the beaches every morning on his ATV, searching for new turtle nests. When he finds a nest, he carefully collects the eggs and transports them to a remote fenced area, where they are protected and incubated under ideal conditions until they hatch. Then the baby turtles are released into the ocean. This is a simple, inexpensive, and remarkably effective program; last year, in fact, was the most successful hatch in the program's history.

May 19

Every spring and early summer, just as the water off the East Cape is beginning to warm up to 75 degrees or so, we get a hard wind from the southwest that blows for two or three days. Contrary to what you might think, that southwest wind is cold, since it passes over the cooler waters of the Pacific. Or at least it's colder than the east wind off the Gulf of California, which is almost always hot. The cold wind rapidly chills the warm surface water, and because cold water is heavier than warm water, it sinks. (That's why the ocean is normally colder the deeper you go.) As the colder water sinks, it causes churning, which mixes relatively warm surface water with colder deep water. Oceanographers call that "overturning," and sometimes in the spring that overturning can be quite dramatic, causing surface temperatures to drop 10 degrees or more in just a few hours.

Last year, in June, we had a severe and very sudden overturning that killed thousands upon thousands of fish, which then washed up on the beaches all across the East Cape. The Mexican government issued a statement calling that incident a *marea roja*, or red tide, which is a die-off of phytoplankton; as the microorganisms decay, they deplete the ocean's oxygen and sometimes release their toxins into the water as well. The government made no mention of the sudden drop in ocean temperature—how would they even know?—but as a surfer who was in the water at the time of the *marea roja*, I can say with certainty that the water temperature dropped dramatically just before the fish died.

Most of the fish that washed up after the die-off were red snappers (*huachinangos*), some of which turned up at local restaurants before the government could issue a warning banning their use. (I didn't hear of anybody getting sick from eating them, but it almost certainly happened somewhere.)

Another fish that washed up in large numbers after the die-off was a strange-looking beast with the tail of an eel, the head of a bass, and an odd little goatee under the bottom lip. I'd never seen anything like it, and it took me days before I finally identified it as a Pacific bearded brotula. They say the brotula has the ability to survive at extreme ocean depths and has even been found alive at 23,000 feet. Why a deepwater fish like that would be affected by a churning of surface waters, I don't know. But it was.

After last year's die-off, the dead fish lay on the scorching-hot beaches until the whole East Cape reeked like a fertilizer factory. The local government finally sent out crews to gather them up, but for some reason they didn't bother with the beaches in Zacatitos—perhaps thinking we gringos had the resources to take care of the matter ourselves. Some of our friends and neighbors talked about organizing a beach cleanup, but I pointed out that every dead fish on the beach now had a sand crab hole next to it. At night the crabs would scramble out of their holes and feast on the abundance that had washed ashore. In crab folklore, an event like that might be remembered as manna falling from heaven. So I told our neighbors, "I don't like the smell any more than you do, and I'm sorry for all the dead fish. But I'm happy for the crabs."

Eventually our neighbors did organize a beach cleanup; they just didn't invite me.

At any rate, the south wind started blowing again three days ago, and the ocean temperature has plummeted from about 75 degrees to 63 degrees in one night. Surfing yesterday in just my trunks and a rash guard, I shivered until I thought I might wash up dead on the beach and bloat in the hot sun like all those *huachinangos* did last year.

Like most surfers, I tolerated cold water more easily when I was younger. Surfing in Santa Cruz back in the sixties, when all I had was a ragged wetsuit top, I would stay out in the frigid waters until I had an ice cream headache. When I moved to San Diego in the seventies, I thought I was living in the tropics, and I wore a wetsuit only in the middle of winter. Wetsuits were vastly improved in the eighties and nineties, but wearing one is still cumbersome, like trying to have sex in a tuxedo, and I figured after moving to Baja I would never wear one again. Over the years, though, my joints stiffened and my tendons tightened, until the thought of plunging into even mildly cold water didn't seem fun anymore.

So this morning, after two days of south wind, followed by the cold overturning, I figured I'd better pull on my old, tattered full-length wetsuit again. As soon as I hit the water, though, I discovered that overnight the ocean temperature had returned to about 72 again, and I stewed all morning.

May 20

When you look at a photo on the cover of a surf magazine showing a surfer relaxed in the pocket of a flawless wave, there's a deceptive and even dishonest simplicity to the scene, as if moments of such dazzling perfection are commonplace in some exotic dimension you might experience yourself if only you were younger, luckier, and had a more fashionable pair of surf trunks. That's why surfers call photography like that "surf porn." If you can't be there to enjoy it yourself, it's just frustrating to look at it. Experienced surfers know that you can wait days, even weeks, for the right conditions to come together, and when they do, there probably won't be anybody there to take a picture.

But today it happened. Everything (except the photo) came together—the wind, the tide, the swell. Except this is a Sunday in May, which means, even on the East Cape, there were too many surfers in the water.

Some of the locals get angry when they see surfers in rental cars appear out of nowhere like that. Personally, I expect it on a Sunday, and I try not to let it annoy me. I've run into a lot of old friends I haven't seen in a while on days like this, made lots of new friends, and had a lot of laughs. Today, though, I needed good surf more than I needed friends, so I drove to an unnamed point break on the East Cape that's hard to get to without an ATV. There were only two other guys out when I got there, both locals I know, and we traded off riding perfect, head-high waves.

After a while, a guy showed up in a rental car and paddled out on a monstrous longboard that must have been 11 feet long. The guy was fifty pounds overweight, and his surf trunks were so small that his pale white gut hung over the waistband. Every time he sat astride his board, we were treated to a peek at the crack of his enormous ass. Well, not everybody can look like they belong on the cover of a surf magazine, including me, so we tried not to notice, or let the disgusting sight ruin our morning.

Every now and then, an extra-big set would push through, and the four of us in the water would have to scramble to get outside in time to avoid getting crushed. On one set, I was the farthest guy out, winded from paddling so hard, and I let the first two waves of the set pass under me. And that fat Barney, sitting out on the shoulder a ways, yelled over at me, "Take one of those, damnit! I don't know where you come from, but it sure as hell ain't from around here!"

I was surprised and offended to hear that guy speak to me that way. Such behavior is common in California, but we don't see it much here. I collected myself, took the third wave of the set, which was perfectly shaped and about 2 feet overhead, and I blew by that plumber-butt like he was waterlogged.

I was angry, I'm ashamed to say, and as I paddled back out, I was determined to paddle over to that guy and ask him if I'd heard him correctly. But then, sadly, I remembered that I'm 63 now, and even though I might still be able to physically challenge him, that course of action would have ruined the rest of my day and resulted in somebody getting hurt— most likely me. So I calmed myself, paddled right by the guy, and ignored him for the rest of the session. My friends in the water did the same, and we all had a wonderful time, except for the plumber-butt, who sat out on the shoulder and bobbed in sad isolation all morning.

It's tempting to think we get wiser as we get older, but I honestly haven't noticed that effect in my own life yet. I like to think I'm beginning to learn to keep my mouth shut, though, which is better than nothing and in this case probably avoided a violent conflict.

We have to be careful, we Baja surf refugees, not to pollute our new land with all our old-country problems. California used to be a paradise too.

May 21

The perfect conditions didn't last long. Overnight the swell has dropped 2 or 3 feet in size. I checked out Punta Espina early but couldn't work up enough enthusiasm to paddle out. Prestigious international surf contests are held in conditions far worse than this, on the theory that a good surfer should be able to make the best of whatever nature is offering on any given day. But the truth is, great surf spoils you for anything less. And I'm spoiled rotten.

May 22

Over the weekend, two of our neighbors in Zacatitos, Duncan and Suzie, were at Shipwreck with their dog Axel, when a little yellow ultralight aircraft flew up the beach and landed on the sand not far away. Axel, a young, goofy, rust-colored lab, had never seen anything that big come out of the sky, and it terrified him. He must have thought it was some kind of predatory bird, or maybe a pterodactyl. Axel bolted off at a gallop before Duncan and Suzie were able to catch him. They drove around for hours looking but couldn't find him anywhere. Later that day, they emailed people all over the East Cape asking them to be on the lookout for Axel.

I recall from my college psychology class that small rodents are terrified of shadows in the shape of a predatory bird, though they will ignore shadows of nonpredatory birds. But how long has it been, I wonder, since dogs, coyotes, or other canines have had to be fearful of aerial predators?

Last summer, I was walking with Kirra through a small town in Colorado when we happened to cross over some railroad tracks just a minute or so ahead of a slow-moving train. Kirra had never seen a train before, didn't understand that they were confined to tracks, and was convinced that this huge, noisy beast was coming to get her. But instead of running away from the train, she headed for our Winnebago, back on the other side of the tracks. Her desperate plan was to run between the wheels of the train in order to reach safety on the other side. She would have followed through with that plan too, if I hadn't managed to catch her just a few feet from the tracks.

Poor Axel's panic must have been something like that. He had never seen pterodactyls before, was horrified to discover that Baja was infested with them, and he had to flee for his life.

Fortunately, we heard via email today that Axel eventually found his way home.

May 25

This morning, returning from our daily walk, we found a pregnant burro lying under the shade of a *palo blanco* in the sandy arroyo below our house. Burros don't lie down very often—they prefer to keep moving most of the time—and when they do rest, they rest standing. So seeing this jenny stretched out on her side, we were fairly certain she was ready to give birth. If so, she had chosen a good spot—hidden, shady, clean, and defensible.

We stopped for a moment to watch her. She looked healthy, well-fed, and not at all bothered by our presence. There was nothing we could do to help her, and she didn't need our help, so we wished her well and moved on.

Later this evening, just before sunset, I went down again to offer her the remains of a watermelon that had sat in our refrigerator too long. But she was gone.

May 26

Last night, around midnight, I had a terrible encounter with a kissing bug—by far my worst encounter with those evil little creatures ever. For a while there I thought we were going to have to make a trip to the hospital in San José.

Kissing bugs, or conenosed bugs, are long, thin insects that suck blood from vertebrates—usually nesting mammals but sometimes birds too. They're native to much of North and South America but favor drier, desertlike climates. In California their native host is the wood rat, or pack rat, but there are far more humans than wood rats in California these days, and the kissing bugs have adapted to sucking human blood. I'm not sure what their native host is here in Baja—possibly the jackrabbit or chipmunk.

When we lived in the Sierra Nevada foothills, I was bitten by kissing bugs many times, so I know them well. After they gain entry to your dwelling through an open door or window, they follow your scent to the place where you sleep, then hide in your bedding or under your mattress. At night they crawl out surreptitiously, suck your blood, then crawl back into hiding. The worst part, however, is that while they're sucking your blood, they excrete, or inject, a protein that acts as a topical anesthetic, so their victim won't feel the bite until it's too late. The protein causes an allergic reaction in many people, and the more times you've been bitten, the worse the reaction can be. For me the reaction has always been bad, but never as bad as last night.

You would think that with two people in a bed, the odds would be fifty-fifty that either person would be bitten. But it doesn't work that way. For some reason, kissing bugs almost always reject Claudia, who is much more succulent. At any rate, I always know when I've been bitten because the reaction wakes me suddenly from my sleep.

I immediately sat up in bed, already in an agitated state,

and woke Claudia. I turned on the light, we got out of bed, pulled back the covers, and there he was, under my pillow. He was about an inch long and brown, rather than the normal black, which perhaps indicates that he wasn't yet fully grown. I pinched him between my finger and thumb and threw him out the window.

But the real trouble was just beginning. Within a couple of minutes, I broke out in big welts on my shoulder, where he had bitten me. Soon after that, I broke out in hives all over my body. I watched the welts on my arms and legs rise up like bread dough. My hands tingled, and I itched all.

I recall from my training as an EMT that by the time a severe allergic reaction begins to cause anaphylactic shock, closing the airways and restricting breathing, it's probably already too late to go to the hospital. In Zacatitos, we're thirty minutes from a hospital anyway. I should have had an Epipen on hand to administer a quick shot of epinephrine, but I didn't. I used to have a couple in my EMT kit, but I used them on other people years ago and never replaced them. Epipens aren't available in Baja, either. So I took two Benadryls and applied hydrocortisone cream to the welts. Then we waited.

Obviously, I lived; however, I might add that anaphylactic shock isn't even the worst possible outcome after being bitten by a kissing bug. That would be Chagas' disease, a strange, incurable ailment with horrible neurological complications. Chagas' can lie dormant or undiagnosed for years before causing death.

May 27

You'd think humans would need more sleep as we get older, that the additional rest would do us good and the pleasure of dreams might offer at least the memory of youth. But as it turns out, just the opposite is true. I've been an insomniac for at least fifteen years now. I know a lot of other people my age are too. Those sleepless morning hours, if left to their natural course, are wasted with worry and regret, reviewing foolish mistakes, lost opportunities, the rancid memory of bad girlfriends, and other apparitions from the past. The best way to avoid such torture, I've learned, is to get out of bed, no matter what the hour, and get on with the day, even if everybody else in the world is fast asleep. This morning I went down to the garage, emptied my gear bag on the floor, and began sorting through a year's accumulation of chaos.

When I was younger, I could leave home for days at a time with nothing but a toothbrush and a little cash. Now I'm afraid to leave the house without my gear bag. The old mountain men called that their "bag of possibles" because when everything went wrong, as they knew it surely would, whatever they had in that bag was what was possible.

I first started carrying a gear bag during my years on a backcountry trail crew. It was just a small pouch then, and it contained a solution to whatever went wrong during my last misadventure: toilet paper, matches, a sewing kit, Band-aids, a scrap of writing paper rolled around a pencil stub, insect repellant, bootlaces, etc. Now my gear bag is the size of a duffel bag, and in addition to all the mountain gear, it includes sunscreen, zinc oxide, rash guard, spare surf trunks, extra fins, wax, an EMT kit, and much more.

Many of my friends and family members have warned me that this is neurotic behavior, that bad things will always happen, and that I will never be able to foresee and prevent every one of them. Which is probably true. But I've already foreseen enough bad things to bail out each of them—some of them many times.

Later today, after surfing, I told my friend Dr. Lynn about my encounter with the kissing bug, the severe reaction I'd had, and my regret for not having an Epipen on hand.

"Go to the Farmacia Dorada," he advised me. "Buy a kit of Celestone. It's a corticosteroid that works great for severe allergic reactions—maybe even better than Epipen because it lasts longer. It comes with a syringe, and you don't need a prescription."

So now I must also add Celestone to my bag of possibles.

May 28

The remnants of the first big hurricane of the year, Hurricane Bud, are spinning raggedly off mainland Mexico, a thousand miles south of us. At its peak, the hurricane kicked up winds in the 90-miles-per-hour range, but that had almost no effect on surf here on the East Cape. In fact, I can see from looking at the surf forecasts today that we're probably going to have a five- or six-day lull, which is unusual for this time of year. And a bit depressing.

Until this morning, I hadn't seen an up-to-date surf forecast for several days because our internet service has been down. Three days ago I called Osmar, our service provider, and let him know the network in Zacatitos wasn't working. Usually he responds immediately, but he was slow this time.

Visitors to Zacatitos often remark how odd it is that we live in a place without electrical lines, phone lines, water lines, or even reliable cellphone service, yet we have high-speed internet. Osmar's service comes to us via radio signals from his tower in San José, relayed to his antenna on the mountain east of Zacatitos, and then beamed down to the small antenna on our roof. His setup is an odd mix of crude equipment with state-of-the-art technology—very Mexican.

A couple of years ago, our neighbor Curtis hiked to the top of the rugged mountain where Osmar's relay antenna is installed. "At first I wasn't sure what I was looking at," he told me later. "I thought maybe I'd stumbled on an old plane wreck. It took me a minute to figure out that this was where we got our internet."

Later, when I climbed the mountain myself, I saw what

Curtis meant. The antenna was a makeshift pole lashed together from aluminum pipes. The guylines holding it up looked like baling wire twisted around the pole on one end and wrapped around rocks on the other. The electricity came from car batteries wedged in crevasses among the rocks, and they were charged by solar panels so old they were scorched brown by the sun. All the routers and relay equipment were housed in what looked like an old war-surplus wooden trunk.

Although I talk to Osmar by cellphone from time to time, I usually see him in person only once a year, when he comes around to collect his annual fee. Because the mail system in Mexico is dysfunctional (the mail personnel open the letters and packages and steal anything valuable), a monthly payment plan is impossible. So Osmar offers only one payment scheme: $600 for the entire year, in cash, prepaid, take it or leave it.

Osmar is a surprisingly young man with a wife and family. Like so many Mexicans, he taught himself English by watching American movies on TV. He studied science and math at local schools, but he tells me that most of what he knows about computer technology he taught himself. "I know I'll never get rich doing this," he said. "Mexico doesn't work like that. But I think maybe I can make a living at it." He has a very strong dose of that Mexican talent for making things work under nearly impossible conditions. He does it with intelligence, hard work, and that Mexican combination of extreme pessimism tempered with extreme optimism. One of my greatest surprises after moving to Mexico was discovering that this country has millions of bright young people like Osmar.

So today, Osmar finally drove all the way out to our house in Zacatitos to diagnose the problem we were having. Using my laptop, he typed a few lines of code that changed settings on his equipment up on the mountain, and suddenly our internet worked perfectly again. It took him all of thirty seconds.

The effect the internet has had on Mexico is already greater than the effect of all its celebrated revolutions combined. Information now is cheap, instantaneous, and irrepressible, and it is fueling the public's demands for greater democracy and political transparency. For people who can't afford internet in the home, there are cybercafes everywhere that provide an hour of internet use for about ten pesos, or 75 cents. The biggest impact of the internet here has probably been on freedom of speech. Anybody can set up a chat room, blogsite, or message board in minutes, and Mexicans participate in these sites with great passion. But the internet has also had a tremendous impact on small businesses. Just yesterday I told our water deliveryman, José, that I had wanted to call him a week ago to order a load of water, but I had run out of minutes on my cellphone.

"You can always contact me by internet," he suggested.

José's truck is held together by surf decals and rust, his pants are held up by a piece of rope, and I had a hard time imagining him sitting at a computer. "You have an email address?" I asked.

He smiled politely at my lack of technological sophistication. "No, I'm on *fa-cey* book," he said. "My picture is the Virgin of Guadalupe. If you send me a *solicitación*, I will *fren* you."

May 29

Driving home alone after my morning surf check, I came across the pregnant burro that had been lying in our arroyo a few days ago. She was standing in the open field across from Zac's Bar and Grill, and behind her was her newborn burrito. It wasn't much bigger than Kirra, though its legs were much longer, knock-kneed, and still wobbly. Its hooves were scarcely bigger than my thumb.

I shut off the Rhino to watch the two for a minute. The mother was chewing on what appeared to be an old, brown head of cabbage, while the newborn was busy learning how to walk. After a minute, the curious newborn took notice of the Rhino and wobbled over to sniff its tail. But Mom wasn't about to tolerate that, and she charged forward to separate us. I agreed with her—it wouldn't do to have a newborn burro bonding with an ATV—so I started the engine and drove away.

May 30

The weather has finally turned warm. The midday highs are around 95, which some people here think is too hot. But it seems to me that 95 degrees is just about perfect for a mammal that's hairless, naked, and lives mostly in the shade.

A lot of the people with homes in Zacatitos are snowbirds. They come down from Canada, Colorado, Idaho, and Oregon to escape the cold winters. And I don't blame them. But many of them have no tolerance for heat. Especially the Canadians. Anything over 88 degrees and they turn lightheaded, their faces flush red, and sweat begins to flow. Most of them can't bear Baja at all after the vernal equinox. They run home to their ice caves and spend the next six months watching snow melt. That's fine with me. This little town becomes quiet and peaceful this time of year.

Cool ocean breezes usually blow all day, but in the evening the onshore flow stops, and things can sometimes get uncomfortable. Air-conditioning is almost impossible for a house running off photovoltaics—we don't have enough juice—but in this dry climate, a ceiling fan over the bed works almost as well. Sometime in the night—often not until early morning—a cold breeze begins to flow down from the north, and we have to turn off the fan and pull our blankets over us again.

That night wind is the cold air falling off the 7,000 foot Lagunas and drawing down the big arroyos all the way to the sea, like an invisible river of cold air. As a surfer, I like to see that north wind blowing at dawn. It's an offshore breeze that might put a nasty bump on the ocean during the night, but it never lasts more than an hour after the sun comes up. Then the surface of the water often becomes glassy, and we might have two, or even three, hours of beautiful calm.

Or that ugly east wind can start blowing hard out of the gulf right after sunrise and ruin the entire day in just a few minutes.

It's not easy being a surfer. All of nature's elements have to come together at just the right time. It would have been easier to take up bowling, billiards, or bridge, where nature plays no role, or perhaps computer games, where you can adjust the weather conditions at the main menu to suit your mood. I can't help it now, though. I chose to become a surfer, and it's too late to change.

The surf forecasts are calling for a big south swell to arrive this Saturday. We will see.

May 31

Like a lot of men, I sometimes get accused of not being romantic. I don't think that's the case, but I must admit I'm not big on wedding anniversaries, Valentine's Day, or second honeymoons. In my experience, couples who need to make a big fuss over their display of affection often have the weakest marriages. Claudia married me at a quickie wedding chapel, so she knew what she was getting into. If she gives me a hard time about it, I remind her that she wore cotton long johns on our wedding night.

But in this, our twenty-fifth year of marriage, I decided I

wanted to do something special for Claudia, something that truly showed how much I love her. So I bought her a Mexican colonoscopy.

I read in the *New York Times* that in recent years many routine health screenings—like those for prostate cancer and breast cancer—have been shown to do more harm than good. Early diagnosis and aggressive treatment sometimes end up costing more lives than they save. But colonoscopies for people over fifty are different. They have been statistically shown to save lives. And I knew it was time for Claudia to have hers.

When we first moved to Mexico, we bought international health insurance, which is relatively inexpensive but has a high deductible. That way, we'll be covered for catastrophic situations but end up paying for our routine care out of pocket. That's okay, though, because in Mexico routine medicine is much cheaper than it is in the U.S.

Sometimes we hear gringos who live in Baja say things like: "If I get sick, don't take me to the hospital, take me to the airport!" To me that sounds like another bit of gringo arrogance. It's true that Mexican doctors have less training than U.S. doctors—a student in Mexico can become a licensed physician just six years after high school. But what good are highly trained U.S. doctors if their services are so expensive that a third of the people in the U.S. can't afford them? From what I've seen, the doctors in Mexico do a very good job, and they do it with far fewer resources. I once watched a Mexican doctor extract a large, stubborn bug from our son's ear using a suction device he fashioned from a hypodermic needle.

Not long ago, I said to Dr. Lynn, "I think it's time for Claudia to have a colonoscopy. If it were your colon, would you have that done here in Baja?"

"Sure, I would!" he said. "Otherwise, you'd have to fly up north, pay several thousand dollars for the procedure, pay even more for the anesthesiologist, then fly back home.

That's a pretty damned expensive enema. Or you can have it done locally in about thirty minutes for forty-five hundred pesos." (About $320.)

"But would you trust the results?" I asked.

"Well, it ain't rocket science!" he said. "Of course I'd trust the results!"

So, following Dr. Lynn's advice, I requested an appointment by email with an endoscopic surgeon in San José who has impeccable credentials, excellent recommendations, and a magnificent name—Dr. Jorge Holguín Aragón. The doctor, who speaks and writes very little English, replied immediately that he would be delighted to see us on Saturday.

Shipwreck Library

Jeff King at Punta Perfecta

June:

The Illusion of Weightlessness

June 2

Dr. Holguin had already sent me the detailed instructions, in Spanish, for Claudia's preparation. They included fasting for a day, then taking two doses of a potent laxative. Claudia followed his instructions faithfully, which meant that neither one of us slept much last night.

Early this morning, we took the beach road into town, and as we rounded the overlook at Punta Gorda, I saw with relief that the big south swell predicted for today hadn't arrived yet.

The office of Dr. Holguin is in one of San José's oldest neighborhoods, and remember, this is a city 300 years old. The area has a vibrant and colorful blend of restaurants, funeral homes, beauticians, astrologers, private residences, and medical clinics. One of our favorite *taquerías*, La Michoacana, where freshly butchered pigs hang for the customers' inspection under the shade of stout mango trees, was just a block away. Gringos, with their obsession for order, often find such neighborhoods confusing, perhaps even distasteful, but in Mexico this is how things are done. Zoning pretensions hold no merit.

Claudia and I arrived early, so we parked on the street and caught a few moments' sleep before Dr. Holguin arrived in his Jeep Wrangler to open his office door.

Dr. Holguin is a few years younger than me a touch shy, with a quiet voice and a surgeon's soft hands. In his office we saw that he had a sentimental affection for owls—their images and ceramic figurines covered his walls and desk. His surgery room, which was in fact the same room as his office but separated by a partition, had a more clinical tone.

Dr. Holguin took Claudia's history; then he and I chatted for a few moments while Claudia changed into her surgery gown. With the arrival of the anesthesiologist, a young man in blue jeans carrying his equipment in a fishing tackle box, we were ready to begin. To my surprise and delight, the doctor graciously invited me to watch the procedure.

With three different monitors, including a new 26-inch Samsung LCD, the secrets of my wife's bowels were revealed in full color. Even without narration or sound track, it was more entertaining than most slick Hollywood productions. Claudia's colon was as brightly lit as a fish tank, and we were the fish, on a wondrous and impossible tour of discovery, seeing things nobody had ever seen before and in splendid detail—every pink undulation, every pristine vein, every throbbing corridor. It was a fascinating and oddly religious experience. How is it possible that in a universe of cold chaos, such beautiful things could have come about?

Our anesthesiologist managed the endoscope's plastic hose, counting off the centimeters of penetration, while Dr. Holguin focused on the endoscope's controls, twisting his body in kinesthetic anticipation of the pathway ahead, shifting his weight from foot to foot, and adding just a touch of body English as he rounded the splenic fixture and gained entry to the transverse colon. The doctor's sense of balance and use of body torque reminded me of surfing. And to my great relief, I saw that our friend Dr. Lynn had been right. This wasn't rocket science. It was more like PlayStation. If there had been a polyp, a cancer, or any other abnormality, it would have had no place to hide. We would have seen it, right there, in 26-inch color.

After the procedure was finished and the doctor had assured me that my wife's colon was in perfect condition, we had nothing to do but kill time while we waited for Claudia to recover from the anesthesia. So I said to Dr. Holguin. "Well, now I've seen a normal colon. But I still have no idea what an abnormal colon looks like."

Dr. Holguin smiled modestly, obviously pleased that I took an interest in his work. He opened up his laptop, and together we reviewed hundreds of photos he had taken of colon abnormalities. I saw a routine appendicitis. I saw common polyps, which looked huge but the doctor insisted were no larger than five millimeters. I saw troubling photos of diverticulitis, a disease that gnaws at the walls of the colon. And I saw dark, horrifying photos of colon cancer, which the doctor assured me his patient might have survived had the disease been detected in time.

As we were leaving, Dr. Holguin handed me a DVD copy of Claudia's colonoscopy. It was a movie I'd already seen, but I thanked him anyway, thinking we might send copies out to family and friends at Christmas.

Claudia hadn't eaten in a day and a half, so on our way home I stopped at a mini-super to buy her a strawberry yogurt drink and a few *dominico* bananas—the small kind with orange flesh and a delightfully tart flavor. Claudia was still a bit groggy, but in a dreamy, Marilyn Monroe sort of way. "Thank you for taking such good care of me," she said.

I kissed her on the cheek. "Just remember, when you think I'm not romantic, nothing says I love you like a colonoscopy."

June 3

That tardy south swell we have been waiting for finally

arrived during the night. Starting around midnight, I could hear it booming all across Zacatitos. By dawn, though, the east wind was blowing in gusts that rattled the coco palms and masked the thunder of the waves, and I was afraid the surf conditions would be impossible.

We drove out to the East Cape before the sun came up, anyway, and I surfed for three hours in ugly chop. The waves were in the 8-foot range, which wasn't as big as I'd hoped, but on this, the leading edge of the swell, they were powerful enough to overcome the rough surface conditions. Often the first wave in the set would be so ragged it was nearly unrideable, but its rolling motion smoothed out the inside section for the following waves, and with a little patience I was picking off some decent rides.

I have a big, cobalt blue 9'6" Kies that I like to ride on days like this. It has a swallowtail, straighter rail lines, and a lot of volume. I call it a big fish. It paddles very well, has enough weight to cut right through most chop, and is extremely fast once I get it pointed down the line. It won't turn as quickly as my smaller boards—especially on cutbacks—but on days like today, the whole game is getting into the waves early and carrying as much speed as possible. So even in these lousy conditions, I managed to have my fun.

June 4

Today we had an hour right after sunrise when the waves were about as clean and glassy as they ever get on the East Cape. Those of us in the water at first light could see the purple wind line half a mile out to sea, though, and we knew those perfect conditions wouldn't last. Everybody was scrambling frantically to get in as many good rides as possible before the door slammed shut.

While I was paddling back out after a long ride, I watched All-Day Ray playing with a gnarled monster of a wave. He started much farther back than we normally do, but he caught the wave while it was steep, which allowed him to pick up speed early, then fly across that long wall at high velocity, carving smooth little top turns all along the lip. It was a beautiful thing to see, and he did it so gracefully. Ray is 6'4" and thin, which makes him look as if he's moving in slow motion. I think tall surfers have an unfair advantage that way. But then sometimes shorter people can be graceful too.

There was a woman in the water today we call Colorado Kim. She's a former world extreme-skiing champion, with tremendous physical talent, but relatively new to surfing. Over the past few years, we've enjoyed watching Kim learn this sport, curious to see what a first-class athlete could do. What we saw were athletic intelligence, natural balance, fierce determination, and a lot of courage. But she still had to learn wave judgment and timing and then practice over and over the motions of coming to her feet and carving a turn at the same time that she's watching the wave develop behind her back. Kim learned fast, though, and today I saw her spot a sizeable wave developing far outside, quickly paddle 200 feet to put herself in good position, then, right at the last second, swing around and take off on one of the biggest waves of the day. And she pulled it off with remarkable grace and poise.

When I watch surfers who are more graceful than I will ever be, I wonder, Where does that come from? How can some people create the illusion of flying? Is there a graceful gene, and you either have it or you don't? Could somebody like me learn it through practice or, as I fear, is that talent hidden so deep inside me that you couldn't even find it with a colonoscopy?

To me, the essence of athletic grace is the ability to make gravity disappear, to become weightless. By the laws of physics, this is impossible, yet great athletes are able to do it: pole vaulters, volleyball players, ballet dancers, wide receivers, gymnasts, cliff divers, ski jumpers, basketball players—I've even seen 300-pound shot-putters who could, for one brief moment, create the illusion of weightlessness. But I don't think any of those athletes come close to being as graceful as a great surfer.

June 6

Unfortunately, this swell is dying fast. There are still shoulder-high waves, but that's pretty dull action after what we've seen over the last couple of days. Still, I paddled out, thinking we might not see anything better for a while.

Powerful south winds have been blowing at night again, and we've had another cold-water turnover. The churning action has caused the water to lose its clear, tropical blue color and replaced it with a murky, greenish brown. Also, the jellyfish appeared today in amazing numbers. Their ugly blobs lined the beach, and when I paddled out I could feel them in the water with my hands, like heavy chunks of Jell-O. The water was still cold enough that I could wear a full wetsuit for protection. Later this afternoon, though, back at home, I developed red and purple welts at my ankles and wrists. And now they're starting to itch.

June 9

We're suffering through one of the longest and most frustrating lulls of this year. The global surf models show a large storm off the west coast of New Zealand, and it's powerful enough to generate large waves, but their northward trajectory is blocked by that island's land mass. There's another large storm off southern Chile, but it's hugging the South American coastline so closely that the chances of its waves striking Baja are almost nil. So winter in the southern hemisphere is spewing out massive fits of fury, but none of that energy is reaching us.

We expect lulls like this in the winter, of course. We keep ourselves busy by puttering around the house, fixing leaking toilets, chasing hairballs behind the refrigerator, and pruning palm fronds. If we get to a point where we just can't stand it anymore, we can always drive over to the west side of the peninsula and surf in the Pacific's frigid waters. But here on the East Cape, in the month of June, we expect big surf, we need big surf, we just don't always get it.

Like a lot of surfers, I'm vulnerable to self-pity. Patience can only get you so far, and then frustration sets in. This morning I woke before dawn, made coffee, then went out to sit on the terrace with Kirra, where I could hear the surf. When we first moved here, surf all sounded the same to me— sometimes louder, sometimes softer, but mostly just random noise. Over time, I learned to listen to the ocean's rhythms and sort out the interval patterns, sound directions and, most of all, energy intensity. What I heard today, though, was a sleepy, insipid drool, like shopping mall music. So I sat in the dark feeling sorry for myself. When Claudia finally came out to join me with her morning coffee, she sat down and said, "What a beautiful day. Gorgeous sky, not too hot, and no wind at all."

"I hate days like this," I replied.

June 12

Finally, we got a break from the monotonous lull that has tortured us for the past week. Nothing on the surf forecasts indicated a change was coming, but sometimes even surfers get lucky. My best guess is that somewhere out in the vast ocean, two mediocre swells combined to create one decent-sized swell packing a fair amount of energy. Plus, the tide was going out and the wind was calm all morning long. It wasn't what I'd call great surf, but it was good enough. I surfed four hours on crisp, hollow, shoulder-high waves.

One unusual thing about today was that there were more women in the water than men. I don't think I've ever seen that happen here before. Back in California, when surfers behaved aggressively, we used to say, "There's a lot of testosterone in the water today." This morning, though, I'd have to say there was a lot of estrogen in the water, and I found it to be a pleasant change. We all chatted politely during the lulls, complimented each other on the way our surf trunks matched the colors of our surfboards, refrained from scratching our crotches, spit only when nobody was looking, got all caught up on the news of our children and spouses, and exchanged many useful beauty and nutrition tips. When the sets finally came, we unselfishly waited our turn.

Colorado Kim shared one piece of information that interested me very much. She said that when she knows she's been stung badly by jellyfish, she shaves her legs, on the theory that the razor scrapes away the microscopic barbs, preventing them from releasing more toxin. She says this definitely helps.

"It's okay for women to shave their legs," I said. "I totally approve. But men can't do that."

"Swimmers do it," Kim replied. "Cyclists do it. Why not surfers?"

I'd always assumed that hairy people, like men, have more natural protection from jellyfish. Now, after just one day of surfing with the girls, I was wondering if I should be shaving my legs.

"I'd rather wear pantyhose," I grumbled, and paddled away.

June 13

The clean little swell from yesterday is holding up fairly

well. Right after sunrise, there were only a few of us in the water, but eventually other surfers, who had about given up on seeing decent surf this week, figured out what was going on. By midmorning, the point was crowded, and some of us started looking around for other options. On the East Cape, there are always waves going unridden somewhere. You just have to go look for them.

Punta Espina is a long right (a wave breaking from left to right from the point of view of the surfer) and well suited to a person who surfs with the left foot forward. But sometimes it's possible to go left there as well. Goofy-footers, who surf with the right foot forward, and are a minority, enjoy days like that. Frontside, facing the wave is always better. Going backside will make most surfers look awkward. So, on most days, that left goes unridden.

I've had the notion lately that I could avoid the problems of going backside by teaching myself to ride goofy-foot. I figured that because I had been a telemark skier for so many years, switching stance on every turn should come natural to me. All I had to do was practice, and today looked as good as any day to start.

In the longboard days of my youth, we used to see guys who were masters at switching stance. They could do it on every cutback, if they wanted to. But switching stance has become a lost art, mostly because it's harder to do on shorter, narrower boards. Plus, the footwork is a bit complicated. To do it with a simple little bird hop sounds easy, but it isn't. I once asked Mike Doyle how longboarders did that maneuver back in his Malibu days. He thought about it for a moment, then showed me an intricate dance in the sand, followed by a shrug of the shoulders. "It was never really my thing," he said.

So I thought to myself, well, I won't switch stance at all. As soon as I catch the wave, I'll come to my feet with my right foot already forward. I figured it would be easier that way. But I soon learned otherwise. On the next four waves, every time I came to my feet, no matter how hard I tried, I just couldn't force that right foot forward. It refused to obey my command. It wasn't really the right foot's fault, either. What was happening was that my left foot refused to relinquish control, even though it made a damned fool of itself on every left-breaking wave. And my right foot was too passive, or perhaps too polite, to assert itself.

One of the greatest advantages of being young is that you don't have to unlearn something old before you learn something new. But change is inevitable, and I figure if we can't at least try, we might as well die and get out of the way.

June 14

Over the past two days, I've accumulated an unreasonable number of jellyfish stings. Everybody has. The water is warmer, which brings out the *aguamalas*, and a full wetsuit is just too damned hot to wear now. I've started wearing a tight-fitting, long-sleeved rash guard, which protects my arms and chest, but my legs have become a raw mass of oozing welts. For some reason, the itching gets worse at night. I had to get up around two o'clock last night and take a long, hot shower. I wasn't ready to follow Colorado Kim's advice about shaving yet, but I liked her logic, so I used soap and a stiff-bristled brush to scrub the welts, in the hope that I might remove some of the barbs. Then I dried off and applied hydrocortisone cream. This allowed me to get back to sleep, but getting up early enough to go surfing was out of the question.

I saw later this morning that the swell has dropped off anyway.

June 17

We're stuck again in another lull. When we first moved to Baja, it seemed as if there was no such thing as a lull. The surf was almost constant—at least in the spring, summer, and fall. I realize now, though, that in those days I was so surf starved I would paddle out in almost any conditions and surf for two hours in ignorant bliss. Small, windblown, or sloppy—I didn't much care. Now I've seen too many days of perfect overhead glass. If my favorite spots don't look like the cover of a surf magazine, I'm not interested.

Over the past couple of days, I've been watching the pair of hooded orioles who built their nest in a coco palm outside our kitchen window. Actually, it was the smaller, drab-colored female who built the nest. That's fitting, since she's the one who will be spending so much time there.

After she'd finished her nest, the oriole laid her eggs in the pouch and burrowed down with just her head poking out. For some reason, she turned fidgety and had a hard time staying put. Now she hardly spends any time there at all, always flying off to some other task or amusement. Maybe in a warm climate like this, it isn't necessary for her to sit on the eggs during the entire incubation period, I don't know. Or maybe she just isn't cut out to be a mother.

What concerned me most about the female oriole's absence was the presence of a couple of aggressive gray thrashers who have been hanging around the coco palms. These are big, noisy, hyperactive birds with long, hooked bills that can do a lot of damage. They're mostly interested in insects, but I've seen them eat small lizards too, so I know they have a taste for meat. Already this spring, I've watched the thrashers raid and destroy a finch nest. Unlike the orioles, the thrashers are wary of swaying palm fronds, but they stay close by in a tall *palo blanco*, waiting for the wind to calm down enough for them to plunder the orioles' nest.

I had assumed that the male oriole had moved on after fulfilling his reproductive role. Why hang around listening to the female complain about the unfair division of labor, or how her nest wasn't quite to her satisfaction, or how she should have chosen a more desirable mate? But then I saw something that surprised me—the male oriole hadn't taken off at all. He'd been watching the nest from a distance. As soon as the thrashers tried to raid the nest, he was there to do battle with them. I watched him relentlessly attack the much bigger thrashers, driving them away from the nest again and again, at great risk to himself, until he eventually forced the thrashers to flee. I thought he did a noble job of representing male orioles, and he made me feel better about myself too.

Is it possible, I wondered, that the bright color of the male oriole isn't to attract a female, as I had assumed, but to serve as a warning to predators like the thrashers that a male protector is on duty and ready to do battle?

June 18

The international G20 economic summit is being held in Los Cabos this week. All the hotels and restaurants are filled, and the highway is clogged with traffic. So we're avoiding San José. Passenger planes have been circling overhead almost constantly, waiting for their turn to land at Los Cabos airport. From our deck here in Zacatitos, we can see the Mexican navy patrolling up and down the coast, and we watched the black helicopters ferrying President Calderón's entourage over from the mainland.

Along with the finance ministers, their staffs, and journalists covering the event, this summit will bring more than 10,000 people into San José. It will be a huge boost for the local economy, at least for those businesses that have some connection to the tourist industry. But as I talk to Mexicans here and read the local newspapers, I am beginning to realize that what the people of Mexico want most from this summit is a little international respect. If I had to name one thing that is harming Mexico the most and preventing it from taking its rightful place in the world, I would say it's a poor self-image.

Mexicans began their modern history as a conquered people. Even after they won their independence from Spain, they suffered the humiliation of losing most of their territory to their rapacious neighbors to the north. And Mexico has always suffered the misfortune of having its economy compared unfavorably to the most materialistic nation the world has ever seen.

But if Mexico were an island nation and free from comparison to the U.S., it would be considered a great economic success. In the G20—by definition the twenty largest economies in the world—Mexico ranks thirteenth. It's the largest Spanish-speaking nation in the world, with twice the population of Spain. Its economy is vibrant and dynamic, its people hardworking and ingenious, and its resources plentiful. In recent years, Mexico has made great strides in modernizing its infrastructure and technology.

So why, Mexicans wonder, does the rest of the world treat us as if we were a third world country? I think Mexicans are truly puzzled by this. They can't understand why the *norteamericanos*, especially, treat them with such contempt. To their great credit—and my almost daily embarrassment— they never seem to despise us in return. They pay us great respect for our popular music, our movies, our technological innovation and, most of all, our personal independence. At the same time, they politely ignore our military aggressiveness, our ignorant and offensive politicians, our religious fanaticism, our self-righteousness, our hypocrisy, and our greed.

I think many Mexicans understand intuitively what most Americans can't: that things have been very good north of the border for many years, but they're now getting worse.

And at the same time, things in Mexico have been very bad for just as long, but they're now getting better. This, to me, explains the optimism I see in Mexico every day. I think Mexicans know a new day is coming. They've worked hard for it, they deserve it, and I'm looking forward to it as much as they are.

June 21

Over the past several days, a tropical storm has been stalled off the coast of mainland Mexico, 500 miles south of us. At one time the storm had an 80-percent chance of developing into a hurricane, but as it meandered north, it found the cold water we've been experiencing all spring and it quickly dissipated. Apparently, though, the storm produced some fairly strong winds, because late yesterday we started seeing decent surf along the East Cape. My guess is that a modest-sized southern hemi passed through that storm, and the storm's wind added an extra punch to the swell. Last night at sunset, the surf looked ragged and disorganized—like storm surf—but this morning the waves looked much cleaner. I surfed for two hours in 8-foot surf, with some sets even bigger.

When it comes to describing surf quality, wave height can be a bit deceptive. Sometimes an 8-foot wave can be so thin it's almost transparent, and getting hit by it is like walking through the spray from a garden hose. These waves today, though, were thick grinders, and getting hit by one was like being in a car wreck without a seatbelt. Just the sound was intimidating.

Once today, a 10-foot wave caught me by surprise. I saw it peaking a hundred feet farther out than anything I'd seen all morning, and I scrambled toward it, hoping to get over the lip before it broke. But I got a sick feeling when I realized I wasn't going to make it and the lurching monster was going to break right on my head.

For me, that's about the worst thing that can happen in surfing. That's how boards and bones get broke. In the days before we wore leashes, in situations like that, we usually tried to hold on to our boards to avoid the long swim in. Sometimes we would try to paddle up the face of the wave, then shove the board over to the other side.

Today I took the coward's escape. I paddled hard until I was sure I was going to get crushed, glanced behind me to make sure no other surfers were close by, and then abandoned my board and dove as deep as I could. Fortunately, the leash held, but I was battered and thrashed and tossed around underwater like a limp piece of rope.

I learned way back in my Santa Cruz days that you can't fight power like that. I tried my best to relax and roll with the flow—that uses less energy and conserves air the longest. When I was finally released and floated to the surface, Colorado Kim, who was watching from about a hundred feet away, called out, "Are you okay? You were held down a really long time!"

"Yeah, I'm fine," I said.

When I was 25 and could hold my breath for more than a minute, I thought it was fun to get hit by a powerful wave like that. I wasn't afraid. Now, I'm still not afraid, but I'm well aware that a wave like that could kill me.

June 22

I'm afraid I might have been unkind in my judgment of the thrashers the other day, when I called them loud and aggressive. I wasn't pleased with their attempts to raid the orioles' nest in our coco palm, but sometimes nature can be cruel, or at least it appears that way to human beings. I'm beginning to see now that the thrashers have their admirable qualities too.

The thrashers spend most of their time picking insects from the cracks and creases of the *cardon* cacti, as well as from the bark of the *palo blancos*, and I'm sure this helps to keep the mosquitoes and other pests in check. In Mexico, mosquitoes carry malaria and dengue fever. While it's true that mosquito populations are fairly small in the desert—or at least in non-irrigated deserts like this one—malaria forced the Spanish settlers to move the location of their village in San José from the banks of the wet *estero* to a drier site farther inland. The Spanish didn't know that mosquitoes spread the disease their people were dying from, but they understood the danger of living by pools of stagnant water, and after they moved inland, their malaria problem was relieved. Of course, during the rainy season, which will be here soon, mosquitoes can breed almost anywhere. So I appreciate whatever help the thrashers can provide.

Another thing I'm learning to admire about the thrashers is their intense energy level. You would think that in a hot, dry environment, they would conserve their energy and body fluids by seeking shade during the day. But that's thinking like a gringo. These are Mexican birds, and like the Mexican people, they become more energetic the hotter the day becomes. Either they don't think the day is all that hot, or they prefer it that way.

What I appreciate most about the thrashers, though, is their amazing ability to imitate sound. I read in one of Claudia's bird books that some thrashers have as many as 3,000 songs in their repertoire. To them, a song can be just about any noise they find interesting. I heard the thrashers screeching and cackling for months before I noticed that one of them had learned to imitate the whistle I use for calling Kirra to dinner. The first time I heard it clearly, I went outside to see if maybe it was one of our neighbors walking up the road to our house.

When I heard it again, I realized it was a thrasher imitating me. I glanced at Kirra, but she rolled her eyes as if to say, "It's just those damned thrashers. Can't you tell?" And when I listened again, I could hear that the whistle wasn't just an imitation, it was a stylized exaggeration, ridiculing my air of stern self-importance. In other words, it was a mockery.

Once I realized what the thrashers were up to, hanging around our house and imitating our sounds, I started paying closer attention. I've heard them imitate my cellphone's ringtone now and Claudia's as well. I've heard them imitate the house finches, the orioles, and the mourning doves, and I've heard them make a good imitation of a rattlesnake too. They imitate the sound of Kirra's squeaky chew toys, and the hum of our water pump.

This afternoon, I heard one of the thrashers working a new song—the most amazing imitation of all. It wasn't a perfect rendition yet, but I was able to recognize it as a sound we'd been hearing for several days from a nearby construction site. The thrasher, from his perch atop a cactus outside our bedroom window, was practicing the sound of an electric drill, starting at low rpm, accelerating up to full speed, warbling in vibrato for a few seconds, and then slowly decelerating to a stop.

You have to love a bird that would even attempt something like that.

June 27

Claudia, along with a few other women in town, attended a ballet recital in San José the other night. I was spared forced attendance this time, but I've been hearing all about how beautifully the children danced. A father here in town—a surfer whose daughter was in the recital—made a mandatory appearance. "Everybody said they'd never seen him in long pants or with his hair combed before," Claudia said. "But he *was* still wearing flip-flops."

I've endured my share of dance performances—those of my sisters, nieces, neighbors, and even my own wife, who is enthralled with ballet. I almost got thrown out of a post-dance-recital party once for saying there should be a maximum age limit for wearing a tutu. If you give Claudia enough wine on any weekend, eventually she'll want to dance. Unfortunately, she married a man who is incapable of dancing with her. I have several excuses: I never saw my own father dance; I was forced to square dance against my will by my kindergarten teacher; my first girlfriend, who tried to teach me how to dance, broke my heart; etc. I've used all those excuses and more with Claudia at one time or another.

The reason I bring up this distasteful subject is that many people over the years have pointed out that surfing can be thought of as a kind of dancing. The similarities are undeniable: rhythm, style, music (imagined or real), practiced steps, colorful costumes, and at least an attempt at grace. I have tried to refute these comparisons by arguing that dancing is for show, a vain public spectacle, almost a neurotic plea for attention. Surfing, on the other hand, is a spontaneous act, a response to the movement of the wave. As soon as a surfer tries to see himself from outside his body, he invites disaster.

It's a weak argument, I know, shot full of holes. Sometimes in my darkest moments of doubt I come dangerously close to admitting that I am, as a surfer, a kind of repressed, or closet, dancer.

During this long and painful lull, many good surfers here on the East Cape have been driven to pitching horseshoes, painting in acrylics, drinking too much beer, and even reading novels. I don't know any who have taken up dancing yet, but then they wouldn't tell me if they had.

Looking forward, the long-range surf models have begun to show a flicker of new activity off New Zealand, and in a few more days we could be looking at some serious surf.

June 30

Zacatitos is almost deserted now. In this town of fifty houses, I suppose only ten or twelve are still occupied. Everybody has left in anticipation of the hot summer and the hurricanes. Yet the weather is still pleasant. The temperature rarely rises above 85 degrees in the day, and at night we need a blanket to stay warm.

The rainy season has officially begun, but still we have no rain. They say this is one of the worst droughts on record for southern Baja, but I'm not sure what that means. Europeans have been living here for only about 300 years, and this is, after all, a desert. Most of the plants act as if they expect the worst every summer. Cacti shrivel and fade, deciduous plants drop their leaves, and even agaves halt all growth. The entire landscape looks gray, drab, and dusty. Every now and then we will see the pink flowers of a coral vine, or perhaps the yellow flowers of a *palo de arco*, in full bloom, standing out in stark contrast to the colorless desert.

The ocean, of course, knows nothing about droughts. If you put on a dive mask and peek under the surface of the water, you might think you were in Hawaii. The rocky reefs are teeming with bass, snapper, clownfish, and many other species of tropical fish. The *panga* fishermen, however, say the fishing for dorado and yellowtail has not been good this year, due to the colder water.

Surfers who have lived here longer than I have say we need a heavy rain to push sand down the arroyos and smooth out our reef breaks. I believe them. I've seen photos from years past that show amazing breaks at places where I've never even seen rideable surf. The problem is that heavy gully washers also wash down the accumulated pollutants, which are mostly animal and human feces. So maybe it's best to stay out of the water for the worst of the rainy season. It's another reason we'll be heading north again soon. If only we could get some great surf before we go.

After checking the global wave models today, I see that the big south swell predicted last week is still heading this way. The swell doesn't show distinctly on the wave-size model, but it can clearly be seen rolling northward on the wave-interval model. I'm hoping for some overhead surf in a few more days.

Steve Sorensen at Punta Espina

July:

Something of a Repulsive Nature

July 1

This is Election Day in Mexico. At El Sacrificio, the beer depository where we buy Pacifico by the case, the owner warned me that I wouldn't be able to buy beer or any other alcohol over the weekend because of the *ley seca*, the dry law that goes into effect just before voting day. The owner complained bitterly that it was going to cost him a lot of money over the weekend. When I picked up a copy of *La Tribuna* so I could follow the latest election news, he pointed out that the issue was a day old. "That's okay," I said. "It takes me a week to read it, so it's all old news by then anyway."

Back home I read one of Josefina Vásquez Mota's final campaign speeches, given to a group of Mayan Indians in Yucatán. Josefina, the PAN candidate, and the first female presidential candidate in Mexico's history, is a wonderful and funny speaker. She told the women in the audience, "Our time has come. It's now or never. Half the voters are women, and the other half have a mother. If you are married, invite your men to vote, and tell them if they don't vote, they will not get the *'loch'* for one month." The Indian women in the audience laughed and applauded at the use of the Mayan word *loch*, which the reporter translated as "intimate embrace."

Some months ago, during a presidential debate, the centrist-right PRI candidate, Enrique Peña Nieto, who is married to a *telenovela* actress, was asked if he knew the current price for a kilo of tortillas. Embarrassed that he didn't, he simply mumbled, "I am not the woman of the house."

Josefina quickly and shrewdly took advantage of the moment by stepping forward and announcing proudly, "I am the woman of the house!"

Although Mexico is indeed a macho country, mothers here are strong and authoritative, and I thought it interesting that the ruling party, the PAN, chose a woman as their candidate. It showed courage and, for a conservative party, a refreshing willingness to embrace change. For a while Josefina was ahead in the polls, but not any longer. Manuel López Obrador, the liberal PRD candidate, who had the most to lose by Josefina's popularity, said, "Mexico does not need another mama." Now Josefina is trailing badly in the polls, and I don't expect that she will win. But it has certainly been fun watching her campaign.

During the final weeks of this presidential race, I was impressed by how impassioned the candidates became, how much humor they displayed, and how articulate their speeches were. I think the days of one-party rule in Mexico are over. I see a young but vibrant democracy growing here, and I don't believe the Mexican people will ever settle for anything less again.

July 2

We woke an hour before dawn to the sound of wind pushing our outdoor furniture across the terrace. I let Kirra inside—she hates a powerful wind because it interferes with her ability to hear and smell. Then I went out in my boxer shorts to secure our belongings and saw, far to the west, that a blood-red full moon was setting over the Lagunas. The air smelled like rain, and out to sea, maybe ten miles away, lightning flashed. But still, not a drop of rain fell.

On our morning walk we saw a *pitahaya* cactus in full bloom. In wet years, the *pitahayas* erupt in flowers about this time, and their seedpods grow heavy with fruit, but this year there are scarcely any in bloom. One brave *pitahaya*, though, had two beautiful, bugle-shaped, pink and white flowers, each maybe four inches long.

In previous years we have tasted the fruit of the *pitahaya*, which is similar to *tuna*, the fruit of the prickly pear, except that the flesh of the *pitahaya* is red and not nearly as sweet. The fruit and seeds of the *pitahayas* were an important source of food for the Pericú, and the way they used the fruit is fascinating. I've tried before to explain this process to people, but I've been called a liar for my efforts. So now I will leave that explanation to a firsthand witness, Padre Johann Jakob Baegert, who was here in southern Baja from 1749 to 1767:

At this point I ask permission of the patient reader to mention something of an exceedingly inhuman and repulsive nature, the like of which has probably never been told of any other people in the world.... I mentioned that the pitahayas contain a great many small seeds, resembling grains of powder, which for reasons unknown to me are not consumed in the stomach but passed in an undigested state. In order to use these small grains, the Indians collect all excrement during the season of the pitahayas, pick out these seeds from it, roast, grind, and eat them with much joking. This procedure is called by the Spaniards the after or second harvest! Whether all this happens because of want, voracity, or out of love for the pitahayas, I leave undecided.... It is useless to try to persuade them to abandon this old practice. They will not give it up.

July 4

Ante Maya Santa! Did we ever get lucky this time! The swell we've been waiting so long for finally arrived in the night. I was up by four in the morning and sat in the dark on the terrace with Kirra, drinking coffee and listening to the sound of powerful waves that had traveled unobstructed for 6,000 miles to crash upon our shores.

I was the first one in the water at Punta Espina. Fireman Tom paddled out on his SUP a few minutes later, followed by all the grizzled, sunburned, jellyfish-stung regulars who have arranged their lives to be ready for days like this one. The wind was calm, but there was still a slight bump on the ocean surface, caused by a tropical storm off mainland Mexico that these waves had passed through. We rode waves that were ten feet high, three hundred yards long, and breaking so fast that the entry had to be flawless, and the line taken had to be drawn with precision, to avoid being closed out and left trapped inside. But we were ready for this. Our shoulder muscles were as strong as they were ever going to be. Our sluggish brains had been slapped awake after twenty years of useless education and forty years of meaningless work, and through long practice, our neural pathways had been rewired for the rhythm and logic of waves. Our injuries and ailments had been patched, medicated, or massaged. And our fears had been compressed into those dark corners where we hide coiled snakes, shadows crossing overhead, and dancing in public. We were ready to surf.

What a wonderful morning we had.

This evening we celebrated American Independence Day at the home of Dr. Lynn and his wife, also Lynn, who live in a beachfront house in Zacatitos. Just about everybody still in town was at the party, the entire assortment of oddballs, cranks, and misfits who have followed California south until there was no place left to go. We have accidental millionaires who live like bowery bums and homeless people with the style and taste of Montecito socialites. We have bikers in gang colors and bicyclists in spandex. We have hapless fishermen, senile pot growers, and lecherous drunks. We have barefoot runners, plastic surgery addicts, tie-dyers, mushroom eaters, goat milkers, and herbal healers. We have woodworkers, weavers, and painters—both kinds, canvas and house. If the people in this improbable little pueblo have anything in common, I would say they're tougher than average, curious, adaptable, irreverent, and have an irrepressible appetite for fun that would get them in trouble just about anyplace else.

Out of pity, we allowed our Canadian friends to celebrate the Fourth of July with us, even though they speak with an odd accent, ramble on incessantly about ice hockey, measure everything in metrics, and can't surf. After one too many beers, I reminded them all that if they hadn't supported King George during the American Revolutionary War, they might have a proper independence day of their own to celebrate. But I must admit that after 240 years of listening to American music, watching American movies, drinking American wine, and driving American cars, they seem to have grasped the error of their ways. They did send us Neil Young as an apology, and I think it's time to let bygones be bygones.

July 5

All morning long the waves were 6 to 8 feet, perfectly glassy, very fast, and with long, steep shoulders. There were three to five waves per set—enough for everybody in the water to grab one if they were in good position—and then there would be a ten-minute break when the ocean turned flat and we could paddle lazily back outside, stretch our shoulders, and catch our breath.

June was a terrible month for surfing—the worst I've ever

seen here—and it was only a matter of time before the odds swung in our favor again. When thinking in terms of global events like massive storms in the southern hemisphere, it's meaningless to talk about luck. The gears will grind full circle. We had this swell coming. Antarctica owed us this one.

The water temperature rose dramatically overnight, going from about 70 degrees to over 80. That's not so unusual this time of year. Fireman Tom told me he once measured a water-temperature shift from 66 to 84 degrees in twenty-four hours. But this may be the last wild temperature fluctuation this year. Every day is getting a little warmer now, and the night temperatures aren't dropping much either.

Fireman Tom has a houseful of teenage relatives visiting from San Diego. They're all hot surfers, but they'd never been to Baja before. Tom said that watching the waves from the height and distance of his terrace, they were acting casually unimpressed. But once they paddled out and saw how great the conditions were, they lost their cool. They were riding shortboards, which usually don't work so well on this wave, but with the lower tide, these kids were dropping into the waves easily, then slashing huge roundhouse turns across the smooth 8-foot faces, spraying water fifteen feet into the air and howling with glee. It was a thrill watching them.

This was probably the best surf I've seen in a year. After three hours in the water, I started telling myself to save something for tomorrow. Don't be foolish, I said. You aren't a kid. Take the next wave in. But I didn't listen to my own advice. I ended up surfing four and a half hours, and when I finally washed up on the beach, I was so tired Claudia had to help me pull off my rash guard.

Claudia knows that when I surf as hard as I did today, I end up with a huge appetite, so tonight she's making a big batch of chicken enchiladas. I can already smell them in the oven.

July 6

Claudia was awake but not out of bed in time to go surfing with me this morning, and seeing I was in a hurry to beat the wind, she told me to go on without her. Downstairs I found Kirra already waiting in the bed of the Rhino, but without Claudia to watch her on the beach while I surfed, I had to leave her behind. She slinked up the stairs to the terrace, glancing back at me as if our friendship had been permanently damaged. So now I had two females mad at me. I felt guilty about leaving without them, but what's a surfer to do?

There's an urgency to surfing that nonsurfers can't seem to grasp. Ocean conditions change every minute, and a perfect swell comes with an expiration date. Serious surfers, the kind who rarely take anything else serious in their lives, know they have to get on it right now, while it's good. The more people and pets involved, the harder surfing gets.

After yesterday, though, today turned out to be a disappointment. The south swell is still in the water, even a bit bigger, but that tropical storm 500 miles to the south is having its way now too. Wind speeds inside the storm have doubled to about sixty knots, and it has veered west. So here on the cape, we're getting a lot of confused cross-swell mixed in with that beautiful southern hemi. In addition, an ugly east wind started blowing early.

I paddled out just after sunrise, and after getting battered, cartwheeled, and held under a few times, I managed to catch a couple of waves in the 10-foot range. Nobody else joined me. I don't know if they were exhausted from yesterday or if, after watching me from the bluff and seeing how I got tossed around in the rough surf, they decided it wasn't worth it.

I saw an unusual number of porcupinefish bobbing around in the water—victims of the big surf—and I've been wondering about these strange creatures all day.

They're called porcupinefish because their bodies are covered with sharp spines. Unlike the blue-gray gnatcatchers that seek shelter among tangles of boxthorn, the porcupinefish wear their protection everywhere they go. They, or a closely related species, are found in tropical waters all over the world, and their flesh, particularly their livers, is extremely toxic. The poison, tetrodotoxin, is said to be 1200 times more poisonous than cyanide. Humans who ingest the poison but survive are rendered temporarily paralyzed, though still conscious. A brilliant ethnobotanist named Wade Davis wrote a fascinating and controversial book called *The Serpent and the Rainbow*, making a case for his belief that the voodoo cult of Haiti is based on the toxin taken from these fish. According to Davis, the voodoo shamans, who perhaps learned their craft from African slaves, used the poison to turn their victims into zombies. The flesh of the porcupinefish is supposedly hallucinogenic and mildly euphoric, if it doesn't kill you. In Japan the flesh is considered a great delicacy, but only trained and certified chefs are allowed to prepare it because it's so poisonous. Still, people in Japan die every year from eating it.

I know nothing about eating porcupinefish myself and have no desire to learn. What I do know is that porcupinefish are the worst swimmers in the ocean. Their plump bodies are the exact opposite of hydrodynamic, and their fins are almost vestigial, like they toyed with the notion of becoming amphibians but lost conviction and abandoned the project halfway to completion. Perhaps their spines and their poison became a defensive afterthought, since they hadn't succeeded in any other evolutionary adaptation. The worst feature of these poorly designed fish, though, is that they have the ability to swallow air to control their depth in the water, but they have difficulty releasing it. So porcupinefish spend much of their lives bobbing around helplessly in a rough ocean, as inept in the water as a tourist just off the plane. Apparently they grow weak from the struggle, because after every big swell we find dozens of them washed up dead on the beach. Yet not only are they not endangered, they actually thrive. What a bizarre chain of mutations it must have been that led to a fish that can't swim.

July 7

The temperature was over 80 degrees before sunrise today, and the air felt like steam. Claudia and I have never experienced humidity like this. It's suffocating us—like taking a deep breath with a hot pillowcase over your head. The ocean temperature is even warmer than the air now, and at Punta Espina this morning, walking toward the shorebreak, I could feel the heat radiating off the water from twenty feet away.

The confused cross-swell from yesterday has disappeared, though, and the surf is much cleaner. In the hazy morning light, the surface of the water looked almost purple. Though the southern hemi has diminished in size and intensity, there were still some clean, head-high waves.

Jeff King was the only other surfer in the water when I paddled out. He has to head north in a few days to have a knee replacement, and with a three- to six-month recovery period ahead of him, this might be his last chance to surf in a long time. A couple of weeks ago, the orthopedic surgeon who will do Jeff's operation was here surfing with us. He cringed when he saw Jeff riding his SUP, and later he told Jeff, "Now that I've seen your X-rays, I can't bear to watch you surf."

Even surfing on one leg, Jeff outperforms most surfers. It's amazing how he always manages to be in the right place at the right time. But he's a shadow of his former self, and he knows it. He's lost much of the fluidity he had when I first saw him surf thirty years ago, and it's easy to see how frustrated he's become. Today between sets, as he tried to sit down on his board to rest, he banged his bad knee against the rail and sat cursing to himself for half a minute before the pain went away.

I said to Jeff, "What's the deal with those bionic knees, anyway? Do they ever work as good as the original?"

"The surgeon tells me you never get it all back," he said. "My goal is to be able to ride a shortboard again, if I can. But it might take me awhile. And I could be looking at a replacement on the other knee in a year or so."

After surfing a couple of hours with Jeff, I moved farther outside, and deeper, hoping to take advantage of the lower tide and maybe catch one more 8-foot wave before this swell faded away. I sat by myself for twenty minutes before the wave I was looking for finally appeared. And it was a real beauty—long, fast, and clean.

As I paddled back out, I passed Jeff and saw that he was grinning. "Nice wave," he said. "I was about to start making fun of you for sitting so far out."

July 9

For the past two months, every time the weather would begin to heat up, the wind would blow from the west, off the cold Pacific, and the East Cape would cool down almost instantaneously. Now, though, the Pacific is heating up too, and the west wind doesn't feel cool anymore.

That heat in the tropical Pacific is the fuel that powers hurricanes, and right now two hurricanes are churning out there at the same time. One has moved 700 miles to the west of us and will no longer be a factor on the Baja peninsula. The other one, Emilia, is about 1200 miles to the south and moving northwest. We're not seeing wind or waves from it yet, and I hope we don't, because we're expecting a new southern hemi tomorrow, and I don't want to see those waves chewed up by hurricane wind. This southern hemi might be the last chance I get to surf until next October. Who knows, at my age it might be the last chance I get to surf at all.

Neither Claudia nor I want to leave Baja, but we know the heat will become intolerable in a few more days. The heat doesn't seem to bother Mexicans, though. Today Brenda, Moisés's wife, asked me brightly, "What do you think about this weather?"

"Hot!" I said.

"But the wind is blowing!" she laughed. "It feels so fresh!"

Mexican construction workers play *fútbol* during their lunch break in 95-degree heat and then go back to carrying buckets of cement up a ladder all afternoon. Along the highway we see laborers in hooded sweatshirts with towels wrapped around their heads, pushing wheelbarrows full of rubble uphill. I can't imagine how they do it.

A few days ago, Claudia cut Kirra's hair short, and every now and then I hose her (Kirra) down to keep her cool. Still, she lies in the shade of our terrace panting most of the day. In San José, though, Mexican dogs trot energetically through their neighborhoods at two o'clock in the afternoon, as if this were just an extended spring and they had someplace important to go.

The parking lot at Mega, the market where we buy our groceries, is about empty now—all winter it was packed with rental cars. The restaurants in town aren't even half full, and some have closed for the summer. I know the off-season can be hard on those Mexicans who make their living from tourism, but I know they secretly look forward to having their town to themselves again too.

July 10

Hurricane Emilia has been upgraded to a category 4, with winds up to 140 miles per hour, but it has moved far to the west now and has no chance of passing over the peninsula. The sky is clear, the wind is calm, and the surf is much bigger today. Some of the sets this morning were in the 10-foot range, and surface conditions were perfect. Nathan, Colorado Kim, and I traded waves for a couple of hours.

Today I was riding my big blue fish, which isn't as maneuverable as my smaller boards but is extremely fast. I was flying across the top of a 10-foot wall at maximum velocity when I reached a slower section, dropped down, and started to carve a big arc across the flat to bleed off that excess speed. Then I hit a patch of whitewater from the previous wave, and my fins couldn't find traction in all that foam. I spun around backwards and got tossed forward about fifteen feet across the flat. I was going so fast, I bounced a couple of times before I could finally claw my way below the surface. Sometimes you can feel so confidant and in control, then get utterly demolished in a fraction of a second by something you never saw coming.

Fireman Tom joined us later on his SUP. He likes to wait farther outside for the biggest wave of a set. Because he's already on his feet, he can take off later than we can, and on that big SUP he can carry more speed across the walls too. Today, though, he was too late on a 10-foot grinder and got absolutely crushed. I couldn't see him after the wave washed over, and because he's been accident prone-lately, I was worried. In surf this big, somebody could be in trouble just 200 feet inside of you and you'd never know it. When SUPs go down in big surf, all that foam volume works against you, and it can be extremely difficult to get back on your feet and start paddling again. Finally, I spotted Tom four hundred yards away, nearly to the beach. He paddled back out slowly, and when he got to where I was, I said, "I lost sight of you there for a while. You must have gotten pounded."

"Oh, yeah," he said, ever cheerful. "I rode the next five waves, though—all underwater!"

I didn't want to go in today. I surfed until every muscle in my body ached and the sweat dripped off my face. On the beach, without Claudia to help me, I had to sit in the shade of a *palapa* and drink water until I had the strength to get up again.

On the way home, at the Tienda Cardon on the bluff above Shipwreck, where I stopped to get a soda, I watched a three-legged dog trying to scratch his ear with the leg he no longer had. He sat there for a moment trying to figure out what was wrong. Then he jumped up, ran to the *tienda*, and scratched his ear against a plywood corner.

Ah, I'm going to miss Baja so much.

July 11

Hurricane Emilia is having her wicked way with this south swell. The waves are still big, but the surface of the ocean is broken and gnarled, and I don't want anything to do with it. Emilia is rapidly moving west, though, and with a little luck, the tail end of this southern hemi could arrive in good shape.

Today we began working on the long list of things that have to be done before we leave Zacatitos: add distilled water to the solar batteries, prune the old palm fronds so they don't get ripped off in the hurricanes, cut back the *bugambilias* so they'll be in full bloom when we return, put out fresh cockroach traps and mouse poison, inflate the truck tires back to their normal 32 psi, clean out the pantry, find Kirra's rabies certificate—and the list goes on. It will take us several days to get ready, and because the weather is so hot, we feel like working only in the cool of morning.

Moisés will come once a week while we're gone to check on the house and water the plants. He has a powerful green thumb that must find expression, so he will insist on fertilizing the *bugambilias*, even though I tell him they don't really need it. Moisés is so conscientious, this spring he was watering some newly sprouted tomato plants for Pete and Pauline while they went north for a couple of weeks; two of the plants turned out to be weeds, but rather than pull them up, Moisés kept watering them until Pete and Pauline returned. Also, Moisés refuses to agree on a price for his services. He says, "When you come back, pay me what you think it was worth. If you don't like what I did, then pay me nothing." Once, he refused to accept what I offered to pay him for a job, saying it was too much, and I had to explain all the reasons why, for me, his work was worth that much and more.

If Mexico would make it easier for foreigners to retire here, young people like Moisés wouldn't have to trek north looking for a way to feed their families—the gringos would come to them. Just a few years ago, Mexico had big plans for hosting more American retirees, but those plans have faded now with the world recession. But in my opinion, the biggest obstacle for retirees here is the Mexican law banning foreigners from owning property within 100 kilometers of the border and 50 kilometers of the coast. That means virtually the entire Baja peninsula is off-limits to direct ownership by foreigners. It's not difficult to understand Mexico's political motivation for this law—after all, the gringos stole half their territory following the Mexican-American War—but the ban is circumvented anyway through a *fideocomiso*, which, in effect, allows a Mexican bank to hold title to your property in trust. So the bad law accomplishes nothing, other than enrich the banks, who collect about $500 per year for this service, and it frightens and annoys *norteamericanos* who might otherwise be happy to own a piece of Mexico.

The Mexican government has a long history of passing politically expedient laws that cause more problems than they solve and become, at any rate, unenforceable. Everybody in Mexico knows there is always a way around a bad law—there must be for people to go about their lives. Unfortunately, the solution often takes the form of a bribe.

Sometimes corruption isn't so much an ethical problem as it is the consequence of bad government.

July 13

For the past two days, the wind has been blowing briskly at dawn. This morning I drove the Rhino to Waimesa for a surf check, even though I knew I'd find nothing but chop. It's too bad, because underneath all this froth there's a good south swell. I'm running out of time now—we're leaving in two days—but I still have hopes that these wretched surf conditions will clean up before we go.

In the meantime, Claudia and I slowly work through our list. Today I cleaned the water filters, burned three months' worth of paper trash, bagged the recyclables, carried the hurricane shutters upstairs, washed the truck, sealed the guest studio, stored the Rhino trailer in the garage, and much more. Claudia cleaned the gas barbecue, cut Kirra's hair even shorter, washed clothes, sprayed her papier-maché fish with a fresh coat of cockroach repellant, and began packing for the road.

Kirra knows by all this activity that we're leaving soon. She's seen this annual migration five times now. Because she's worried we might leave her behind, she follows either Claudia or me everywhere we go.

July 14

Before sunrise I drove as far as Shipwreck but didn't like what I saw. There was a powerful swell running, but the hurricanes out to sea had confused things so badly that the wave periods were less than ten seconds, and there were no breaks between sets at all. In addition, the night wind off the Pacific had torn up the ocean surface. I watched for an hour, hoping conditions might improve after sunrise, but I finally gave up and headed home.

Halfway to Zacatitos, I met Doyle coming the other way. Besides the three surfboards stacked on top of his car, he had his kiting equipment with him too. We stopped and shut off our engines. This time of year, the East Cape road has hardly any traffic, so we sat in the middle of the road comparing observations.

"You know, things might look better out at Boca de Tule," Doyle said. "This swell is coming from about180 degrees, which is fairly rare. But Boca likes that direction. And sometimes this west wind isn't quite as bad out that way."

"You think?"

"You never know," he shrugged. "Maybe I'll go take a look."

Doyle is a master at reading surf conditions, and I should have listened to him. But Claudia and I had a hundred things that had to be done around the house, and feeling just a twinge of surfer's guilt, I headed home to do my share.

July 15

Today was our last day in Zacatitos, so, recovering my true natural form, I left my wife to finish packing while I went surfing for three hours.

At Shipwreck the surf looked a bit rough and disorganized, but the farther east I went, the better the conditions looked, and by the time I reached Punta Espina, the surf looked promising. The tide was too high but dropping quickly, so I paddled out and surfed alone for an hour, hoping everything would eventually come together.

Colorado Kim watched from her house on the bluff, and when I finally started getting decent rides, she paddled out to join me.

"I went out to Boca de Tule yesterday," Kim said.

"Yeah? How was it?"

"Big and scary. Maybe ten-foot and barreling. I didn't even paddle out. But there were a bunch of hot shortboarders there ripping it up. There weren't any breaks in the sets, and they had to duck dive every wave just to get outside."

Fireman Tom joined us later, but not on his SUP—he was riding his ten-foot gun. I hadn't seen him belly paddling in a year, so I knew he must be fully recovered from his injuries. "Boca was big and pumping yesterday," he said. "I thought maybe I'd see you out there."

"I should have listened to Doyle," I replied. "He called it early in the morning. Was it crowded?"

"Lots of guys who looked like they'd just gotten off a plane," Tom said. "And they brought their California attitudes with them. But it was still worth it."

By eight o'clock, the tide had dropped enough that the waves were breaking more crisply; they were still a foot or more overhead, and we had no wind at all. By nine o'clock the three of us—Kim, Tom, and I—were getting some long, exceptional rides.

At times I can be as hapless as any surfer in the water, but today everything seemed effortless, as if my thoughts were actions in themselves—I imagined what I wanted to happen and it became reality. I could drop into these waves with just a couple of paddling strokes, and with a quick top turn I was launched down those transparent walls one fraction of a second ahead of destruction, which is all the time you need. I've never felt more in control, more at ease, more alive.

Once again I surfed until I was exhausted.

Back at home, though, it didn't matter if I was exhausted or not. I had to finish putting up the hurricane shutters, turn off the gas, disconnect the internet antennae in case of a lightning strike, drain the gray-water holding tank, take the battery out of the Rhino, and many more last-minute chores. It was so hot and humid, I stripped down to my boxer shorts, but I still had to hose off every half hour or so. The one good thing about this kind of heat is that it reminds us why we're leaving, and that we're making the right choice.

Kirra followed me constantly. I don't know why she's so insecure—we've never left her anywhere. Finally, I opened up the truck door, lay her rug out in the backseat, and she jumped up there and took a nap.

On our way out of town, we pulled off the road just past Punta Gorda to check out the surf one last time. The swell was still pumping, and it sorely grieved me to leave the East Cape while there were waves to be ridden. We'd been sitting there a minute when a woman pulled up in a rental car. She rolled down her window, pointed to our front license plate, and practically screamed at us, "Did you really drive here all the way from South Dakota?"

"Yes, ma'am," I nodded. "We really did."

The woman started to say something, but her words became strangled in her throat. She paused for a moment to let the spasm pass. Her expression was one of disgust. Kirra—always on the lookout for erratic behavior, poked her head out the rear window and barked twice at the woman to warn her that her attitude was not acceptable. Finally, the woman was able to spit out her thought. "Are you crazy?" she asked.

"No, ma'am," I said. "We're surfers."

We drove as far as Ciudad Constitución, about 200 miles from Zacatitos, arriving just before dusk. If a tornado picked up a dusty farm town in the San Joaquin Valley and plopped it down in the center of southern Baja, it would look exactly like Ciudad Constitución. The place is hot, flat, and ugly, and it usually smells of white onions and cattle feed. Like farm towns everywhere, the local boys are into fast cars, drinking beer, and smoking marijuana, while the girls are pretty and tend to have their children young.

We pulled into the dirt parking lot of our favorite hotel to find that the place had been converted to a motel. In Mexico, a motel is something different from a motel in the United States. I discovered this many years ago after stopping at a motel in Ensenada and having the price for the room quoted to me as an hourly rate by a woman behind bulletproof glass. In addition, each room at that motel had its own secluded carport, so the guests' vehicles couldn't be seen from the highway. This doesn't mean—as you might suppose—that a motel in Mexico is the same as a house of ill repute. It just means that the rooms are available for those customers requiring an extra measure of privacy, for whatever purpose, be it adultery, homosexuality, or a peaceful evening of X-rated movies alone.

Claudia and I were tired, and we didn't want to go looking for another place to spend the night. This motel was fenced and secure, the management had always accepted dogs, the rooms were basic but clean, and we had spent many comfortable nights here in years past. So I told Claudia, "Wait here. I'll go inside and see what the deal is."

The nightly prices posted in the office were almost double what they had been in previous years, but at least they weren't hourly rates. Condoms were sold at the front counter now, and the woman behind the desk smiled at me with a hint of mischief. "Can I help you?" she asked.

"I'd like a room for the night, please."

"How many people?" she inquired, peeking over my shoulder.

"Just two," I said. "Uh... my wife and me."

"One bed or two?"

"Just one, please."

"With vibration, or no?"

Now I knew she was having fun with me. "That's not necessary," I replied.

She glanced at the keys hanging on the wall, trying to decide which room would be most appropriate for an older married couple. "Would you like to have all the TV channels?" she asked.

I didn't understand right away. "I'm sorry … all the channels?"

She pointed to a plastic-coated brochure on the counter that advertised the X-rated channels available.

"Oh, no, I don't think so. The regular channels will be fine."

The woman studied the keyboard again, then made her decision. "Room seven," she said. "It's in the back. It's very quiet and," she paused, her eyes twinkling, "*muy romántico.*"

When I went back to the truck and explained the situation to Claudia, she laughed and said, "Maybe tonight you'll even dance with me."

That evening we sat on the bed drinking beer and watching a Mexican soap opera while eating a bucket of chicken from the Pollo Loco and tossing the scraps to Kirra on the tile floor. I must have been tired, because I don't even remember falling asleep.

July 16

Over the years I've probably driven the 1,050 miles of the Transpeninsula Highway thirty times. Once, I drove the entire distance by myself in eighteen hours straight. Sometimes, just for the hell of it, we make excursions on dirt side roads that parallel the coast or cross the rugged mountains from one side of the peninsula to the other. At other times we like to stay for a night or two in our favorite towns along the way, like San Ignacio or Cataviña. Most often, though, we make the journey in three days, covering about 600 miles on the second day, driving from dawn to dusk.

This afternoon we stopped in Cataviña long enough to say hello to a gringo panhandler we call Rockefeller who has been working that little desert town for the last five years or so. At various times he presents himself as Marilyn Monroe's brother; the inventor of plastic bottles, the hula hoop, and the paint roller; a child actor who played in the Tarzan movies; or heir to the Rockefeller fortune. He stands out in the Baja sun every day, with no hat, begging for a peso or two, but always offering in return an outrageous tale, delivered with charm and good cheer, almost like an old vaudeville actor. If you challenge his facts, he just adds layer after layer of detail, with no more regard for the truth than a novelist, until you surrender to his version of reality. I suppose in the U.S. he would be considered insane and put on medication. Yet he is always remarkably cheerful, rattling off his latest fantasies and delusions with great gusto. I find it difficult to feel sorry for him, because he's so much happier than most people considered sane.

We found Rockefeller standing at his usual place, beside the highway, next to the children selling gasoline in plastic jugs. (There are no gas stations between Jesús María and El Rosario, a distance of more than 200 miles, which gives the locals a chance to earn a little money.) His skin looked as brown and hard as a desert tortoise, and his hair and beard were matted like an old horse blanket. I rolled down the truck window and gave him a handful of change. His odor was outrageous. With the sun behind him, his face looked ghastly— almost purple—but he was grinning like a time-share salesman about to close a deal. Kirra, who is usually deeply offended by people who smell, rose from her blanket and wagged her fanny, hoping to make a new friend.

Every remote desert town I've ever known, both in the U.S. and Mexico, attracts people like Rockefeller. Most desert folks are tolerant of eccentricity, having stood on the abyss of insanity themselves once or twice. And it's possible that the residents of Cataviña saw Rockefeller as a valuable asset, like a plaster dinosaur or a Cadillac Stonehenge, who enticed the gringos to slow down long enough to throw a few dollar bills out their car windows. It certainly worked on us, because we stopped at the little market there to buy sodas and a block of ice.

Then, as we were about to leave, I said to Rockefeller, "You've been standing out in this sun for a lotta years now. We see you every time we pass through. Tell me, how come the *federales* haven't run you out of here by now?"

"Oh, they wouldn't dare," he growled. "I own most of the land around here. And besides, they know I invented Coca-Cola."

July 17, Carlsbad, California

It was nearly a three-hour wait at the Tijuana border. When we were younger, the customs agents always eyed us suspiciously, asked where we'd been in Mexico, how long we'd been there, and why. Quite often they would send us to the secondary inspection area and go through everything in our car. While traveling with a backpack through South America, I was subjected to a complete body-cavity search at a few border crossings. Now, though, the agents glance at our gray hair, smile with amusement at my preposterous lie about being a 63-year-old surfer, and wave us through. Another advantage of growing older, I suppose.

One look at those sparkling concrete highways and Claudia said she was sort of happy to be back in the U.S. Like always, I had mixed feelings. After spending months in Mexico, the U.S. doesn't feel real to me. Everything is too clean, too organized. The place looks false. Almost pretentious. So much green grass and freeway landscaping, so many imitation waterfalls, as if San Diego weren't a desert too, just like Baja. I find the affluence difficult to trust, and the blank stares I see on people's faces confirm my suspicions. I see entire neighborhoods in which every house is painted some shade of beige—not a single raspberry, mango, or lime green house in sight. And where, I wonder, are these people hiding their broken-down cars? Why aren't there dead cows alongside the road? You mean to tell me that cows don't die in the USA too, just like they do in Mexico? And where do they keep their chickens? Why can't I smell cooking food? Don't gringos eat? Why do drivers stop at every single stop sign, even though they can see that nobody is coming the other way? Are they nearsighted?

The U.S. looks lifeless to me, colorless, and bland.

August 11, Mammoth Lakes, California

Claudia, Kirra, and I have retreated to the Eastern Sierra Nevada, where we will pass the summer in our Winnebago, moving once a week or so from one campground to another, gorging on views of distant snow-covered peaks and dark green ponderosa pines swaying in the wind. At night Claudia and I will snuggle under three or four blankets to ward off the cruel chill of a *norteamericano* summer.

On the satellite radio today, we heard the astonishing news of Mexico's winning the gold medal in men's *fútbol* at the London Olympics. Mexico has long had world-class divers, boxers, and a few track athletes. The martial arts, as well as cycling, are growing in popularity as well. But no sport in Mexico comes even close to being so important to the national psyche as *fútbol*. Our first thought upon hearing the news was regret for having missed that celebration—fireworks, all-night parties, and dancing in the streets. But on second thought, we realized that in Mexico such a celebration might very well last until we get back in October.

This morning, at the grocery store in Mammoth Lakes, I watched as a young Mexican immigrant and his wife loaded their shopping cart with fresh produce. Being a ski resort in the winter and a popular vacation destination in the summer, Mammoth Lakes has a great need for ski lift operators, cooks, dishwashers, laundry workers, and maids—almost all of them Mexican immigrants. Sometimes America's affluence looks like a painted Hollywood prop held in place by the labor of people like this young couple.

The Mexican man was wearing new Wrangler jeans and a freshly ironed cowboy shirt; his pretty wife had on a purple fleece jacket. It was Saturday morning, and Mexicans like to dress up on their day off.

"This corn is very cheap," the man said in Spanish to his wife.

"Maybe it's not good corn," his wife replied.

In Mexico the state of consumer protection is about where it was in the U.S. in the 1950s. Metal parts of all kinds rust and corrode like a sugar cube dissolving in tea. Plastic and rubber goods crumble and break. Red potatoes taken home and boiled will lose their red dye. And an ear of Mexican corn—that ancient country's great gift to the world—is often inedible. So this young woman had good reason to be skeptical. And because Mexicans work so hard for their money, they spend it shrewdly. The man picked up one ear of the corn and shucked it partway down to see for himself—as any sensible buyer in Mexico would. "It looks good to me," the man said, and he shoveled a dozen ears into his cart.

Watching this simple act made me hopelessly homesick for Mexico, and I couldn't resist sharing a word or two with this couple. "Look," I said, "mangos at only a dollar apiece!"

The man laughed, understanding my joke—in Mexico mangos in season can be bought for a few pennies apiece, and in Baja most people gather them for free from the trees growing in their yard.

Nowadays most Americans are suspicious of a stranger trying to make small talk. And who can blame them? America has become a very dangerous place. But Mexicans are different. For this man it would have been impolite to ignore a harmless, gray-haired fool like me wearing a tattered Pacifico T-shirt.

"You know Mexico?" the man asked.

"My wife and I live in southern Baja, near San José del Cabo," I replied.

The man was surprised—even a bit confused. "You mean you moved to Mexico? Why would you do that?"

"Well," I shrugged, "everybody can't live in the United States. Somebody has to go the other way."

By now the man's wife had concluded that I was crazy, and she was gently tugging her husband by the arm. He was curious, though, and not ready to give up on me yet. "But do you really want to live there?" he asked.

I pointed to the fresh fruit and said, "Well, I'm not going to pay a dollar for a mango!"

All we know about Baja these days is what we read in emails from our friends in Zacatitos. In one three-day tropical storm, something like eight inches of rain fell on the East Cape, blowing out culverts, washing out roads, causing mudslides, trapping cars in the flooded arroyos—but also replenishing the badly depleted aquifers. From what we hear, our house has weathered the storms without damage, but we won't know that for sure until October.

I've seen enough tropical storms now to know the damage they can cause. But I also know that after a wet summer like this one, the entire Baja landscape will bloom. Beautiful flowers will cover the _malvarrosa, palo de arco,_ and _palo adan._ The _cardon, pitahaya,_ and _la choya_ will fatten and swell, as will the bellies of the cows and burros. The fine grass, for which our town of Zacatitos got its name, will grow thick and green. Vines of all kinds will grow over and entangle everything, until the entire landscape will appear lush, almost as if the desert had retained a memory of the jungle it once was.

Author Profile

Steve Sorensen was born in San Francisco, grew up in the San Joaquin Valley, and graduated with a degree in English from California State University at Fresno. He spent fifteen years supervising a backcountry crew in Sequoia-Kings Canyon National Park and conducting winter snow surveys. After being warned by his college professors that it would be impossible for him to earn a living as a writer, he sold the first feature story he ever wrote to the *San Diego Reader* and spent the next twenty years writing for that same paper. He's an avid surfer, climber, and kayak fishermen. He and his wife Claudia, who have three grown sons, now live on the east cape of Baja California Sur. His other books include: **Morning Glass***: The Adventures of Legendary Waterman Mike Doyle*, and **A Branch of the Sky:** *Fifty Years of Adventure, Tragedy, and Restoration in the Sierra Nevada.*

Steve and Claudia Sorensen

Heap of Bones

Made in the USA
Middletown, DE
20 November 2019

79103644R00182